Moscow and the Ukraine
1918-1953

Moscow and

BASIL DMYTRYSHYN

the Ukraine

1918-1953

A STUDY OF RUSSIAN BOLSHEVIK
NATIONALITY POLICY

BOOKMAN ASSOCIATES

New York

To the Memory of
My Mother

Preface

The overwhelming majority of Westerners think of the Soviet Union as one economic, political, and cultural entity. Comparatively few know that this "monolith" consists of sixteen union republics, several autonomous republics, a number of autonomous regions, and various other political units. Still fewer realize that each of these units is inhabited by people who differ in language, custom, tradition, history, etc. Viewed from this standpoint, the Soviet Union represents not a monolith, but a polyglot state welded together and maintained by force. Of the over 200,000,000 population of the Soviet Union, the Russians comprise over half, the Ukrainians about a fifth, and the remainder is divided among more than a hundred other nationalities.

In this, what is doubtless one of the most variegated nationality patchworks of the world, the Ukrainians occupy a vital place. In addition to being the second largest ethnic group, they inhabit a territory which, although comprising only about 2% of the entire Soviet Union, has been of paramount importance both economically and strategically. The Ukraine's fertile soil and abundance of natural resources (coal, iron, manganese, etc.) have played a significant part in the industrialization of the Soviet Union, while its geographic location has been quite instrumental in Moscow's acquisition of a firmer hold on the Balkans. Furthermore, the Ukraine has been used as a laboratory for many national, social, and economic experiments. Aware of its strong potential role, the Ukraine has tended to act as one of the most powerful centrifugal forces within the Soviet Union. That role, however, has been obscured by works which have attempted either to minimize or to exaggerate its importance.

5

The object of this study, which originally was submitted as a doctoral dissertation at the Institute of Slavic Studies, University of California, Berkeley, is to provide a comprehensive treatment of the Russian Bolshevik nationality policy in the Ukraine from 1918 to the death of Stalin in March, 1953. This inquiry is based primarily on documentary evidence—stenographic reports of Party Congresses, Plenums of the Central Committees, resolutions, directives, government laws and decrees, and speeches and pronouncements of responsible Party and government spokesmen. This information, in turn, has been supplemented by semi-official publications and other studies pertinent to the problem. To avoid hopeless entanglement in the various versions produced by the notorious practice of "doctoring" evidence to fit the changing Party line, it was felt advisable to use the wording of many documents as they were originally reported in official newspaper and other accounts.

Though treated as one unit, this study can be said to consist of two parts. The first, and the main part, which includes Chapters I through VI, traces chronologically and analyzes the political side of the Russian Bolshevik nationality policy in the Ukraine. The second part, which includes Chapters VII through IX, plays a supporting role. Chapter VII evaluates the role of the Ukrainian economy in the economy of the USSR, and its influence on policy making. Chapter VIII treats the development of federal relations between the UkSSR and the USSR as reflected in their constitutions. Chapter IX traces the evolution of the national and social composition of the membership of the CPU.

The author desires to acknowledge his great indebtedness to Professor Robert J. Kerner, Director of the Institute of Slavic Studies at the University of California, Berkeley, who suggested the subject of the study, guided its completion, and contributed trenchant counsel and sustained encouragement.

The author wishes to express his deep appreciation to Professor John M. Letiche, Department of Economics, University of California, for his stimulating and invaluable advice on varied problems. He is likewise grateful to Professors Raymond H. Fisher, Department of History, University of California at Los Angeles, and

Julian Towster, Department of Political Science, University of California, Berkeley; Mr. George C. Guins, formerly of the Department of Political Science, University of California; and Professors Charles Jelavich and the late George V. Lantzeff, Department of History, University of California, for the generous contributions of their knowledge and experience. The author alone, however, assumes full responsibility for the views expressed.

His thanks are extended to the Inter-Library Loan staff of the University of California Library for its helpful service. He is grateful to the staff of the Hoover War Memorial Library, Stanford, California, and in particular to Mr. Witold S. Sworakowski. He is also thankful to the Slavonic Room of the Library of Congress, the Columbia University Library, and the Slavonic Room of the New York Public Library for extending to him their excellent research facilities.

The author is deeply indebted to his wife, whose patience, understanding, and devoted assistance not only made this study possible, but also contributed to the shaping of every paragraph.

Basil Dmytryshyn

Portland State College, Oregon
Summer, 1956

Contents

CHAPTER I

The Evolution of Theory

Ever since Communist seizure of power in Russia in 1917, their theoreticians have persistently asserted that the Communist movement, from the very beginning, has had a clear-cut program regarding the nationalities.[1] They have claimed that this program has been consistent; that the Communists alone defend the right of national self-determination and support the development of each minority; and that they, and they alone, have found the solution for national minorities within the framework of their own state— often referred to as "a multinational state," "a voluntary federation of nationalities," "a voluntary unification of equal Soviet Socialist Republics," etc.

A careful examination of the development of Communist views on the nationality problem not only annuls many of these self-satisfying assertions, but also points out that in Communist theoretical writings the national problem has gone and continues to go along a most zigzagging path. Furthermore, a critical evaluation of numerous pronouncements the Communist leaders have made on the nationality problem indicates that these pronouncements, pregnant with high-sounding ideals, were nothing but meaningless double talk, concealed in carefully chosen phraseology and intended to confuse, not to clarify, and to arrest, but never to solve the national problem.

The Russian Communist attitude toward the national problem in general, and toward the Ukrainian problem in particular, was influenced by several factors. It was determined in part by the ideas and writings of Russian revolutionary intellectuals of the XIX century. The majority of these considered the Russian empire a political and economic entity, and in their struggle against Tsarism

11

they directed their efforts primarily toward changing Russia's political, economic, and social system. Though aware of Russia's multinational nature, they ignored the national problem and considered the struggle of nationalities as something narrow, limited, and insignificant in comparison with their own high and noble ideals. Within Russia, their attitude toward the national problem was if not outright hostile at least negative. Abroad, however, especially in the Balkans and Austria-Hungary, many Russian intellectuals posed as the most outspoken defenders of national rights.[2] This contradiction corresponded in part with the official Russian government policy of vigorously russifying national minorities at home while taking advantage of the national problem abroad.

The Russian Communist attitude toward the national problem was likewise influenced by the ideals and principles of socialism. The latter, which found many adherents among Russian intellectuals, maintained that the interests of human progress demanded the amalgamation of small nations and small economies into one large unit embracing the entire world. Since, in their opinion, nationalism tended to prevent effective concentration of production, socialists adopted a negative attitude toward the national problem, ignoring it at times, utilizing it on other occasions, but always treating it as a barrier against their own interpretation of progress.[2a] Because of these and other considerations, the legitimate and moderate national demands (viz., equality, local self-government, the right to use the native language, etc.) that began to emerge in Russia during the latter part of the XIX century went unanswered. Russian unwillingness to take national requests into consideration only paved the way for increased demands.

V. I. Lenin, as the organizer of the Russian Communist movement, the founder of its doctrine and the creator of its national policy, was greatly influenced by these approaches to the national problem. As a pupil of Russian revolutionary thought, Lenin, in his early days of political activity, accepted many of its ideas and traditions. He viewed the Russian Empire as one political and economic whole, and almost completely ignored its national differences. As a student of Marxism, Lenin neglected the national prob-

lem and centered his attention on theorizing the capitalist development of Russia. Both as a Russian and as a Marxist, Lenin was
favorably inclined toward the historical development of Russian
imperialism, as he believed that this development was beneficial to
the theory of economic and territorial centralism. Both as a Russian idealist and as a Marxist Utopian, Lenin failed to comprehend
the inner nature of national problems and demands, viewing and
solving them in accordance with the interests of the center rather
than with those of the periphery.

Although, in 1894 and 1899, Lenin paid some lip service to
national equality irrespective of race or religion, it was not until
February, 1903, that he made his first basic pronouncements on
the national problem. In clear Marxist terms, Lenin declared that
it was not the business of the proletariat "to propagate either federalism or national autonomy," or make similar demands, which
in the end would only result in creation of an autonomous class
state. The aim of the proletariat, he declared, was not itemization,
but as close as possible unity of all workers of all nationalities, "for
a struggle in a *possibly wider arena* for a democratic republic and
for socialism"; not self-determination of peoples or nations "but of
the *proletariat* of every nationality." As a result, he concluded,

> the fundamental and always obligatory program of Social Demo-
> crats of Russia should consist of demanding only full equality of
> citizens (irrespective of sex, language, religion, race, nationality,
> etc.) and their right for a free democratic *self*-determination.
> With regards to the support of demands for *national* autonomy,
> then this support is not a permanent program or obligation of the
> proletariat. This support can become for it [the proletariat] indis-
> pensable only in separate, exceptional cases.[3]

The essence of Lenin's arguments entered into the Party's program in the summer of 1903. It announced that as its political
objective, the Party planned the overthrow of Tsarism. Its place
was to be taken by a democratic republic whose constitution among
other things was to safeguard: local self-government; equality irrespective of sex, religion, race and nationality; the right to use the
native language in education, conversation, meetings, and in state

institutions; and the right of nations to self-determination.[4] The last item, the co-author of the Party's program, G. V. Plekhanov, explained in the Party's organ *Zaria,* had to be included in view of the adoption of the same point by the International Social Democratic Congress in London in 1896. "If we forgot about it or neglected to bring it forth, fearing to incite national superstitions of our Russian compatriots, then the fighting slogan of international social democracy: 'Proletarians of all countries unite,' would become a very bad lie." [5]

Lenin was more straightforward in explaining the meaning of self-determination as included in the Party's program. "Unconditional recognition of the struggle for freedom of self-determination," he declared,

> does not at all obligate us to support every demand for national self-determination. Social democracy, as the party of the proletariat, places as its fundamental and main task the realization of self-determination not of peoples and nations, but of the proletariat of every nationality. We ought always and unconditionally to strive for a *very close* union of the proletariat of all nationalities and only in separate exceptional cases can we accept and actively support the demands aimed at the creation of a new class state or at the substitution of full political unity of the state by a weaker federal union.[6]

Lenin's explanation of self-determination leaves no doubts that not self-determination, but centralism and amalgamation, were to become the official policy of the Party as long as he was the chief spokesman. One of the by-products of this interpretation was the split in the ranks of the Russian Social Democratic Workers' Party (RSDRP) into the Bolshevik and the Menshevik factions. Another by-product of Lenin's interpretation was a long and bitter polemic war waged between Lenin on the one hand, and the Jewish Bund and Polish Socialists on the other.

Although the national problem was indirectly referred to in connection with various unifications of national organizations of the RSDRP(b), the national problem as such was not considered by the Party at its congresses or conferences until August, 1913, when Lenin suddenly brought the matter up for discussion at the Conference of the CC of the RSDRP(b). Lenin's sudden interest was not motivated by any desire to solve the national problem. Far from it. It was the force of nationalism as a potential weapon to be utilized in bringing about a socialist world revolution that attracted his attention. This was explicitly stated in a resolution on the national problem adopted by the conference. "The debauchery of the Black Hundreds nationalism, the growth of nationalist tendencies among the liberal bourgeoisie, the strengthening of nationalist tendencies among the upper layers of the oppressed nationalities—bring the national problem at the present time to a conspicuous place." [7]

The resolution further made clear that the bringing up of the national problem for the conference's consideration was due to various attempts on the part of non-Bolsheviks to solve the national problem not only in theory, as Lenin had done to his own personal satisfaction, but also to solve it in practice. If, stated the resolution, national peace is possible under capitalism, it can prosper far better under socialism where neither privileges nor discriminations will exist, and where broad autonomy and self-government, to be determined by local population, national composition and economic conditions, will prevail. However, alongside these concessions to the national problem, the resolution stressed centralist features by declaring that the interests of the working class demanded the amalgamation of all workers, irrespective of nationality, into single proletarian organizations—because only the unity of the working class could cope with capitalism and "reaction." [8]

The resolution expressed the same dualism regarding the problem of the right of national self-determination. On the one hand it stated that "with regard to the right of self-determination of nations oppressed by the Tsarist monarchy, i.e., the right to separation and the creation of independent states, the Social Democratic Party ought to support that right." This support, it was argued, was demanded by the fundamental principles of international democracy, as well as because of Tsarist oppression of the Russian and non-Russian peoples. On the other hand, the resolution made

important qualifications regarding the Party's agreement to support
the right of self-determination—qualifications which annulled the
concessions and exposed the Party's favoring of centralism.

> The problem of the right of nations to self-determination (*i.e.,*
> the safeguarding by the constitution of the state of full, free and
> democratic means of deciding the problem of separation) cannot
> be mixed with the problem of expedience of separation of this or
> that nation. The latter problem, the Social Democratic Party
> ought to decide in every separate case totally independently, from
> the point of view of the interests of social development and inter-
> ests of class struggle of the proletariat for socialism.[9]

Lenin's ambiguity on the national problem reached a high
point in his letter of November 13, 1913 to an Armenian Social
Democrat, S. G. Shaumian, who had interpreted the Party's duplicity on self-determination as the right to separate, the right to federal
ties, and the right to autonomy. "In principle," Lenin wrote, in
attempting to clarify for Shaumian the Party's stand,

> we are against federation [because] it weakens economic ties, [and
> because] it is an unworthy type [of system] for one state. . . . We
> favor autonomy for all parts; we favor the right of separation (but
> we are not in favor of the separation of all). Autonomy is our
> plan of construction of a democratic state. Separation is not our
> plan at all. We do not propagate separation. In general we are
> against separation, but we stand for the right to separate in view
> of the Black Hundred Great Russian nationalism which destroyed
> so much the question of national co-operation that it will receive
> more unity after free separation.
>   The right of self-determination is excluded from our general
> support of centralism. This exclusion is of course necessary in
> view of [nationalist and deviationist opportunist danger]. But the
> exclusion cannot be interpreted as being solved. Nothing, abso-
> lutely nothing except the right of separation is there and can be
> there.[10]

However negative and confusing Lenin's stand on the national
problem may have been, he was shrewd enough to recognize the

potential force of any national movement, and did his utmost to utilize it to his own advantages and objectives with or without justification, even if this utilization contradicted his previous stand. "We would be very poor revolutionaries if, in a great liberating war of the proletariat for socialism, we were unable to utilize *every* national movement against *separate* negative forms of imperialism in order to sharpen and broaden the crisis." [11] Between 1913 and 1917, Lenin wrote a whole series of articles on the national problem.[12] These articles show, on the one hand, Lenin's ignorance, and above all his misunderstanding, of the national problem— perhaps because he approached it from the point of view of a dominant nation and tried to fit the national problem into his own centralist schemes which were determined purely by economic thinking. On the other hand, these articles show, as pointed out above, his realization that nationalism was a potential force.

It was during this period, 1913-1917, that Lenin worked out an important two-part tactical scheme in an effort to utilize national movements without departing from centralism—a scheme that is still in full force. One part of these tactics was destined to guide the proletariat of the dominant nation, whose entire efforts were to be directed along centrifugal lines, *i.e.*, toward breaking up the multinational states. Those who opposed this scheme were to be labeled as enemies. "Russian socialists who do not demand the separation of Finland, Poland, the Ukraine, etc., conduct themselves as chauvinists, as lackeys, covered with blood and dirt of imperialist monarchies and imperialist bourgeoisie." [13] "We have the right to, and should, consider every Social Democrat of the ruling nation who *does not* conduct such propaganda [freedom of separation] an imperialist and a scoundrel." [14] Lenin made it clear, however, that separation was not his objective. "When we demand freedom of separation for the Mongols, the Persians, the Egyptians, etc.,—and for *all* subjugated and unequal nations without exception, it is not that *we favor their separation* but *only* that we stand for a *free, willing* unity and merger, and not for a forceful one." [15] "The aim of socialism consists not only of the destruction of the separations of mankind into small states, and [of the destruction of] all par-

ticularities of nations, not only of the understanding of nations, but
of their amalgamation." [16]

An important role in the process of amalgamation—the second
part of the tactics—was assigned by Lenin to the proletariat of the
non-privileged nations. They were, without violating their obligations as internationalists, to stand for independence of their nations
and for their inclusion into neighboring states, especially if the
latter should be under proletarian control. At the same time they
were to struggle against petty bourgeois narrowmindedness, seclu-
sion, peculiarity, and were to subordinate particular interests to the
interests of the whole.[17] The role of the proletarians of the non-
privileged nations was therefore a triple one. They were to co-
operate in the destruction of the state, together with their comrades
of the privileged nations; they were to sabotage any constructive
work undertaken by forces other than those under their control;
and finally, they were assigned the role of "real" builders of a new
economic, political and social order. By advocating these tactics,
Lenin hoped to effect the destruction of a state without destroying
its territorial integrity, which was to serve as a base for future
operations; to turn world war into civil war; and to bring ruin
and prepare states for a proletarian seizure of power.[18]

It was only natural that with Lenin's turning toward the national problem in 1913-1917, he should turn some of his attention
to the Ukraine. Though he took some notes on the Ukrainian
problem as presented by Russian as well as by Ukrainian writers,[19]
basically Lenin's treatment of the Ukrainian problem before the
revolution is only a part of his polemics with the Russians, and
represents his own views on the national problem in general and
on the Ukrainian in particular, as opposed to the views held by
his opponents.[20] Lenin's lack of sufficient interest in the Ukrainian
problem, and his casual treatment of it, was the product of a prevailing belief in Russian liberal circles, which maintained that the
Ukrainians, attracted by a superior Russian industrial culture, were
being easily assimilated; hence there was no need to worry about
the Ukrainian problem.[21]

Before the outbreak of World War I, Lenin, in his arguments with his opponents, treated the Ukrainian problem from a purely economic standpoint. For him, the Ukraine economically and politically, as well as historically, represented an integral part of Russia. On several occasions, however, Lenin did denounce Tsarist mistreatment of Ukrainians in the cultural field, since this mistreatment in his opinion sharpened the Russo-Ukrainian animosity, created hatred between these two peoples and blocked the process of Russo-Ukrainian natural amalgamation which, in Lenin's opinion, was well under way.[22] For this reason Lenin insisted that there be a united action between Ukrainian and Russian workers, as he held that only such action was capable of bringing the Ukraine freedom. This freedom he interpreted in the economic and not in the political sense. "The freer the Ukraine and Great Russia will become, the *wider and faster* capitalism will develop and the stronger it will attract workers of all the districts of the state and the working mass of all neighboring states (if Russia should happen to be a neighboring state of the Ukraine) into the cities, into the mines and into the factories." [23]

While Lenin never abandoned these views, he nevertheless made some important modifications regarding the potential value of the Ukrainian national movement. This re-evaluation was due primarily to the increasing blunders on the part of the Russian Imperial Government in its policies toward the Ukraine. Of particular interest and significance was, for example, the government's denial of permission to celebrate the centennial of T. H. Shevchenko's birthday in March, 1914—a denial which made many Ukrainian peasants nationally conscious, even though prior to this act they had been almost totally indifferent to it. As a shrewd agitator, Lenin recognized at once the effect of this denial.

The denial of celebration of Shevchenko's Day was such a first class successful measure from the stand-point of agitation against the government that one cannot imagine a better one. I think that all of our best social democratic agitators against the government could never have achieved such complete success in so short a time as this measure alone has attained. After this measure, millions and millions of "dwellers" began to turn into conscious citizens convinced in the righteousness of the saying that Russia is "the prison of nations."[24]

Lenin was not the only one to recognize the effect of this blunder. Speaking in the Duma on the results of this measure, which he bitterly denounced, Paul N. Miliukov analyzed the Ukrainian national movement in these words:

> The movement exists, and you can neither suppress it nor alter its significance; the sole question is whether you wish to see this movement as inimical or friendly. That will depend upon whether the movement will regard you as friends or enemies. There is as yet no separatist movement in Ukraine, and if the beginnings of one exist they are very weak. But such a movement can be developed and those who are actually developing it, the true "separatists," those who are really working on behalf of Austria are Mr. [A. I.] Savenko [leader of the Ukrainiophobes in the Duma] and his political friends.[25]

The collapse of the Tsarist Government in February, 1917, and the accelerated revival of national ideas and national demands in the face of the Provisional Government's inability and unwillingness to cope with national problems, created for the Bolsheviks, and for Lenin in particular, an opportunity to utilize the national problem as a means of completely discrediting his opponents in the eyes of the non-Russian people, and at the same time, to bring about final territorial dismemberment of old Russia. Directions on the Party's nationality policy were provided by the Seventh (April) All-Russian Conference of the RSDRP(b). A resolution on the national problem declared that all nations comprising Russia should be given the right to free separation and the creation of independent states. The denial of such rights and the non-acceptance of appropriate measures guaranteeing practical realization of this right, the resolution stated, could but mean support of an annexationist policy.

Along with this somewhat hopeful tone, the resolution also underscored centralism, stating specifically that "the question of the right of nations for free separation cannot be mixed with the problem of expediency of separation of this or that nation at this or that moment. The latter question, the Party of the proletariat ought to decide in each separate case completely independently, and from the point of view of the whole social development and of the interests of class struggle of the proletariat for socialism." Thus, on the one hand the Party expressed its demands for wide autonomy, including separation, elimination of privileges, inequalities, etc.; while on the other hand it declared that "the interests of the working class demand the amalgamation of workers of all nationalities of Russia" into proletarian organizations, for only then could the proletariat be successful in waging a war against outside and internal enemies.[26]

To realize the scheme which the Party, under Lenin's direction, had set forth, it was necessary to have a large organization, politically mature and numerically strong. In the beginning of the Revolution, none of these prerequisites was met satisfactorily. However, Bolshevik weaknesses found great compensation and a source of strength in the successive political blunders and considerable administrative incapacity of the Provisional Government in many phases of its activity. The shortsightedness, which the Provisional Government demonstrated in its policy toward the Ukrainian problem, is very striking and represents only one of many blunders.

In Kiev, following the February, 1917 Revolution, there was organized the Ukrainian Central Rada, among whose members were representatives of all walks of Ukrainian life. In a resolution which the Rada, upon its organization, submitted to the Russian Provisional Government, a demand was made for autonomy of the Ukraine based on the Pereyaslav Act of 1654. The delay and indecision on the part of the Provisional Government, which had adopted the principle that nothing should be decided without approval of the Constituent Assembly to be convened sometime in the future, increased Ukrainian demands and impatience. In May, 1917, Struve suggested to the Ukrainian delegation an Autonomy Statute, on the basis of which Ukrainian administration was to be introduced in the Poltava, Kiev, Chernigov, Volyn, and Podolie

Gubernias. Since Struve's suggestion excluded Ukrainian administration from industrial regions (the Donbass, the Krivoy Rog, and the Black Sea areas), the Ukrainians rejected it, arguing that such exclusion would make the Ukraine completely dependent on the will of the central authorities.[27] On June 10, 1917, the Central Rada issued its First Universal—a manifesto which, while declaring that laws governing the Ukraine specifically were to be made in Kiev, solemnly stated that the Ukraine would not in any form break from the Russian Republic.[28]

The First Universal brought a crisis in the Provisional Government. Several of its members, including Miliukov, resigned over the issue, to the great rejoicing of Lenin and his followers.[29] Commenting in *Pravda* on the Ukrainian demands, Lenin, enthused by the Ukrainian decision not to separate from Russia, wrote that "not a single democrat, to say nothing of a socialist, can decide to reject fullest legality of the Ukrainian demands. Not a single democrat can reject the *right* of the Ukraine for free separation from Russia." He further argued that not rejection, but unconditional acceptance of this right, would preserve the unity and pave the way for a free union between both peoples; as well as a break with the not-too-glorious past in Russo-Ukrainian relations.[30]

Two days later in *Pravda*, Lenin again criticized the irresolute Provisional Government and all the parties it represented. He declared that the rejection of Ukrainian demands, which in his opinion were moderate and properly legal, was "an unheard of shame, wild insolence of counter-revolutionaries, [and] a real expression of the policy of Great Russian *derzhymorda*."[31] To the apologists who tried to justify the government's denial of Ukrainian autonomy, Lenin answered that such a denial was unrealistic, and argued that it was hypocritical to insist on legal guarantees and legal procedures in the Ukrainian problem alone at a time when no one respected, adhered to, or even mentioned legal procedure in other spheres. Common sense, he concluded, dictated that the Russians yield to these demands. "With force you will not keep but only anger the Ukrainians. If you yield to the Ukrainians you will then open up the road to trust between both nations, to their brotherly union as equals." [32] This policy was fully embodied in a resolution of the June, 1917 Conference of the Front and Rear Military Organizations of the RSDRP(b), which declared that "all nations of Russia have the full right to self-determination and independent decision of their fate including full separation [and] that in particular the Ukraine has the full right to realize its autonomy without waiting for a Constituent Assembly." [33]

The importance of these pronouncements cannot be underestimated. Their prime objective was to discredit the incapable Provisional Government. However, they were also directed toward, and fell upon the very receptive ears of, the numerically small and wavering radical Ukrainian intelligentsia. The latter, in view of these developments, began to consider the Bolsheviks the only political group in Russia not opposed to the creation of an independent Ukrainian state, completely overlooking the subtle and hidden centralist features of these pronouncements. In accordance with the Bolshevik pro-Ukrainian stand, and on Lenin's personal orders, Georgii Piatakov, the spokesman for the Bolshevik organization in Kiev, entered the Government of the Ukrainian Central Rada where he pledged that the Bolsheviks were ready to support Ukrainian independence against Russian imperialism and colonialism in the Ukraine; [34] a pledge that was operative as long as the Bolsheviks were not in power.

The relatively easy Bolshevik seizure of power in October, 1917, transferred the national problem from a theoretical sphere into reality. Overnight the national problem, which for several years had been the subject of academic hair-splitting, and of a multitude of proposed solutions, forced itself to the fore, and became the central problem around which began to revolve not only a whole series of events, but also numerous problems (economic, political, social, cultural, etc.). The very same national problem whose existence in the Russian Empire had been questioned, and whose significance had been constantly lowered by the Tsarist as well as the unofficial press, became the focal point around which the future history of Russia was to be written.

CHAPTER II

Theory *versus* Practice

One of the most important repercussions of the Bolshevik *coup d'état* of November 6, 1917, which thus far has received very little attention, was the territorial dismemberment of the Russian state. In some instances this dismemberment was the logical outcome of the disappearance of the legal government of Russia. In others it was a product of the reaction to the *coup*. In still others it was the work of the Bolsheviks themselves, whose leaders, on November 15, 1917, issued in the name of the Russian Republic "The Declaration of the Rights of the Peoples of Russia." This solemn document proclaimed: 1) The equality and the sovereignty of the peoples of Russia; 2) The right of the peoples of Russia to free self-determination, even to the point of separation and formation of independent states; 3) The abolition of any and all national religious privileges and disabilities; and 4) The free development of national minorities and ethnographic groups inhabiting the territory of Russia.[1]

However noble, hopeful, and promising this vague "Declaration of the Rights of the Peoples of Russia" may have been, it remained an empty phrase and a "scrap of paper." This was because, on the one hand, of its sponsors' failure to reject the centralist philosophy, which was an antithesis to the proclaimed principles and, on the other hand, because of Bolshevik imperialism which, under the disguise of "socio-economic unity," decided to crush the seceding states one by one. As far as the Ukraine was concerned, the November 15, 1917 Declaration was, for all practical purposes, inoperative because of the prevalent attitude among the Bolsheviks toward the national problem in general and the Ukrainian problem in particular. "For the majority of our Party members," Mykola Skrypnyk, the acknowledged spokesman for the Ukrainian Bolsheviks, observed in retrospect,

the Ukraine as a national unit did not exist. There was Little Russia, an inseparable part of one unbreakable Russia; something not very clear by its very nature; by its relations with Russia; as well as by its territory and even language. As a last resort a considerable part [of our Party members] recognized the existence of Little Russia, and some even of the Ukraine, but only within the framework of the so-called Western Lands, *i.e.*, Kiev, Volyn, Podolia, and Poltava Gubernias. Kherson, Ekaterinoslav, the Donets and the Krivoy Rog Basins, because of the knowledge of the strength of the working class [there] and its Bolshevik Party, [were considered] a territory beyond the Ukraine. That territory had to be set against the Ukraine.[2]

In addition to these factors, the "Declaration of the Rights of the Peoples of Russia" was inapplicable to Ukrainian conditions, for the Ukraine possessed its own, quite effective self-governing body, the Ukrainian Central Rada. The Rada's responsibility as well as authority, since its organization in March, 1917, had increased continuously in proportion to the decline of power of the Provisional Government. In answer to the Bolshevik *coup d'état* in Petrograd on November 6, 1917, the Ukrainian Central Rada formed a "Committee for the protection of the Revolution in the Ukraine" on the following day. It unequivocally expressed itself against the Bolshevik *coup,* declaring that it was ready to fight with all means at its disposal against any attempts to introduce the rule of the Soviets in the Ukraine.[3] The Bolshevik armed insurrection in Kiev from November 11 to 13, 1917, was accordingly suppressed. As a result the Rada emerged not only more supreme, but, in addition, felt strong enough to refuse recognition of the Bolshevik-sponsored Soviet Government as the federal government of Russia.

It was in accordance with this stand that the Rada, in answer to the vague November 15, 1917 "Declaration of the Rights of the Peoples of Russia," issued its Third Universal on November 19, 1917. Therein, deploring the reign of "anarchy," "chaos,"

"sanguinary civil strife and complete decline" in the regions of
Russia under Bolshevik domination, it declared a Ukrainian People's Republic, "in the name of the establishment of order in our
country [and] in the name of the salvation of all Russia." "Not
separating from the Russian Republic, [and] preserving union with
it, we stand firmly on our land so that we can help all Russia
with our forces so that the whole Russian Republic may become a
federation of free and equal peoples." Assuming full authority and
responsibility over the territory it considered ethnically Ukrainian,[4]
until the convocation of a Ukrainian Constituent Assembly—whose
meeting was set for January 9, 1918—the Rada, acting as the
supreme legislative organ in the Ukraine, abolished without compensation the "property rights on landlord's estates and in other
agricultural land which is not farmed by the labor of its owners,
in monastery, Crown and church land." It decreed an eight hour
working day. It established "state control over production in the
Ukraine, respecting the interests both of the Ukraine and of all
Russia." It pledged itself to a speedy conclusion of peace in full
cooperation with other peoples of Russia, and until such time, it
decreed that all citizens of Russia were to stay firmly at their present posts—be they "in the front or in the rear." It abolished the
death penalty and granted complete amnesty for all political of-
fenders. It also decreed the broadening of the rights of local self-
governing bodies; and reaffirmed the preservation of all liberties
gained by the February, 1917 Revolution, namely, "freedom of
speech, press, faith, assembly, unions, and strikes, immunity of persons and dwellings, the right and possibility of using local language
in relations with all institutions." For all minorities inhabiting the
Ukraine, the Third Universal recognized "the right of national personal autonomy, in order to guarantee them the right and freedom
of self-government in matters of their national life." And finally,
"in the name of the People's Ukrainian Republic, and of Federative Russia," the Rada summoned all citizens "to a decisive struggle
with disorder and destruction and to vigorous great upbuilding of
new state forms, which will give the great and weakened Republic
of Russia health, strength and new power." [5]

This Ukrainian challenge, which one observer labelled as being tantamount to a declaration of war against the Soviet regime,[6] produced no immediate reaction from the Bolsheviks, who, at the time, were extremely busy entrenching themselves in power in Petrograd. As long as the Bolshevik power was militarily weak and politically insecure, relations between Kiev and Petrograd remained in a *status quo*—neither normal nor hostile. When, however, the power of the Bolsheviks began to reach a certain degree of stability, Ukrainian-Soviet relations began to grow rapidly worse and it soon became apparent that a conflict between the two was unavoidable. It became inevitable not only because of opposed ideologies, but also because of the economic and strategic importance of the Ukraine to Russia in particular, and to the success of world revolution in general.

Though territorially small when compared to the rest of Russia, comprising only about 2% of the latter's territory, strategically and economically the Ukraine represented a very vital region of the Russian Empire. Thanks to the possession of the Ukraine, Russia had lengthened her frontiers with the Dual Monarchy; obtained her only territorial link with the Balkans; increased her preponderance on the Black Sea; and furthered her ambitions toward the ever-vital Straits. As an agricultural region, the Ukraine was interchangeably known as the "breadbasket of Europe" and as the "granary of the Empire," providing food for domestic needs and contributing a great share for export. In addition to rich coal, iron, manganese ore, salt, and other mineral deposits, which comprised the basis of Russian industry, the Ukraine possessed a considerable part of Russia's industrial enterprises, and a large portion of the Russian railroad network. In view of these, as well as many other factors, and in spite of their contradicting promises, it became apparent that the Bolsheviks would not tolerate either Ukrainian national aspirations or separation any more than would any other Russian political party or government. Thus, because economically and strategically the Ukraine was extremely vital to the success of world revolution, it became the first victim of Bolshevik aggression, and hence the laboratory for "a noble experiment."

The Ukrainian problem first came under serious consideration by the Soviet of People's Commissars, the Sovnarkom, in the early part of December, 1917, at which time strategy as well as tactics for the seizure of power in the Ukraine was formulated. While re-affirming the Party's stand on the national problem as set forth in the April, 1917 thesis, and at the same time stressing the principles expressed in the November 15, 1917 declaration, the Sovnarkom decided to call in Kiev, in the middle of December, 1917, a congress of representatives of Workers, Soldiers, and Peasant Deputies, with or without the participation of the Rada. It was hoped that, once convened, the Congress would replace the Rada as the supreme organ of power in the Ukraine, thus deciding not only future relations with Russia, but also the extent of Ukrainian territorial ambitions. Accordingly, calls were sent to local organizations of the RSDRP(b) in Kiev, Odessa, Kharkov, Ekaterinoslav and other cities in the Ukraine "to start immediate work on the calling of such a congress." [7]

The task assigned to the un-coordinated groups of the RSDRP (b) in the Ukraine was beyond their capabilities, for as regards their strength, unity, or influence, these organizations had never been outstanding. This can be seen from an observation made by one of their own spokesmen.

Even in 1903, at the first formulation of the Bolshevik and the Menshevik factions at the Second All-Russian [Party] Congress, the South [i.e., the Ukraine], with its organizational dispersion and political indecision, represented the fundamental group of Martov. In 1905, at the Third Party Congress there were represented mainly the metal and the textile [workers] of the North, while the Mensheviks' Conference of 1905 represented Kharkov, Ekaterinoslav, Odessa, and other southern organizations. In 1912, when the Mensheviks . . . were expelled from Party positions, they were able quite easily to preserve their organizations and ideal bases in the main working centers of the South [the Ukraine].[8]

The revolution, aside from allowing these small and uncoordinated groups of the RSDRP(b) in the Ukraine to work openly instead of in the previous secrecy, brought no important changes to their organizational disunity, political indecision and numerical weakness. It has been estimated that shortly before the revolution their total numerical strength consisted of 1,060 members,[9] of whom only a very small number were of Ukrainian origins; the overwhelming majority representing mainly Russian and Jewish city intelligentsia. The membership of these organizations was never permanent, or as Skrypnyk characterized it:

> One of the most negative characteristics of the development of the Bolshevik Party organization in the Ukraine is the absence of permanent Party forces. When you examine now the lists of Party Committees from before the revolution, you will note that almost all of the workers in the Ukraine during the revolution were only temporarily on the territory of the Ukraine. . . . The entire revolutionary struggle of Ukrainian organizations [before the revolution] consisted of the fact that from the lower ranks of the Party there came forward new workers who grew up on the assignment and then directed their sails toward the wide sea of Russian organization, thus failing to form any all-Ukrainian center.[10]

In addition to organizational disunity, political indecision and numerical weakness, local organizations of the RSDRP(b) in the Ukraine, before and after the revolution, were permeated with the feeling of suspicion, jealousy, power ambition, and above all lacked a common policy on the national problem. The Kharkov, Krivoy Rog, the Donets and the Ekaterinoslav Party organizations, whose members subscribed to the idea of extreme centralism and anti-Ukrainian sentiment, considered anything Ukrainian as an "expression of counter-revolutionary chauvinism." Only in the Kiev Party organization did the Ukrainian sentiment receive any consideration,[11] and there only in order to neutralize Ukrainian opposition to Bolshevik rule and to gain badly needed popularity.

In spite of their numerical weakness and disunity, each organization of the RSDRP(b) in the Ukraine tried to claim for itself the exclusive right to speak in the name of the entire "South" before the central organs of the Party in Petrograd. Lenin, quite sus-

picious of the Ukrainians,[12] at least for the time being, welcomed
this disunity since it presented an opportunity for him to exploit
the situation to the fullest extent, play one group of "leaders"
against another, and by means of various compromise tactics bring
them into complete submission.

When on December 15, 1917, the First All-Ukrainian Congress
of Soviets convened in Kiev, the representatives of the RSDRP(b)
displayed a rare demonstration of unity, no doubt under heavy
pressure from Petrograd. Nevertheless, from the first it was apparent that the hopes which the Sovnarkom and the CC of the
RSDRP(b) had placed in the Congress were doomed to failure,
for the Bolshevik faction controlled only from 60 to 80 delegates
among more than 2,000 peasant delegates, the remainder being
firm supporters of the Ukrainian Central Rada. Overwhelming
peasant approval of the policies pursued by the Rada only widened
the gulf between the two groups of delegates, and a firm Ukrainian
peasant decision not to submit to the dictates of nationally and
socially alien elements pointed to the inevitable break. At the Second Session of the Congress, seeing their failure in all attempts to
impose their will on the peasant majority, the Bolshevik delegates
charged the Congress with misrepresentation of the "will of the
masses," and bolted to Kharkov where, together with the self-
appointed spokesmen for the Krivoy Rog and the Donets Soviets,
they declared themselves the "legitimate" and the only power in
the Ukraine, which they proclaimed a Soviet Republic.[13]

The rare unity which the organizations of the RSDRP(b) displayed during the creation of the UkSSR was both short-lived and
incomplete, for the spokesmen of the Ekaterinoslav Party organization, being extremely hostile to the Ukrainian idea, refused to
attend the proclamation ceremony and instead declared a republic
of their own in the early part of January, 1918. The spokesmen
of the Donets and Krivoy Rog Party organizations, though present
at the proclamation, immediately thereafter withdrew their support, joined the Ekaterinoslav group, and formed the Krivdonbass
Republic.[14] As a result of this jealousy and ambition, there were
proclaimed on the territory of the Ukraine between December,

1917 and January, 1918, five Soviet Republics with Kiev, Kharkov, Krivoy Rog, Odessa, and Ekaterinoslav as respective centers of each republic, each acting as a counter to the other. It was not until February, 1919, however, that Lenin abandoned his stand on the territorial division of the Ukraine and ordered Stalin to dissolve the Krivdonbass Republic which had been re-created as a result of the second Bolshevik invasion of the Ukraine in December, 1918.[15]

While these events were taking place, Lenin, then fully aware of the failure to seize power in the Ukraine from within, drafted a "manifesto-ultimatum" to the Ukrainian Government on December 16, 1917. Speaking in the name of the Sovnarkom, this strange document declared on the one hand that it supported "the right to self-determination for all nations which had been oppressed by Tsarism and Great Russian bourgeoisie, including the right of those nations to separate from Russia." In accordance with this stand, the manifesto-ultimatum recognized the Ukrainian People's Republic, "its right to full separation from Russia" or whatever form of relationship with Russia it might choose. It also acknowledged, unconditionally and without limitations, national rights and national independence of the Ukrainian people. On the other hand, however, this strange document charged the Ukrainian Government with pursuing a "two-faced bourgeois policy" concealed behind "nationalistic phrases." It specifically accused the Rada of non-recognition of the Soviets and the Soviet regime in the Ukraine; of disorganization of the front by recalling Ukrainian units; of disarming Soviet troops in the Ukraine; and of "supporting the Kadet-Kaledin conspiracy and uprising against the Soviet Regime," while at the same time *"refusing to let through* [Soviet] *troops against Kaledin."* Labelling these charges an "unprecedented treason to the revolution," the manifesto-ultimatum, speaking for the Sovnarkom and quite clearly contradicting that body's previous stand, declared that as a result of these actions "the Rada would have compelled us, without any hesitation, to declare war on it, even if it were the formally recognized and indisputable organ of supreme state power of the independent bourgeois republic of the Ukraine." In accordance with this war-like spirit, the manifesto-ultimatum demanded from the Rada: 1) A formal promise to abstain from attempts to disorganize the front; 2) An assumption of "the obligation in the future not to permit any military units bound for the Don, the Urals, or for other places, to pass through its territory without the consent of the Supreme Commander-in-Chief"; 3) A pledge "to support the revolutionary troops in their struggle with the counter-revolutionary Kadet-Kaledin uprising"; and 4) A promise "to stop all its attempts to disarm the Soviet regiments and the workers red guards in the Ukraine and to give back immediately arms to those from whom they were taken away." In the event that a satisfactory reply to these demands was not received within forty-eight hours, the Sovnarkom was to consider "the Rada in a state of open war against the Soviet regime in Russia and in the Ukraine." [16]

Because, in the opinion of the Ukrainian Government, Lenin's manifesto-ultimatum lacked both "sincerity" and "logic," the Ukrainian Government in its timely reply categorically repudiated it. It argued that it was impossible "to recognize simultaneously the right of a people to self-determination, including separation, and at the same time to infringe roughly on that right by imposing on the people in question a certain type of government." Pointing to economic and political anarchy created by Soviet rule in the northern regions of Russia, the Ukrainian Government, in its reply, underlined that it did not wish to lead the country along such a path and unequivocally declared that if Bolshevik followers in the Ukraine were dissatisfied with the composition of the Ukrainian Government, they were welcome to leave the country and "go back to Great Russia where their national sentiments will receive the desired satisfaction." Passing from the general to the specific accusations made against it by the Sovnarkom, the Ukrainian Government, in its reply, acknowledged that it had disarmed Soviet bands and promised to continue their disarming in order to prevent the spread of anarchy. As regards the charge of the withdrawal of troops from the front, the Ukrainian reply noted that it was the Sovnarkom which had first ordered the withdrawal of its troops from the front for their utilization elsewhere; therefore, the Ukrainian reply argued, it was foolish to demand that Ukrainians maintain the front with their own forces. With respect to the question of allowing Soviet troops to cross Ukrainian territory, the Ukrainian reply insisted that, like Russia, the Ukraine stood for complete self-determination, and therefore opposed any form of imposition of rule against the will of the people. And finally, concerning the last Soviet demand, the Ukrainian reply, while arguing against a war, stressed that "on the territory of the Ukrainian People's Republic, all power belongs to Ukrainian democracy and therefore any attempt to overthrow that power by force will be met by force." [17]

In addition to its reply, the Ukrainian Government dispatched to Petrograd an additional statement calling upon the Sovnarkom to reconsider its threat of war against the Ukraine by agreeing in principle to the following conditions: 1) To recognize the right of the Ukrainian Republic and to pledge complete non-interference in its internal affairs; 2) To separate Ukrainian military units from Russian units for exclusive employment in the Ukraine; 3) To agree on the payment for food and other resources; 4) Not to interfere with Ukrainian military administration; 5) Not to decide the problem of general peace without Ukrainian participation; and 6) To agree on a federal government for all of Russia with the participation of all socialist parties wherein the Ukraine would receive about 1/3 of the representation.[18]

However wide a base for compromise the Ukrainian reply, and especially its additional note, offered, in the opinion of the Sovnarkom it was unacceptable. Commenting on the Ukrainian conditions, *Pravda,* speaking in the name of the Sovnarkom, stated that while the Ukrainian modified statement represented a noticeable change of the Rada's original stand, it was

> unsatisfactory to the Soviet of People's Commissars because it avoids the fundamental problem on the relations of the Rada toward Kaledin-Kadet counter-revolution. Therefore the Soviet of People's Commissars, while welcoming possible peaceful negotiations with the Rada, considers that these negotiations could be possible only under the condition that the Rada reject uncondi-

tionally and categorically all support of the Kaledin-Kadet threat on the Don.[19]

The Sovnarkom's rejection of the Ukrainian attempt to settle the Ukrainian-Soviet differences, by means other than unconditional acceptance of Soviet conditions, was accompanied by a wave of smearing propaganda against the Ukrainian Government. High Party spokesmen and the Party's official press accused the Ukrainian Government of "selling the Ukraine to counter-revolution" and foreign capital. They not only charged it with initiation of hostilities against Russia; with conspiracy and with treason to socialism; with anti-peace activity; with war-mongering; and all other known "crimes," but they also called for its overthrow and its replacement by Soviet rule. "Only a new Rada, a Rada of the Soviets of the workers, soldiers and peasants of the Ukraine," wrote Stalin at the time, "can protect the interests of the Ukrainian people from the Kaledins and Kornilovs, the landlords and capitalists." [20]

This campaign for total annihilation of the Ukrainian Government was greatly aided and in fact was made possible by the timely-planned establishment of a Soviet Government in Kharkov and the proclamation of a Ukrainian Soviet Socialist Republic on December 24, 1917, to act as a rival to the Rada in gaining control of the Ukraine. On December 22, 1917, two days before the formal proclamation of the UkSSR, *Pravda* extended its greetings to the newly-created republic,[21] while on December 29, 1917, the Sovnarkom officially acknowledged its own creation, the UkSSR, and promised "the brotherly Republic complete and all possible support in its struggle" with the Rada.[22] Accordingly, the Soviet Government severed its relations with the Rada, and ordered its armed forces, and food and requisitioning brigades, which by now were ready for action, to advance against the Ukraine in full force— to move in their first aggression in the expansion of the territorial base of the revolution. The first practical application of the Bolshevik self-determination theory was thus put to a test.

Although the forces under the Rada's command had, on several occasions, demonstrated heroism in their efforts to stop the invaders, they were, because of being outnumbered, inadequately equipped and disorganized by revolutionary ideas, no match for Bolshevik forces which on their southwesterly move had occupied one Ukrainian city after another. On January 10, 1918, Ekaterinoslav was taken; on January 23, Zhmerynka; on January 30, Odessa; on February 4, Nikolaev; and on February 9, after several days of street fighting and bombardment, Kiev was captured, and the Rada was forced to evacuate to Zhytomir.

The critical situation in which the Ukrainian Government found itself as a result of these events, and of which it made no secret, also received much attention from the German Military High Command as well as from the German Foreign Office, whose representatives were at the time engaged in endless arguments with the Bolshevik delegation at Brest-Litovsk. To evaluate properly German anxiety, it is necessary to review briefly some of the causes that led to it.

Ever since the outbreak of the Russian Revolution in March, 1917, and especially following the Bolshevik seizure of power in November, 1917, which was accompanied by the initiation of a policy of "no annexation, no indemnities, and the right of self-determination" if possible, "but peace at any price if necessary," the Germans had very carefully followed the developments in Russia. German military experts, the servants of their profession and tradition, measured these developments in the East not in political but in military terms. They were anxious to conclude any kind of peace settlement in the East in order to concentrate all of their forces in the West.[23] In accordance with this strategy, on December 1, 1917, military operations had ceased all along the Eastern Front, and two weeks later a thirty days' armistice was signed at Brest-Litovsk between Germany and Soviet Russia. On December 22, 1917, the first peace congress of World War I was under way. On the same day, the Ukrainian Secretariat for Foreign Affairs, in a note to all belligerent and neutral countries, expressed its willingness to participate in the peace conference at Brest-Litovsk on the basis of no annexation and no indemnities without the direct consent of the people concerned. With little preparation the Ukrainian delegation arrived at Brest-Litovsk on January 7, 1918, on German invitation.[24]

From the very beginning, the appearance of the Ukrainian delegation at the peace conference was controversial as well as perplexing. For the Austrians, whose internal and external difficulties demanded peace as soon as possible with a minimum loss of territory, the Ukrainians were an annoyance.[25] The Ukrainian demands for Galicia, Bukovina, and Kholm as *conditio sine qua non* outraged the Austrians. Submission of the Austrian representatives to Ukrainian demands would have meant not only an affront to Austria's prestige, but also Austrian recognition of a principle dangerous to the Dual Monarchy—the right of national self-determination. Momentarily, therefore, the Austrians rejected Ukrainian demands and opposed the idea of a separate treaty with the Ukraine. Later, however, the Austrians gave in on this point when they realized that they could obtain the much needed Ukrainian grain only through a separate treaty with the Rada's representatives, who were fully aware of the Austrian plight.[26]

At first, Leon Trotsky, the head of the Soviet delegation, recognized the delegates of the Ukrainian Government as participants in the negotiations and representatives of an independent state. But he reversed himself when he realized the danger of a separate treaty between the Ukraine and the Central Powers. He recognized that such a move might not only force him to sign a separate peace treaty with the Central Powers, but also that it would put both Germany and Austria in a position to obtain food and other vital necessities, thus emasculating the danger of the Allied blockade, as well as causing the loss of Ukrainian resources to Soviet Russia.[27] To prevent this from happening, Trotsky tried unsuccessfully to introduce a Soviet Ukrainian delegation, which was brought to Brest-Litovsk for that purpose, as the "real" government of the Ukraine.

Only the Germans welcomed Ukrainian participation at Brest-Litovsk, for it presented them with not only an additional means of keeping their Austrian partners in check, but also it provided a strong weapon against the Bolsheviks, whose fear of a separate treaty did not escape the notice of the representatives of the Supreme Command.[28] In addition to these considerations of potential usefulness of the Ukrainian delegation, the Germans viewed very seriously the importance to themselves of the Ukrainian economy.[29]

Pressed by these motives, as well as by the prevailing food shortage then being publicized by the German Food Ministry, the representative of the German High Command, General Max Hoffmann, "received the Ukrainians with pleasure." [30] From the very beginning he encouraged them to discuss their plans and "being as able a tactician at the conference board as on the field . . . he gained their confidence and respect." [31] With the consent of Count Ottokar Czernin, the Austro-Hungarian Foreign Minister, Hoffmann opened private negotiations with the Ukrainians, removed the obstacles that separated the Ukrainians and Austrians from a peace settlement, and on his own authority promised the Ukrainians his support.[32]

As a result of these negotiations, which the Bolsheviks were unable to control and which seriously menaced their position, the German High Command achieved a separate treaty with the Ukrainian Republic, which was signed on February 9, 1918. As a result of this treaty the Ukraine was recognized by the Central Powers as an independent Republic. It received the disputed territory of Kholm and also a promise that the Ukrainian provinces of Galicia and Bukovina, which remained with the Austro-Hungarian monarchy, were to receive linguistic rights. In the event the Ukrainian Government failed to fulfill its promises, Austria-Hungary was to be released from her obligations. In return, the Ukraine agreed to place its surplus of foodstuffs and agricultural products at the disposal of the Central Powers. Furthermore, Article VII, Section I, of the treaty provided for the formation of a joint commission which was to meet in Kiev to determine the amount of surplus in the Ukraine, which the Ukrainian delegation had guaranteed to be not less than 1,000,000 tons. Accordingly, then, a supplementary economic treaty was signed on the same day, making thus the Ukrainian Republic a political granary and a storehouse of the Central Powers.[33]

In view of the considerable anti-Russian feeling in Germany, the Germans welcomed the formation of the new Ukrainian state, and more so the *Brotfrieden*. The German press, in particular, expressed great enthusiasm, stressing economic, political, and military importance of the Treaty. Except for the Independent Socialists, who denounced the Treaty, the spokesmen for all German political parties at the Reichstag debates on the Treaty expressed great satisfaction.[34] As far as the German Government was concerned, the Treaty with the Ukraine was of great value. By signing it, Germany not only liquidated partially the danger in the East, but she was likewise breaking the iron ring of the Allied blockade, opening for herself a road Eastward for possible economic exploitation, and was no longer afraid of defeat through starvation.

Bolshevik occupation of the Ukraine greatly endangered these advantages, and above all, the food supplies which Germany had been promised by the Treaty. To save these from destruction and plunder, German military intelligence urged immediate military intervention.[35] Prompted by this advice, inspired by the favorable attitude of the German press and the Reichstag toward the Ukrainian Treaty, as well as antagonized by Bolshevik failure to reach an agreement with Germany, the Supreme Command decided to ignore the ethics of self-determination. On February 16, 1918, it denounced the armistice in the East, which was subject to seven-day notice, and two days later, in the name of humanity, but for the sake of security and conquest, military operations were resumed all along the Eastern Front. This turned the Bolshevik "victorious" march into an inglorious, and disorganized, rout, which finally culminated not only in the complete loss of the Ukraine for the Bolsheviks, but which also led to the signing of the Soviet-German Treaty of Brest-Litovsk. By virtue of this Treaty, in return for the maintenance of a territorial base, the Bolsheviks agreed to all German demands. Under German pressure the Kharkov group was forced to dissolve itself on April 14, 1918, at the Preparatory Conference in Taganrog, transferring its political seat to Moscow. Two weeks later, under German supervision, the moderate Rada too, was dissolved and replaced by the rule of

Hetman Pavlo Skoropadsky. With these changes, most of the achievements of the Great Russian Revolution in the Ukraine disappeared. The triumph of the extreme Left and of the extreme Right took the upper hand.

The first temporary occupation of the Ukraine by the Russian Bolshevik forces from late December, 1917 to March, 1918, aside from providing badly needed food and fuel resources, was very instructive in that, for the first time, it proved in actual test the incompatibility between their nationality theories and practices— a contradiction which continues to the present day.

The contradiction began to show vividly when, to counter the representation of the Ukraine assumed by a few non-Ukrainian members of the RSDRP(b) as well as to attract Ukrainians toward Communism, a group of Ukrainian Social Democrats, under the direction of Vasyl M. Shakhrai and S. Mazlakh, attempted to form, in January, 1918 in Poltava, an independent Ukrainian Communist Party.[36] The brevity of the Bolshevik stay in the Ukraine prevented the realization of this ideal. Though this attempt failed to produce the desired results, its repercussions were felt strongly in the RSDRP(b). The idea of an independent Ukrainian Communist Party was favorably received only by a small pro-Ukrainian group within the RSDRP(b), which believed that such an action might neutralize Ukrainian opposition to Bolshevik rule in the Ukraine. The idea of an independent Ukrainian Communist Party, which could act as a possible competitor for power, drew bitter criticism and denunciation from the Russian centralist faction of the RSDRP(b) in the Ukraine. Its members, aside from labelling everything Ukrainian as an "expression of counter-revolutionary chauvinism," [37] accused the pro-Ukrainian faction of being responsible for the loss of the Ukraine and for all the Bolshevik failures. An open clash between these two views came at the Taganrog Preparatory Conference of the RSDRP(b) in mid-April, 1918, wherein future strategy as well as a new name for the Party in the Ukraine were considered. While, in principle, both groups agreed on vital strategic points, the tension between them over the name of the Party was so great that only the personal intervention of

Lenin prevented a break-up. After bitter debates, a compromise was reached whereby neither a Russian nor a Ukrainian Communist Party was created, but a Communist Party (bolshevik) of the Ukraine—a name which the Party retained until October, 1952. The compromise reached at the Taganrog Conference was officially acknowledged by the CC of the RCP(b) on May 18, 1918, in a special resolution, which recognized the CP(b)U as an independent Communist Party with the right of membership in the Comintern, provided the Ukraine existed as an independent state.[38]

Even this conditional recognition of an independent status of the CP(b)U has never been realized. This is not only because of the centralism of the Party, but also because in the framework of the Soviet system, aside from a vague spirit of cultural independence, the usual attributes of state independence were, according to one Bolshevik theoretician,

> more of a slogan rather than a fact because there could not have been any talk about economic and military independence of Soviet Republics. Such independence did not exist even for a single day, either for Georgia or for the Ukraine. It was absent thanks to the conditions of civil war in which the birth of new republics took place, and which from the beginning needed help from the elder sister, the RSFSR, in order to strengthen themselves. It was absent thanks to the general conditions of the struggle with chaos and capitalist encirclement in which all Republics found themselves.[39]

The problem of the independence of the CP(b)U, its name, and the entire nationality policy received full treatment at the First Congress of the CP(b)U held in Moscow in the early part of July, 1918. The very same arguments and bitterness which had reigned at the Taganrog Conference were re-played in Moscow, and ended only by the personal intervention of Lenin, who as host, in order to bring an end to the seemingly endless arguments, sided on the one hand with the views of the pro-Ukrainian faction, but, on the other hand, staffed the CC of the CP(b)U with the opponents of the Ukrainian idea, and charged them with elaborating and carrying out the nationality policy in the Ukraine.[40] This "compromise" received additional assurances from Skrypnyk, who, at a closed session of the Congress, told the delegates that the RCP(b) would continue to be

> that source wherefrom we all take a lesson of revolution and which we, all the workers and poorer peasants of the Ukraine, have to take, as an example of how to go, and which way to conduct one's struggle . . . Every action we take . . . we should take first of all from the Russian Communist Party . . . I am underlining: in reality the Russian Communist Party with its central organs will be before us and we shall follow and imitate her actions in our construction further and further. Slogans with which we shall go will come from the Russian Communist Party. Formally, . . . our Party will be separated, but this is only a formal side—it has no value for us, the adherents of the revolutionary international . . . Comrades, besides a written constitution there is an unwritten constitution which for us has much more weight, and this constitution says that we are members of the Communist Party. The Russian Communist Party is the leading example which shows us how we should go and fight.[41]

Skrypnyk suggested, and the First Congress of the CP(b)U approved, a resolution, of which point 4, sections *b* and *c* read that "the Communists of the Ukraine in all of their activities are united with the Russian Communist Party (bolshevik) and this unity must remain no matter what the formal side of the Party's organization may be"; and that "Communists of the Ukraine in all of their activities must support the realization . . . of the policy of the Russian Communist Party [and] they must live up to the general decisions of the Central Committee and of the Congresses of the RCP . . ." [42] A few months later, in March, 1919, the VIII Congress of the RCP(b), in its resolution on the organizational problem of the Party, confirmed this action. It recognized the temporary existence of the Ukrainian Soviet Social Republic, but at the same time it rejected categorically any thought that the Party should organize itself along federal lines, forming independent Communist

Parties. Accordingly, the VIII Congress of the RCP(b) decreed that there was a need for the existence of only

> *one* centralized Communist Party with one Central Committee guiding all the work of the Party in all parts of the R.S.F.S.R. All decisions of the RCP and its leading organs are unconditionally binding on all the branches of the Party, irrespective of their national composition. Central Committees of Ukrainian, Latvian, and Lithuanian communists have the rights of *oblast'* committees of the Party and are completely subordinate to the CC of the RCP.[43]

The victory of the centralist faction at the VIII Congress of the RCP(b) relegated the principle of self-determination into the background. This relegation, aside from demonstrating total ignorance and misjudgment of the forces of nationalism, demonstrated quite vividly the cynical opportunism of the Party and its spokesmen in their attitude toward and in their consideration of the national problem. Recognizing the potential force of nationalism, the RCP (b), in its official program, announced that its aim was the continuous utilization of national movements in future revolutionary struggle. To make this utilization more effective, the program of the RCP(b) declared that it was necessary "to abolish all privileges of any national group, to proclaim the fullest equality of all nationalities, and to recognize the rights of *colonies and oppressed nations to political separation.*" For the same purpose, and as a temporary measure toward achieving the unity of nations, the Party program suggested "a federative combination of all states organized on the Soviet basis." [44]

Even greater opportunism than that expressed in the Party's program governed the speeches of many high Party officials. Speaking for a good many Party members, Piatakov maintained that self-determination united more non-workers than workers. He insisted that the Party "ought to reject completely the slogan of the right of nations for self-determination, and also ought to abandon the slogan of self-determination of the toiling masses of every nation, and stand firmly on the road of strict proletarian centralism and proletarian unity." [45] N. Bukharin, reflecting the views of a large segment of Party membership, and with his mind on the strategy of the Comintern, argued that while in the RSFSR (in Russia), the Party could not afford the maintenance of the slogan of self-determination, it would not lose anything by retaining the slogan of self-determination for Hottentots, Bushmen, Negroes, Hindus, etc.[46] A similar stand was taken by Stalin who, even as late as 1920, placed himself on record as favoring

> the secession of India, Arabia, Egypt, Morocco, and other colonies from the Entente, because secession in this case would mean the liberation of those oppressed countries from imperialism, thus undermining the position of imperialism and strengthening the position of revolutions. We are against the separation of the border regions from Russia since separation would here involve imperialist servitude for the border regions, thus undermining the revolutionary power of Russia and strengthening the position of imperialism.[47]

The opportunism of high Party spokesmen, and the confirmation of centralism as the official policy of the Party, found full reflection in the Ukraine, which at the time, was experiencing the second Bolshevik invasion. Drunk with victory, and having abandoned various promises of toleration and equality, Party organizers in the Ukraine, in their composition basically non-Ukrainian and in their sentiment strongly anti-Ukrainian, tried to subordinate completely the national problem in practice to the principle of centralism. Considering anything Ukrainian as reactionary and bourgeois, they attempted with great impatience to destroy everything Ukrainian, or as a resolution of the July, 1926 Plenum of the CC of the CP(b)U expressed it, "In the beginning the Ukrainian Party organization underestimated the significance of the national problem in the revolutionary struggle in the Ukraine, and some comrades even came to the point of rejecting the very existence of the Ukrainian nation." [48]

Thanks to this opportunism and misjudgment as well as to the policy of mass requisitioning of food without appropriate compen-

sation, the second Bolshevik invasion and occupation of the Ukraine
produced a very strong anti-Bolshevik sentiment among the Ukrainians. The resentment expressed itself in numerous un-coordinated,
but extremely bloody, peasant uprisings.[49] "The peasantry in its
mass," wrote the nominal head of the UkSSR, Khristian Rakovsky,
in retrospect,

> considered itself Bolshevik because it saw in us the only party
> which could free it from the landed nobility. But that was as far
> as the co-operation between the proletariat and the peasantry
> went. As soon as the Ukrainian peasants saw themselves freed
> from the *pomeshchiki* they did not want to hear anything about
> communism. Their aim was a *peasant* republic. Soviet laws and
> decrees as well as Soviet rule met opposition from Ukrainian vil-
> lages already in the second half of 1919. A number of peasant
> uprisings made our task difficult . . . Among peasant masses there
> took place some kind of insanity. 'We favor the Bolsheviks,' they
> said, 'but we are against communists.' [50]

Peasant uprisings and the bankruptcy of the Bolshevik national
policy were the most important factors that paved the way for the
hasty retreat of the Bolshevik bands before the advancing forces of
General A. I. Denikin. It was only because of the latter's inability
to comprehend peasant needs and desires—a factor upon which
the Bolsheviks placed their hopes[51]—that Denikin's victory faded
as quickly as it had arisen, proving the Bolshevik gamble a correct
appraisal.

The misjudgment of the Ukrainian national problem and the
underestimation of the forces of the Ukrainian national movement
by the RCP(b), which had led to the Bolshevik fiasco in the
Ukraine in 1919, caused the Ukrainian situation to receive serious
consideration by the CC of the RCP(b), and by Lenin in particular. In December, 1919, he personally drew up a resolution on the
Ukrainian problem which he submitted to, and which was first
approved by, the CC of the RCP(b), and later by the VIII All-
Russian Conference of the RCP(b).[52] The resolution began by
emphasizing that the RCP(b), believing in the principle of self-

determination of nations, maintained "a point of view of recognizing the independence of the UkSSR." At the same time it stressed that the danger of imperialism demanded the closest union among Soviet republics, the forms of which were to be determined by the Ukrainian workers and toiling peasants at some future date. In an attempt to prevent possible repetition of previous blunders by Party members, the resolution obligated "all members of the Party to try to eliminate all barriers in free development of Ukrainian language and culture."

Taking into consideration the century-long Ukrainian oppression which had created nationalistic feelings, the resolution likewise obligated Party members to treat the Ukrainians "with great patience and care, extending toward them a word of kindly explanation of unity of interests of the toiling masses of the Ukraine and of Russia." All Party members on the territory of the UkSSR were to employ in all Soviet institutions the Ukrainian language. They were to study the Ukrainian language, and by every means they were to try to prevent all artificial attempts to reduce the Ukrainian language to a secondary plane, and were to turn it instead into a weapon of Communist education. Soviet institutions were ordered to employ sufficient numbers of persons capable of speaking Ukrainian.

In addition to the problem of the Ukrainian language, the resolution of the CC of the RCP(b) devoted considerable space to the peasant problem and the Party's policy toward the peasantry. It decreed that the peasantry be encouraged to participate in local Soviet organizations and institutions, thus making it possible for the Soviet rule to gain their confidence. The resolution likewise called for the adoption of modified methods, applicable to Ukrainian conditions, in carrying out food collections. These were to be greatly limited in order to remove the prevalent belief that "the aim of Soviet Russia is export of bread and other food produce from the Ukraine to Russia." To strengthen Party ties with the peasants, the resolution called for complete liquidation of private ownership which had been restored by Denikin; the granting of land to the landless; the creation of state farms only in extreme

cases, taking into account the interests of the local peasantry; and
strict avoidance of the use of force in creating peasant communes
and artels.[53]

While being quite liberal toward the Ukrainian culture and
language in general, and while expressing itself favorably toward
the Ukrainian peasantry, the resolution of the CC of the RCP(b)
called for extreme caution toward the Ukrainian city intelligentsia.
It asked for the adoption of measures to bar "the overflowing of
Soviet institutions by elements of Ukrainian city population, alien
in the understanding of conditions of life of the broad peasant
masses, and frequently covering itself with slogans of Communism."
Their participation was to be allowed only on the condition that
they be very carefully screened as regards their qualifications, their
devotion to the interests of the working people, and their willingness
to fight. Those meeting these qualifications were to be placed
"under strict class control of the proletariat."

The importance which the RCP(b) attached to the Ukraine
can be seen from the fact that a few weeks after the resolution of
the CC of the RCP(b) was adopted, Lenin sent a personal appeal
to Ukrainian workers and peasants,[54] wherein he promised them
complete liberation from oppression. Written at the peak of the
Bolshevik campaign against Denikin, Lenin's appeal, in order to
gain Ukrainian support, dealt at length with Ukrainian sovereignty.
He emphasized that the RCP(b) and the Soviet government recognized Ukrainian independence, and declared that it was up to
the Ukrainian workers and peasants to decide the future course of
their state—"Whether to unite the Ukraine with Russia or to leave
the Ukraine an independent and sovereign state, and in the latter
case what federal ties should be established between that republic
and Russia." To make sure that the Ukrainians chose the right
solution, Lenin suggested that, in view of the international scope
of capitalism, the interests of the toilers demanded complete trust
and a close union among the toilers of various countries and of
different nations. "We," he went on, "are opponents of national
animosity, national differences, national peculiarities. We are internationalists. We strive for a close union and complete amalgama-

tion of all workers and peasants of all nations of the world in one world Soviet republic," without national oppression, based on complete trust, on unity, on complete agreement—a union which can be accomplished only with hard work, extreme caution and patience, so as not to arouse suspicion of the masses.

In accordance with these principles, Lenin called upon members of the RCP(b) and of the CP(b)U to exercise extreme caution in the Ukraine. He warned Russian members of the Party to avoid overemphasis of the policy of Russo-Ukrainian unity, to prevent their being accused of Great Russian chauvinism; to be extremely careful in their display of Russian nationalism; and to be considerate in disagreements with Ukrainians "if their differences concerned state independence, its form of union with Russia, and the national problem in general." At the same time Lenin advised Ukrainian members of the CP(b)U to avoid overemphasis of the economic independence of the Ukraine from Russia, in order to prevent their being accused of narrow nationalism. Mutual distrust, Lenin concluded, would always result in unilateral defeats, and to prevent this he called for close unity between the Soviet Ukraine and Soviet Russia, for, as he stated, "if we shall be unable to preserve closer union between ourselves, union against Denikin, union against capitalists, and union against the kulaks of our country and of all countries, then all of our efforts will definitely collapse for many years, because the capitalists will succeed in choking and destroying both the Soviet Ukraine and Soviet Russia."

The resolution of the CC of the RCP(b) and Lenin's appeal to the Ukrainian workers and peasants, though ineffective and inoperative in reality because of their non-rejection of centralism, nevertheless represent important documents in the study of the Russian Bolshevik nationality policy in the Ukraine, for on the basis of their treatment of and approach to the national problem, many future pronouncements were to be made. Lenin's letter, in particular, became an example which was imitated, widely quoted, and variously interpreted. As such it became the source of much controversy. On the basis of this letter, the All-Ukrainian Revolutionary Committee issued a proclamation to the Ukrainian peasantry, wherein it heavily underscored the unity between the Ukrainian peasantry and the Russian workers and peasantry as a prerequisite of continuous victory.[55] On the basis of Lenin's declaration and the resolution of the CC of the RCP(b) of December, 1919, the Sovnarkom of the UkSSR, on September 21, 1920, ordered the Commissariat for Education to work out a plan for introducing the Ukrainian language into all educational institutions. By virtue of this order, study of the Ukrainian language became obligatory in all educational institutions, with Ukrainian as the language of instruction. The State Publishing House was directed to supply a sufficient amount of books in Ukrainian. Every gubernia capital was to have a Ukrainian language newspaper, and state employees who were unable to converse in Ukrainian were to attend evening courses.[56]

Lenin's unity thesis served likewise as a foundation for a resolution on Russo-Ukrainian relations adopted by the V Conference of the CP(b)U in November, 1920, which declared, after heated arguments between the opponents and supporters of centralism,[57] that "a complete separation of these two states [the Ukraine and Russia] is merely an artificial process, in contradiction with the entire past and future struggle of the Ukrainian workers and peasants." The resolution likewise maintained that "complete national separation of the Ukraine will inevitably lead to an internal national struggle within the Ukraine, and to the magnification of the economic demoralization both in the Ukraine and in Russia." [58]

Lenin's call for unity as a prerequisite to the maintenance of victory, and his usage of outside danger as a means of keeping that unity effective, entered very heavily into the thinking of his successor, Stalin, who, even during Lenin's lifetime had completely, but logically, subordinated the national problem to the principle of centralism and world revolution. Writing on the eve of the X Congress of the RCP(b), which adopted important decisions on the nationality policy, Stalin argued that Central Russia—"that hearth of world revolution"—could not "hold out long without the assistance of border regions which abound in raw materials, fuel, and foodstuffs." To utilize successfully these natural resources of the border regions for the cause of world revolution, Stalin held that there was an imperative need for "an intimate and indestructible union" between the center and the periphery. In view of this, he excluded from practical realization the problem of secession, for he maintained that it would run counter not only to the principle of centralism, but also to the interests of the peoples concerned. "The interests of the masses," he declared, "render the demand for secession of the border regions, at the present stage of the revolution, a profoundly counter-revolutionary one."

Stalin tried to argue, however, that his rejection, in practice, of the secession of border regions was not a final word on the subject, for the border states, in his opinion, retained the right to secede. He likewise attempted to demonstrate that the center had not only promised but that it also was supporting national autonomy. He admitted that this autonomy, which was designed to connect the center with the periphery, was intended, and tried, to bring to the masses of the border regions "the material benefits of the revolution"—by abolishing all privileges; by introducing universal education in order to "create spiritual ties"; and by recruiting native population to local administration, courts, economic organizations, etc. These concessions, he said, were far greater than those people had asked for, or even hoped to receive. He insisted that these concessions be accepted by the Party, for without them "the real sovietization of these regions, [and] their conversion into Soviet countries closely bound with Central Russia in one integral state is inconceivable." [59] Thus, Lenin's appeal for unity between Ukrainian workers and peasants in order to remain victorious, became, in Stalin's interpretation, an excuse for one-sided economic exploitation of the border regions which, in return for "material support of the revolution," were to receive political, military, and organizational benefits and protection against outside powers,[60]—an exchange that placed the border regions at the shorter end of the bargain.

Although Stalin's concept of unity, which he re-emphasized in his report to the X Congress of the RCP(b) in March, 1921, was unacceptable to many Party members, some of whom denounced

it because of its grant of concessions to border regions[61] and others
because of its abandonment of previously promised rights,[62] it was
accepted without any major changes as a resolution and became
the official policy of the Party on the national problem.[63] After
citing numerous examples of national oppression, of national prejudice, and of national inequality in the capitalist world, and after
stating that "the bourgeois society has proved to be utterly incapable
of solving the national problem," the resolution declared that "the
victory of the Soviets and the establishment of the proletarian dictatorship are a fundamental condition for abolishing national oppression, establishing national equality, and guaranteeing the rights
of national minorities." The resolution went on to assert that the
solution of the national problem under the Soviet system, and the
creation of Soviet Republics, was "a deadly menace to imperialism." This was not only because these territories broke away from
imperialism to become independent states, thus shrinking the territorial base and source of revenue of capitalism, but also because
by their very existence these republics strengthened the proletarian
dictatorship and also became examples to be imitated and followed
by nations still under the oppression of imperialism. The latter
factor, the resolution pointed out, was the all-responsible cause for
"imperialist" intervention in Soviet affairs in an effort to isolate
Soviet Russia economically. Accordingly, the resolution argued
that "in the present state of international relations [and] in the
conditions of capitalist encirclement, not a single Soviet Republic,
standing alone, can regard itself as insured against economic ex-
haustion and military defeat by world imperialism."

Since none of the Soviet Republics, except the RSFSR,[64] was
in a position to exist as an independent state, reasoned the resolution, they had to unite or perish one by one. The necessity for unity
"as the only means of salvation from imperialist bondage and national oppression," stated the resolution, was demanded by common interests of defense, "the task of restoring the productive
forces destroyed by the war," and the "necessary assistance the
grain-growing Soviet Republics must render those which do not
grow grain." The unity, which was to assume a federal form and

which was to be based on common military and economic interests, was: 1) "to insure the integrity and economic development of each individual republic and of the federation as a whole"; 2) "to embrace all the diversity as regards manner of life, culture, and economic condition of various nations and nationalities," which were at different stages of development; and 3) "to arrange the peaceful coexistence and fraternal co-operation of the nations and nationalities which, in one way or another, have linked their fate with that of the federation."

The Party, as the nucleus of power, was ordered by the resolution to: 1) Help the toiling masses of the non-Great Russian peoples to catch up with Central Russia; 2) Develop and strengthen their Soviet statehood in forms corresponding to the national complexion of these peoples; 3) Set up their courts, administration, economic organizations and organs of power employing the native language and staffed with local people familiar with the manner of life and customs; and 4) Develop their press, schools, theaters, recreation clubs, and cultural and educational institutions in the native tongue. In addition, the Party was to help eliminate the survivals of the past among the non-Russian peoples, and was to draw them into Soviet construction, create among them strong Communist organizations that would be capable of utilizing the experience of Russian workers and peasants in their own construction, and help the national minority groups "to make fullest use of their guaranteed right to free development."

However, the resolution warned Russian Party members, who "did not suffer national oppression," to proceed cautiously in their work, and neither to underrate nor to ignore the importance of specific national features. Above all they were not to vulgarize and "distort the Party's policy on the national question," as such action might lead to "a deviation from Communism to a dominant nation and colonialist outlook, [and] to Great Russian chauvinism." At the same time the resolution warned native Communists neither to overrate nor to confuse the interests of the working people with "national interests" of that nation, since this might lead to "a deviation from Communism towards bourgeois-democratic national-

ism." Though the resolution condemned both these deviations, it
considered that "the deviation towards a dominant-nation, colonialist outlook" represented special danger, and accordingly called
upon the Party members to overcome their prejudice, as only then
would it be possible "to build up in the border regions strong,
genuinely Communist organizations linked with the masses and
founded on internationalism."

The outbreak of the Kronstadt rebellion, which occurred during the meeting of the X Congress of the RCP(b) and for whose
suppression many delegates were dispatched, prevented discussion
of these vague and ambiguous promises of federation and equality
and of the call for unity and centralism, which was justified by the
threat of capitalist encirclement. In the Ukraine, where forces of
centralism had always been strong and where hatred toward
Ukrainian statehood among Party members was extremely great,
vague promises, in themselves of temporary nature, were overlooked and only the centralist features and call for the elimination
of the past were underscored. The prevailing attitude among the
members of the CP(b)U had been formulated by Rakovsky when,
at the end of 1920, he wrote that

> The tendency of Socialist revolution is political and economic
> centralism, provisionally taking the form of international federa-
> tion. Of course, the creation of this federation cannot be effected
> by the stroke of a pen, but is the result of a more or less extended
> process of elimination of particularism, provincialism, democratic
> and national bourgeois prejudices.[65]

In accordance with this philosophy, the years 1919 to 1923 may
be characterized as the years of elimination or absorption of Ukrainian political, economic, trade union and cultural organizations as
independent institutions. Of major significance was the silencing
of the *Borot'bisty,* when, in the early part of 1920, they were absorbed into the CP(b)U. The problem of the *Borot'bisty* is quite
perplexing. Until 1918, they represented the radical wing of the
Ukrainian Socialist Revolutionary Party, which exercised considerable influence over the Ukrainian peasantry. Following the Ger-

man occupation of the Ukraine in 1918, the *Borot'bisty,* finding themselves in disfavor with the authorities, entered into contact with the Russian Bolsheviks, and established themselves as an independent Party. Although they stubbornly held to their own program, especially insisting on the unconditional independence of the Ukraine, they accepted the fundamental points of the Russian Bolsheviks' international program and helped the latter considerably in their second conquest of the Ukraine.[66]

Because of their influence among the peasantry, which was dissatisfied with Bolshevik agrarian policies and practices, the *Borot' bisty* became an important asset to the RCP(b) as well as to its subsidiary, the CP(b)U. At the same time, because of their insistence on the practical application of various theoretical pronouncements on the national problem, they became a constant annoyance to the RCP(b).[67] Since, from Lenin's point of view, it was unfeasible to declare open war on them, thus revealing prematurely the actual policy of centralism, it became his objective to pacify the *Borot'bisty,* by arguing that the differences existing between the Bolsheviks and the *Borot'bisty* could not be the cause for a break between the two. In his appeal to the Ukrainian workers and peasants in December, 1919, Lenin made the following remark on this problem:

> The Borot'bisty differ from the Bolsheviks chiefly in that they stand for the unconditional independence of the Ukraine. The Bolsheviks do not make *of this* an issue of disagreement and disunity; *in this* they do not see any obstacle to united proletarian work. Let there be unity in the struggle against the capitalist yoke and for the dictatorship of the proletariat; over the question of national borders and federal and other ties between the states, Communists must not disagree. Among the Bolsheviks there are advocates of complete independence of the Ukraine, advocates of a more or less federal tie and still others in favor of a complete fusion of the Ukraine with Russia.
>
> These questions should not create insurmountable differences. They will be decided by the All-Ukrainian Congress of Soviets.[68]

Simultaneously, Lenin planned, by absorbing the *Borot'bisty* into the CP(b)U, to utilize their popularity and at the same time to neutralize them politically as rivals. He revealed this plan at the IX Congress of the RCP(b) in March, 1920, when, accused of yielding to the *Borot'bisty,* Lenin replied:

> Comrade [Andrei S.] Bubnov has said here that he is closely associated with the Ukraine, revealing thereby the true identity of his views. He said that the CC [of the RCP(b)] was guilty of strengthening the Borot'bisty. This is a very complicated and important problem and I think that in this significant problem, where maneuvering was needed, and a very complicated [maneuvering at that] we came out the victors. When we spoke in the CC [of the RCP(b)] about maximum concessions to the Borot'bisty, they laughed at [us]; they said that we were not going straight. However, a head-on collision is possible only when the enemy follows a straight line. When, however, the enemy employs zigzags, and not a straight line, then we must follow him and catch [him] at all the zigzags. We promised the Borot'bisty maximum concessions under the condition that they conduct a communist policy. By this we have demonstrated that we have great patience. And that these concessions were made correctly is demonstrated by the fact that all of the better elements of the Borot'bisty have entered into our Party. We have re-registered that Party and, in place of a Borot'bisty uprising, which was inevitable, we have received, thanks to the correct line of the CC [of the RCP(b)], excellently executed by c.[omrade] Rakovsky, that what was the best in the midst of the Borot'bisty who had entered into our Party, under our control, with our consent, and the remainder disappeared from the political scene. This victory is worth two good conflicts [*i.e.,* military victories]. To say, therefore, that the CC [of the RCP(b)] is guilty of strengthening the Borot'bisty, means not to comprehend the political line in the national problem.[69]

The need for the maintenance of an alliance was not a one-sided one, for many of the *Borot'bisty,* seeing that by their own efforts they were in no position to realize their program, were quite willing to take Russian Bolshevik promises at their face value and to join the ruling group in order to become not only leaders but the builders of a new Ukrainian statehood.[70] Their hope vanished as fast as it had arisen, for following the Kronstadt rebellion, only 119 out of about 4,000 members remained in the CP(b)U;[71] the remainder, having been charged with inciting the rebellion,[72] was either expelled from the CP(b)U or transferred to Central Russia. The vacancies were filled by Party officials from Central Russia.

The subtle elimination of the *Borot'bisty* was due, in addition to their connections with the rebellious peasantry, to their stubborn defense of Ukrainian cooperative, trade union, and cultural institutions,[73] wherein many of their members had been employed, and which, in the opinion of the centralist faction of the CP(b)U, had to be eliminated because of their particularism and provincialism. On the Party's orders in 1920, the entire structure of Ukrainian cooperatives, which included the *Dniprosoiuz,* the *Tsentral,* the *Ukrainbank,* and the *Koopstrakh,* was reorganized; subordinated to Party organs, and transferred from Kiev to Kharkov, hence under entirely new personnel supervision.[74] A similar fate met some Ukrainian trade union organizations (cf. the Poltava Society of Workers in Cooperatives, and Ukrainian Teachers' Association) which, following the revolution, had attempted to establish themselves for the first time as independent institutions, for the purpose of protecting Ukrainian workers in cities in which the majority of the population was non-Ukrainian in composition and anti-Ukrainian in sentiment.[75]

However contrary to the announced slogans these centralizing actions may have been, they did not arouse as much popular antagonism as did the Bolshevik attempt to liquidate the Ukrainian schools and cultural organizations, the *Prosvity.* Since February, 1917, these had spread throughout Ukrainian territory, developing enthusiastic and unprecedented cultural activity in the villages by organizing libraries, lectures, theatrical performances, various courses for adults, and by founding Ukrainian primary and secondary schools. Because most of these cultural organizations had begun their activity during the period of the Central Rada, in the eyes of impatient Centralist members of the CP(b)U they had bourgeois connections and had to be liquidated. Thus were destroyed the

Poltava Cultural Union, the Kharkov Cultural Union, the Kiev Society for Schools, and many others.[76] The liquidation of these institutions was justified in the Party's eyes by Article 12 of the program of the RCP(b), which stipulated that the task of the Party was to transform "the schools from an instrument of class domination of the bourgeois into an instrument for the abolition of the class division of society, [and] into an instrument for a Communist regeneration of society."[77] The impatience with which the process of liquidation was carried out greatly antagonized the Ukrainian population, and still further separated it from the ruling group. It also served as another indicator demonstrating the incompatibility between Russian Bolshevik theories and practices.

CHAPTER III

Ukrainization Policy

The impatience which many members of the CP(b)U had demonstrated in their attempt to achieve the Communist state, their overzealousness in liquidating everything Ukrainian in the name of that future Utopia, and their tolerance of almost anything Russian as an expression of proletarian achievement, proved to be a boomerang. Having once experienced the benefits of education in their native language, which before the revolution had been forbidden by law, the Ukrainian peasantry was in no mood to return to its previous status. Accordingly, the forceful imposition in the name of Communism of Russian culture and language on the Ukrainian peasants, as the culture and the language of the proletariat, meant an attempt to turn history backwards. This action exposed Russian Bolshevik intentions in the Ukraine. It likewise revealed in almost total nakedness their complete ignorance of the national problem as well as their misunderstanding of peasant psychology. Finally, it demonstrated once again the total bankruptcy of their nationality policy, which, together with economic difficulties during the reconstruction period, presented a grave crisis for Communism.

The seriousness of the crisis in the Ukraine was vividly exposed by Trotsky at the VII Conference of the CP(b)U in April, 1923, where he spoke as the representative of the CC of the RCP(b). In a lengthy speech, Trotsky expressed surprise that many members of the Party in the Ukraine, as well as in Russia, took the view that the national problem had been solved; and hence that there was no need for its consideration by the Party. "We should recognize," Trotsky declared, that we have not solved the national problem similarly as we have not solved any economic or cultural problem. We have created only revolutionary prerequisites for the solution of the national problem. We have destroyed the Tsarist prison of nations, the prison of nationalities. But it is not enough to proclaim national equality. It is necessary to show to the oppressed in deeds—because he is full of suspicion—that we are with him, that we are behind him, and that we serve his interest not by general phrases but by deeds and work.[1]

While Trotsky agreed with the anti-national groups of the Party that nationalism was not the aim of the RCP(b), he reminded them at the same time not to forget that they lived in a world of reality and facts which they could not overlook. "Our fundamental aim," he stated,

is not the problem of nationalism. Our aim is communism. Social and not the national problem is the foundation upon which we stand. But, neither is the peasant economy our aim; but socialist, centralized production, high technique, etc. Yet, nevertheless, peasant economy is a fact—not a program, not an aim, but a fact . . . [which, because of its numerical force] could turn our entire program upside down. The same thing exists with the national problem. These two problems—the peasant and the national—are closely tied.[2]

Viewing nationalism as a potential force in world revolutionary strategy, Trotsky warned the delegates of the VII Conference of the CP(b)U not to impose the official language of the state—Russian—on the Ukrainian population. He believed that such an act could produce dangerous results, especially because of the numerical weakness of the CP(b)U in the Ukraine. He cautioned Party members not to antagonize the peasantry along national lines, for he considered that peasant dissatisfaction was dangerous in itself, and when colored with national ideology that it was "one hundred times more dangerous." He defined national ideology as "that exploding force which in some cases is revolutionary and in others counter-revolutionary, but in both a powerful, exploding force." Trotsky pleaded with the Conference delegates for moderation, understanding, and patience in dealing with the national problem in the Ukraine, and placed his hopes for solving the national problem on the future Soviet federal system.

Words of warning regarding the national problem in the Ukraine were also sounded by Nicolai N. Popov, a Secretary of the CC of the CP(b)U, in an article published on the opening day of the VII Conference of the CP(b)U. Like Trotsky, Popov associated the national problem with the peasant problem. He argued that because of the peasant numerical strength, their non-Russian origin, and the efforts of the Bolsheviks' enemies, the policy of the CP(b)U should be directed toward the creation of unity between the working class and the peasantry. The realization of this unity, he stated, was very important in the Ukraine, Turkestan and the Caucasus —the non-Russian regions—where "we have been unable up to the present time, in the sixth year of the revolution, in spite of the strengthening of Soviet rule, to suppress political banditism, about which central Moscow gubernias have forgotten a long time ago." [3] Since Popov considered that the national question in the Ukraine was a question of conquering the Ukrainian village by the Party, which in its decisive majority was Russian with respect to language and culture, he condemned those Party members who, for reasons of the Party's "purity," barred peasant membership in the CP(b)U thereby preventing Ukrainian elements in the Party. Popov also assailed those Party members who suggested Russification as a means of conquering the Ukrainian countryside. He likewise attacked those who denied the existence of Ukrainian culture and language, and those who stated that Ukrainian villages needed no Ukrainian schools, newspapers, etc., maintaining that the peasants did not understand the Ukrainian language. Finally, he condemned those who, while agreeing to the existence of the Ukrainian people and culture, tried to limit the Ukrainian idea to villages and prevent its spread into the cities.

These denials, Popov said, meant non-recognition of the strong peasant nationalism, which had been so violent in the Ukraine from 1917 to 1923. They also represented the intentional forcing of the peasantry under the leadership of Ukrainian nationalists. Because of the Ukrainian numerical superiority, Popov argued, Ukrainian culture must, and would, reflect on the city, which was growing at the expense of the village surplus population. He pleaded, therefore, that not the suppression of Ukrainian publications, not the denial of higher schools with Ukrainian as the language of instruction, and not the intentional non-compliance with Party resolutions, but a wide usage of the Ukrainian language and employment of Ukrainian cadres in Party work should be the adopted policy of the CP(b)U. "We shall conquer the Ukrainian peasant," Popov concluded, "only if we are able to transact the Party and the cultural work in the Ukrainian language." [4]

The warnings of Trotsky, Popov, and a few other spokesmen of the Party, sounded at the VII Conference of the CP(b)U in the early part of April, 1923, were a prelude to the re-examination of the entire nationality policy and the warnings issued by the XII Congress of the RCP(b), which met in mid-April, 1923. Many of Trotsky's and Popov's arguments were embodied in a thesis on the national problem which was approved by the CC of the RCP(b) and made public at the end of March, 1923. This lengthy document, which was adopted by the XII Congress of the RCP(b) as a resolution and as its official policy, openly admitted that the Party's doctrines, which had been so ardently proclaimed, were not working. It disclosed that the solution of the national problem which was to have been found in the Soviet multinational state was not developing, and that as a result the Party would attempt to return to its earlier theories and try to carry them out. One observer of Bolshevik affairs, after examining carefully these admissions, came to the conclusion that perhaps "in no other resolution of the communist party or of the soviet organs has the program outlined for the future so well shown existing conditions." [5]

The resolution of the XII Congress of the RCP(b) began by presenting the causes which had led to the formulation of the national problem, and pointed to the "inability," "helplessness," and "impotence," of the bourgeoisie in finding a correct approach to the solution of the national problem. In contrast, the resolution went on, the Bolshevik Party, having recognized the force of the national movement, from the very beginning had based its policy on "the right of nations to self-determination, [and] the right of peoples to independent state existence." Accordingly it had repudiated coercion, recognized "the equality and sovereignty of peoples in determining their destinies," and had taken the stand that "a permanent union of peoples"—the goal of Communism—"can be achieved only on the basis of co-operation and voluntary consent." The adoption of such a policy, the resolution recognized, was greatly responsible for the support and sympathy which the Party had received from oppressed nationalities, before and during the revolution. Without that support, neither the victory nor liberation of the oppressed nationalities would have been possible. It was in this support and co-operation, the resolution asserted, that the proletariat had found "the key to correct solution of the national question," which "had assumed the character of a military, economic, and political union of peoples into a single multinational Soviet state."

However, the resolution went on, finding the key to correct solution to the national problem did not automatically give the solution "concrete and practical shape," for there were many inherited obstacles which had to be surmounted. Thus, rather than the centralized nature of the administrative system, as well as the centralized control of political and economic life, the inherited obstacles became the scapegoat for the improper functioning of the Party's nationality policy.[6] One of the inherited obstacles, the resolution stated, was to be found "in the survivals of a dominant-nation chauvinism," which was a reflection of the former privileged status of the Great Russians. The remnants of this survival were alive in the psychology of many Party and Soviet workers, as well as Party and state institutions. Practical manifestations of this survival, the resolution declared, were evident in "the contemptuous and bureaucratic attitude of the Russian officials toward the needs of the national republics"; in their unfamiliarity with the habits, customs, and local language; in their underrating of the specifically national features and the national language in Party work; and in their arrogant and disdainful attitude towards specific features of the language. A visible manifestation of this survival, the resolution stated, lay in the Great Russians' consideration of the Union Republics "not as a union of equal states, . . . but as a step toward the abolition of republics, *i.e.*, toward the formation of the so-called 'one and indivisible.' " [7]

Another inherited obstacle, the resolution acknowledged, was contained "in the economic and cultural inequality of the nationalities composing the union republics"—an inequality whose roots lay in the history of these peoples as well as in the policy of past governments, which had aimed at converting these border regions "into areas of raw materials exploited by the industrially developed central districts." As a result of past circumstances, these republics and peoples had not yet passed through the stage of capitalism; had no proletariat of their own; had remained backward; were unable fully to utilize their rights and the possibilities afforded them by the revolution. They would be unable, without prolonged economic and political assistance from Central Russia, "to raise themselves to the highest degree of development, and thus place themselves on equal footing with the nationalities which have forged ahead in this respect."

Still another inherited obstacle, according to the resolution, was "the survival of nationalism among a number of nations which had borne the heavy yoke of national oppression and could not forget the feeling of old national grievances." Practical manifestations of this survival were to be found in national aloofness, lack of confidence in measures originating from the Russians, overrating the specifically national features, and underrating the class interests of the proletariat. The resolution condemned both the local nationalism and the Great Russian chauvinism, as well as all other obstacles on the road to realization of "the actual union of peoples into a single state." It called upon the Party members to overcome these inherited obstacles, and to staff local organs of administration "with people from among the local inhabitants who know the language, manner of life, habits and customs of the people concerned." The resolution further recommended the creation of an organ within the Soviet system that would "represent all national republics and national regions without exception, on the basis of equality." It charged the CC of the RCP(b) with: (1) The formation of advanced Marxist study circles among local Party workers of the national republics; (2) The development of literature in the native languages based on Marxist principles; (3) The establishment of a group of instructors recruited from among local Party members; (4) The development of a new Party literature for the masses in the native languages; (5) The increasing of Party educational work in the republics; (6) The intensification and promotion of work among the youth in the republics; (7) The promulgation of special laws that would safeguard the employment of local language in all state institutions; (8) The intensification of educational work in the Red Army in the spirit of brotherly solidarity; and (9) The adoption of practical measures for organization of national military units.[8]

The treatment of the national problem as expounded in the resolution, and Stalin's defense of the views expressed therein,[9]—between which there was very little difference—produced a lively discussion on the national problem during the XII Congress of the RCP(b). The Georgian and the Ukrainian delegations were the most outspoken in their denunciation of the treatment of the national problem. Their resentment was chiefly motivated by Stalin's attempt to compare the danger of Great Russian chauvinism with local nationalism. Speaking for the Ukrainian Bolsheviks, Skrypnyk charged that such a comparison would only encourage the Russians, under the pretext of fighting local nationalism, to intensify their policy of Russification. Accordingly, he bitterly assailed Russian chauvinism, forcible Russification of the Ukrainians, and Russian inability to recognize existing facts or changes that had taken place. To substantiate his arguments, Skrypnyk cited the Red Army as the best example and the strongest instrument of Russification of all nationalities and pointed out that for 60,000 recruits from the Ukraine nothing was being done in the army in the cultural field. He also singled out the Russian treatment of Ukrainians in the RSFSR as another example of Russification. In Siberia, he said, there lived 1,202,000 Ukrainians; in the Kuban, 2,273,000; in the Volga Regions, 2,786,000; and in Central Asia, 654,000. But, he charged, between 1921 and 1923, the Government of the RSFSR had published only two pamphlets in the Ukrainian language for all these people. One of these was a decision of the First Congress of Soviets and the other a collection of songs—a rather impressive testimony to the contradiction between Russian Bolshevik words and deeds. Skrypnyk complained that there was "a very deep-rooted centralist inertia not only in the Soviet apparatus but also in the very heart of the Communist Party." He deplored the fact that there was only theoretical recognition of national equality but that when it came to action, Party members showed "neither will nor force." "Great state fiction," Skrypnyk charged,

> . . . has become instinctive among many comrades. We need only
> to recall how many of our comrades were painfully touched when
> our Congress accepted the name of the Union of Soviet Socialist
> Republics and not Russian Soviet Socialist Republic. They con-
> sidered it an insult to, and a digression from tradition, when some
> argued that the Russian Communist Party should be changed into
> the Communist Party of the Union of Soviet Socialist Republics.[10]

In his opposition to Stalin's treatment of the national problem, Skrypnyk received support from Rakovsky, who warned the proponents of centralism that an improper and hastily improvised solution of the national problem was very dangerous to the Party as well as to the state. "It is one of those affairs," he said, "which —and we might as well say this clearly and honestly—promises us internal war if we do not display sufficient feeling and understanding."[11] Passing from this general observation to specific problems, Rakovsky stated that the two-chambered legislative system for the USSR proposed by Stalin not only failed, in his opinion, to provide safeguards and guarantees for individual republics, but that it strengthened the centralized system which was then in operation. Comparing the two systems, he remarked that the only difference between them lay in the fact that, whereas previously it had 280 out of 360 seats in the Central Executive Committee, under the new system the RSFSR would have 64 to 70 seats as against 16 for the other republics. He reasoned, therefore, that since all autonomous republics of the RSFSR had one central budget, one central administrative system, and were automatically tied with the RSFSR, it was hypocritical to maintain "that in one room of the All-Union Central Executive Committee they would follow one dotted line and then they would go to another room and say that they were independent and separate republics." Rakovsky insisted that if the RSFSR wished "to give an example of liberalism and democratic nationalism" it should create a second legislative chamber in its own Central Executive Committee, but on the Union level should allow only the state entities to be represented.[12]

These and many other criticisms of Stalin's machinations drew a bitter reply from Stalin himself, who, on April 25, 1923, accused his critics of overemphasizing the significance of the national question, of overexaggerating it, and of allowing "it to overshadow the social question; the question of the working-class power." While he expressed agreement that the Party should not offend national minorities, Stalin held that the overemphasis of border regions meant placing the Great Russian proletariat in a position of inequality in relation to the formerly oppressed nations. "It is clear," he said,

> that the political basis of the dictatorship of the proletariat is primarily and chiefly the central, industrial regions, and not the border regions, which are peasant countries. If we exaggerate the importance of the peasant border regions, to the detriment of the proletarian districts, it may result in a crack in the system of the dictatorship of the proletariat. That is dangerous, comrades. We must not exaggerate things in politics, just as we must not underrate them.
>
> It should be borne in mind that in addition to the right of nations to self-determination, there is also the right of the working class to consolidate its power, and the right of self-determination is subordinate to this latter right. There are cases when the right of self-determination conflicts with another—a higher right—the right of the working class that has come to power to consolidate its power. In such cases—this must be said bluntly—the right of

self-determination cannot and must not serve as an obstacle to the
working class in exercising its right to dictatorship. The former
must yield to the latter.[13]

The bitterness over the national problem which prevailed at
the XII Congress of the RCP(b), the clash of personalities, etc.,
was the open beginning of the struggle for power among high Party
officials. Though it seemed that the differences over the national
question could not be reconciled, by the end of the Congress an
outward compromise had been reached and all disagreements ban-
ished. The Congress adopted a resolution, which set before the
CP(b)U the following tasks: 1) Mastering of the Ukrainian language by members of all Party organs in the Ukraine; 2) Studying of socio-political conditions and history of the Ukraine; 3)
Active and organic participation of the Party in the construction
and guidance of Ukrainian culture; 4) Recruiting into active work
of Ukrainian workers and peasants in order to build up Ukrainian
Party cadres; 5) Strengthening of the Ukraine as a state organism
and also strengthening its ties with the entire USSR; 6) Recruiting
of the native population into state and economic construction; and
7) Bringing the state apparatus to the masses by means of appoint-
ing to various posts people "who know the language, conditions,
habits and customs of the local population." [14]

These directives of the XII Congress of the RCP(b) received
further elaboration at the IV Conference of the CC of the RCP(b),
which met in June, 1923, to work out practical measures for im-
plementing the resolution on the national question adopted by the
XII Congress of the RCP(b). Since the Ukraine was recognized
by the participants of the Conference as the second weakest point
of Soviet power—the first being Turkestan—the Ukrainian problem
received thorough treatment. Speaking as the representative of the
CC of the RCP(b), Stalin recognized that the situation in the
Ukraine as regards culture, literacy, etc., was very unsatisfactory
and alarming. The alarm, he said, was due to the fact that, on
the one hand, the state apparatus in the Ukraine was "as remote
from the language and manner of life of the people as it is in

Turkestan [sic]," while on the other hand, the Ukraine was strategically very important and had the same significance for the peoples of the West as Turkestan had for the peoples of the East. The alarm, he continued, was also a result of the fact that the proletariat in Ukrainian industries was not a product of natural development or of local origin, but had been introduced and "artificially implanted from outside"; and hence in its language was non-Ukrainian.[15] As a result of the national differences, the Ukrainian cities exercised very little cultural influence over the Ukrainian countryside; a factor which in Stalin's view hindered very greatly the unity between the non-Ukrainian urban proletariat and the Ukrainian peasantry. In spite of all these difficulties, Stalin argued, unity between the two not only had to be accomplished but also, because of its "enormous significance for the peoples of the West," it was absolutely essential to tranform the Ukraine into a "model republic." [16]

What Stalin and other high party spokesmen failed to mention was their complete ignorance of peasant psychology. They spoke in terms of the *smychka* between the city and the village, between "the higher" and "the lower" cultures, ignoring the fact that these cultural achievements of the city, about which they spoke and endlessly argued, were not only unreachable, but also unintelligible and alien to peasant psychology. For the peasantry, which in the Ukraine formed over 80% of the population, the city was and remained an enemy, the center of political and economic control, full of various traps, full of alien bureaucrats, of unintelligible laws, and the center of intellectual vagrants who sat on the peasants' shoulders.

To transform the Ukraine into a "model" Soviet Republic, and other border regions into Soviet strongholds, the IV Conference of the CC of the RCP(b) in June, 1923, adopted a resolution which directed the Party apparatus: 1) To rear and develop young Communist organizations composed of proletarian and semi-proletarian elements of the local population; 2) To help those organizations stand firmly on their feet; 3) To acquire a real Communist education and to unite the genuinely international Communist cadres, even though they may be few at first; 4) To meet halfway the revolutionary democratic elements, or even those who were simply loyal to the Soviet regime, in order to win the support of the toiling masses of the local population; and 5) Since there were very few local intellectuals in the border regions, who in addition differed in many respects from the intelligentsia of the central regions of Russia, the Party was directed to make all the efforts to "win every one of them to the side of the Soviet regime," in order to strengthen Communist organizations there.[17]

In pursuance of these directives as well as of those of the XII Congress of the RCP(b), the Government of the UkSSR, on August 1, 1923, issued the first Ukrainization decree. It stated that since the fury of war had ended, the government was ready, by means of Ukrainization of the state apparatus, to liquidate the existing inequality between Russian and Ukrainian cultures for the purpose of strengthening the unity between workers and peasants, and to bring "the state apparatus [closer] to the needs, customs, and language of the Ukrainian people." [18] In its preamble, this decree explicitly stated that the elevation of the Ukrainian language to equality with the Russian in no way tended to reduce the significance of the latter. The Russian language was to remain the language obligatory for all state employees, not only as the language of the largest minority group of the Ukraine, but also as the language of the worldly significant Russian culture. The preamble also acknowledged that the previous formal recognition of the equality of languages had proved to be unsatisfactory because of the insufficiently developed Ukrainian schools, culture, lack of equipment, absence of qualified personnel, etc.

Taking all these factors into consideration, the Government of the UkSSR, in its Ukrainization decree, announced several general principles on which Ukrainization was to be based. It decreed that on the territory of the UkSSR all languages were to be equal; that every citizen, irrespective of nationality, had the right to employ his native tongue in his dealings with the government; that the Ukrainian language was to be made the official language of the state; that the Russian language, because of its extensive employ-

ment in cultural and political spheres, was to be made equal with
the Ukrainian; that the government of the UkSSR could employ
either or both languages in its official business; that in all public
meetings every citizen had the right to use his native tongue; and
that in territorial administrative units and cities, the language of
the majority in a given area should be employed; while in places
where no definite majority could be established, the language of
the largest group should be used without violating rights of minority groups.

On the basis of these fundamentals, the Ukrainization decree
stipulated that in the forthcoming year, 1923-24, the following
government institutions were to change their official language from
Russian to Ukrainian: 1) The Administration of Affairs of the All-
Ukrainian Central Executive Committee; 2) The Administration
of Affairs of the Sovnarkom of the UkSSR, both central and local
offices; 3) Peoples' Commissariats for Education; 4) Agriculture;
5) Justice; 6) Internal Affairs; 7) Production; 8) Social Security;
9) Local tax organs of the Commissariat of Finance; 10) Local
organs of the Post and Telegraphs; 11) Regional organs of the
Commissariat of Health; 12) Inspection of Rural Labor; 13) Commissariat of Labor; 14) Military Administration and its district
offices and Regional and Gubernia Military Commissariats. Each
of the above mentioned institutions was to work out its own plan
and system of transition from Russian to Ukrainian language.

The gubernia, the *okrug,* and the *rayon* offices of the above
mentioned branches of administration were to employ in their
official transactions the most widely used language, either Russian
or Ukrainian. The *rayon* offices, in their relations with villages,
were to employ the most widely used language of the *rayon.* In
the inter-Republican and All-Union transactions, the Russian language was to be employed. However, in answering requests of
citizens, central and local organs of administration were to use the
language in which the request had been made. Public documents
emanating from the gubernia and *okrug* offices were to employ the
two most widely used languages, while documents originating in
the *okrug* and *rayon* offices were to be published in Ukrainian and

any other widely used language of the area. A similar procedure was to be followed in all legal acts, and also in the court system.

The Ukrainization decree further stipulated that persons unable to converse in the two languages (Russian and Ukrainian) were to be barred from state employment—except by special permission from either the Commissariat or from the gubernia office concerned, and then only with the understanding that the person entering the state service would learn the second language within six months. The decree obligated those who were already in the state service to learn the second language within a year or be dismissed. In the cases of those dismissed, the decree provided that the person could be re-employed without learning the second language only by special permission from the Sovnarkom of the UkSSR. To make the learning of the Ukrainian language possible, the Commissariat of Education of the UkSSR was ordered to organize at all institutions concerned, three and nine months' courses of instruction in the Ukrainian language.

This was the extent of the basic objectives of the first Ukrainization decree of August 1, 1923, which inaugurated the policy of the same name. From a legal point of view the Ukrainization decree was an absurdity because nationalization of social, political, economic, and cultural activities within the UkSSR was presupposed by its constitution, which had been adopted in March, 1919, and which declared the Ukraine an independent state. Viewed from this perspective, Ukrainization could scarcely deserve the characterization of being a "bold stroke of statesmanship on the part of the ruling Communist Party." [19] It would be perhaps more appropriate to describe Ukrainization as a grave crisis of Bolshevism and above all as a vivid demonstration of the total bankruptcy of the Bolshevik nationality theories.

That it was a grave crisis can be seen from various appraisals and definitions of Ukrainization given by highly responsible spokesmen of the CP(b)U. Speaking at the Third Session of the All-Ukrainian Central Executive Committee in 1926, Lazar Kaganovich, at the time the General Secretary of the CP(b)U, in answer to various charges that the Ukrainization policy was a submission to alien and non-proletarian elements, declared that, while Ukrainization was not desired by the Communist Party, it could not be labelled a submission to anyone. It had, he said, been called forth by the interests of the revolution and by the interests of the construction of socialism, and only those interests guided the Party in the matter of Ukrainization. "For us, Communists," Kaganovich declared, "Ukrainization represents one of the fundamental links, one of the fundamental means of the construction of socialism; that is why we conduct and will continue to conduct Ukrainization." [20]

Skrypnyk, a long time advocate and an ardent supporter of the Ukrainization policy considered it as a prerequisite of socialist construction. Speaking at the June, 1927 Plenum of the CC of the CP(b)U, he stated that Ukrainization was not only the means for the narrowing of gaps between the workers and the peasantry, but that it also was *"the method of guiding the entire Ukrainian cultural process and one of the prerequisites of socialist construction."* To narrow Ukrainization down to the simple mechanical meaning of the *"smychka,"* Skrypnyk argued, meant complete misunderstanding of the role of the Party and that of the proletariat; hence it also represented a nationalist deviation.[21] Identical views were expressed by Skrypnyk's long-time friend, E. F. Hirchak, who in his polemic with the opponents of Ukrainization, argued that Ukrainization was "neither a decoration, nor a diplomatic play nor a joke," but a means of strengthening the alliance between the working class and the peasantry. He called it "a mighty weapon of socialist construction of Soviet Ukrainian culture"; "a weapon of cultural revolution in the Ukraine"; and "a very serious policy dictated by the interests of the ruling proletariat of our country, by the interests of the construction of socialism, [and] by the conditions of the struggle with the class enemy." [22]

S. V. Kosior, for a number of years the First Secretary of the CC of the CP(b)U, speaking at the XIV Conference of the Kiev *okrug* Party organization on December 20, 1928, argued that Ukrainization was one of the component elements and one of the mightiest means of socialist construction, and not simply a narrow isolated task. Since the Party of the working class, Kosior reasoned, was the builder and the organizer of the Ukrainian state, the Party was responsible for the entire socialist construction of the Ukraine including cultural construction. It was therefore the duty of the Party to elevate culturally the masses of the Ukrainian workers and peasants in order to introduce them practically into socialist construction.[23]

Almost identical arguments were used by V. P. Zatonskyj, a long-time member of the CC of the CP(b)U and for a number of years the Commissar for Education of the UkSSR. Speaking at the May, 1926 Plenum of the CC of the Ukrainian Comsomol, Zatonskyj argued that to build socialism, especially with the peasantry, command in itself was not enough. He maintained that it was necessary to penetrate into the peasant soul; that it was necessary to understand him in order that he might understand the worker. In this process, Zatonskyj stated, it was imperative that Ukrainian culture, which had some peasant, some bourgeois, and some proletarian heritage, be utilized in order to become a "proletarian weapon, and not simply a weapon for directing, for naked directing, for command of the proletariat over the peasantry. That would be madness [and] harm to the revolution—but through the elevation of [Ukrainian] culture, [we could] give the Ukrainians a possibility, the proletarians as well as the peasants, to comprehend faster in their native tongue Leninism, so that we could build up socialism without unnecessary difficulties."[24]

Popov, a long-time advocate of a realistic and practical approach to the national problem, putting aside all the vagueness and ambiguity so characteristic of all the pronouncements on, and definitions of, Ukrainization, expressed the meaning of Ukrainization in these simple but very striking words:

As far as we are concerned Ukrainization never was and is not an end in itself. It is only a method for establishing a contact with the Ukrainian masses. Without this, the Party cannot operate. The principal function of Ukrainization is to draw the Ukrainian masses into the orbit of Communist influences. The organic development of the Ukrainian movement has its own course, and if this is not taken into consideration the position of the Soviet Government and of Communism in general may become dangerous indeed. Not knowing the Ukrainian language, Party cadres must remain outside Ukrainian national development. This is the source of the weakness of the Communist Party on the Ukrainian ideological front. This leads to the strengthening of dangerous elements. Herein lies the danger.[25]

It becomes quite obvious from these and many other pronouncements that the movement which became known as Ukrainization was an anti-Bolshevik movement. Some high Party spokesmen, having realized the potential force, as well as danger, but being unable to crush it by force, resorted to the application of a "liberal" and "soft" policy in order to divert this strong anti-Bolshevik movement in the Ukraine along such lines as would in the end produce favorable results for the Party.

In the field of education, Ukrainization meant a considerable increase of schools, both elementary and secondary as well as higher institutions of learning, with Ukrainian as the language of instruction. In many cases these increases are striking in view of the fact that from 1919 to 1923 Ukrainian schools had been on the downward trend. Thus, for example, according to data released by the People's Commissariat for Education of the UkSSR, in the Kharkov Gubernia alone, the number of elementary schools declined from 1,907 in 1920 to 1,296 in 1923.[26] The situation in the Donets Gubernia was not much better, where, it was reported, elementary Ukrainian schools in 1922-3 formed only 0.35% of the total, at a time when the population of the Gubernia was more than half Ukrainian.[27] Thanks to the adoption of the Ukrainization policy, as well as general improvement under the NEP, the situation improved greatly. According to Zatonskyj, the number of elementary schools in the UkSSR rose from 16,004 with 1,575,538 pupils and 46,717 teachers in 1923-4, to 20,032 schools, 2,529,936 pupils and 74,383 teachers in 1928-9.[28] A school census in December of 1927, conducted by the Commissariat for Education of the UkSSR, placed the national composition of 2,380,698 pupils of elementary schools in the Ukraine in 1927 at the following: Ukrainians: 1,828,025, or 77%; Russians: 241,858, or 10.1%; Germans: 39,194, or 1.6%; Jews: 173,537, or 7.3%; Poles: 47,640, or 2%; Moldavians: 17,245, or 0.7%; and others 33,184, or 1.3% [sic].[29] In 1928, the distribution of 19,620 elementary schools in the Ukraine, according to the language of instruction represented the following: Ukrainian: 16,172, or 82.4%; Russian: 1,314, or 6.7%; German: 574, or 2.9%; Jewish: 469, or 2.4%; Polish: 325, or 1.7%; Moldavian: 113, or 0.6%; and others, 653 or 3.3%.[30]

In addition to changes in the elementary education, Ukrainization greatly influenced higher institutions of learning. According to an official statement, there were in the Ukraine in 1922-3, only 8 of the total of 41 Institutes, 32 of 160 Technicums, and 13 of 466 Professional Schools, wherein the language of instruction was Ukrainian.[31] In 1923-4, the first year of Ukrainization, the number of Institutes using the Ukrainian language for instruction rose to 10, Technicums to 53, and Professional Schools to 193.[32] Between 1925 and 1929, the distribution of the Institutes and of the Technicums according to the language of instruction was as follows:[33]

INSTITUTES

Language of Instruction	1925		1927		1928		1929	
	Number of Schools	Number of Students	Number of Schools	Number of Students	Number of Schools	Number of Students	Number of Schools	Number of Students
Ukrainian ..	6	3,512	9	3,983	11	6,218	14	11,197
Russian	8	7,639	3	3,512	1	1,822	2	3,442
Jewish	—	—	—	—	—	—	—	—
Ukrainian-Russian	21	16,054	25	20,712	24	22,675	19	18,727
Russian-Ukrainian	—	—	—	—	—	—	4	3,186
Others	—	—	—	—	2	2,691	3	4,338
Total ..	35	27,205	37	28,207	38	33,406	42	40,890

TECHNICUMS

Language of Instruction	1925		1927		1928		1929	
	Number of Schools	Number of Students	Number of Schools	Number of Students	Number of Schools	Number of Students	Number of Schools	Number of Students
Ukrainian ..	43	6,438	50	9,475	46	10,100	52	13,979
Russian	30	5,583	31	5,572	18	3,072	9	1,211
Jewish	5	557	3	454	3	588	2	300
Ukrainian-Russian	63	12,595	32	6,193	34	8,114	25	5,876
Russian-Ukrainian	–	–	24	6,779	20	4,419	15	4,316
Others	4	458	6	846	5	603	4	661
Total ..	145	25,631	146	29,319	126	26,896	107	26,343

From the above table it becomes quite clear that increases in
the number of Ukrainian schools meant corresponding decreases
in Russian schools. The change in favor of the Ukrainians would
have perhaps been greater, had it not been for the lack of teaching
personnel, which, because of revolutionary circumstances, as well
as numerous other causes, was basically non-Ukrainian (Russian,
Jewish, Polish, German). Percentage-wise, the national composition of teaching personnel at various institutions of higher learning
presented, at the times indicated, the following picture:[34]

	Ukrainians	Russians	Jews	Others
City Trade Schools, Dec. 15, 1927	59.1	20.1	13.7	7.1
Village Trade Schools, Dec. 15, 1927	84.1	6.3	2.7	6.9
Professional Schools, Dec. 1, 1925	54.8	25.2	14.9	5.1
Technicums, Dec. 1, 1925	43.7	36.7	13.3	6.3
Institutes, Dec. 1, 1925	35.5	40.8	19.5	4.2

The most important single factor, which influenced the increase
of institutions of higher learning with Ukrainian as the language

of instruction, was the increase of Ukrainian attendance at those institutions. According to official data, as of June 24, 1923, there were in the Ukraine 39,002 students in the institutions of higher learning. Of those, Russians comprised 39.3%; Jews 27.5%; Ukrainians 25.2%; and others 8%.[35] The distribution of this student body according to profession was quite different. In the industrial-technical education, for example, the Ukrainians comprised 1,108, or 15.5% of the total of 7,154 students; in agricultural education, 1,696, or 49% of 3,461; in pedagogy, 3,121, or 32% of 9,754; in medicine, 3,070, or 22.9% of 13,407; in socioeconomic studies, 412, or 10.6% of 3,887; and in art, 253, or 18.9% of 1,339.[36]

As time went on, the Ukrainian attendance increased in all institutions of higher learning. In the Institutes and in the Technicums, for example, the national composition of the student body presented the following picture for the years 1925-9.[37]

INSTITUTES

Year	Ukrainians	Russians	Jews	Poles	Germans	Others
1925	45.1	20.3	34.4	0.5	0.2	0.5 [sic]
1927	51.8	18.7	25.7	0.6	0.6	1.6 [sic]
1928	53.5	16.6	25.0	0.7	0.7	3.5
1929	56.1	15.8	23.3	2.0	1.5	1.3

TECHNICUMS

Year	Ukrainians	Russians	Jews	Poles	Germans	Others
1925	57.9	18.2	20.1	1.3	1.0	1.5
1927	58.0	15.3	21.2	1.5	1.1	2.9
1928	61.5	14.7	18.1	1.7	1.1	2.9
1929	66.2	13.4	14.3	1.5	1.4	3.2

In 1929, when the student body in the Institutes was 40,890 (of whom 22,939 were Ukrainians, 6,461 Russians, 9,527 Jews, and 1,963 others), and in the Technicums 26,778 (of whom 17,727 were Ukrainians, 3,588 Russians, 3,829 Jews, and 1,634 others), its national composition along the lines of specialization, presented the following picture:[38]

Institutes	Ukrainians	Russians	Jews	Poles	Germans	Others
Agricultural	73.6	11.7	7.6	3.1	2.1	1.9
Industrial-Technical	40.2	27.5	26.4	2.7	1.9	1.3
Socio-Economic	51.0	12.5	33.6	1.2	0.9	0.8
Medical	45.8	15.6	34.3	2.3	1.2	0.8
Pedagogy	64.9	10.3	21.0	1.2	1.5	1.1
Art	46.9	20.5	28.9	1.2	0.9	1.6
Technicums						
Agricultural	83.1	4.3	7.7	2.0	0.6	2.3
Industrial-Technical	46.5	24.4	24.2	1.4	1.2	2.3
Construction	25.9	24.7	46.6	0.8	0.4	1.6
Transport	55.4	34.8	5.2	0.9	0.8	2.9
Socio-Economic	54.7	33.1	8.3	—	0.6	3.3
Medical	37.9	14.0	45.1	0.3	0.6	2.1
Pedagogy	80.4	14.5	7.5	1.8	1.9	3.9 [sic]
Art	36.4	24.6	32.3	0.4	1.8	4.5

This table shows that attendance of Ukrainians in the Institutes and the Technicums, while growing and quite impressive, was channeled or limited to agricultural and pedagogical schools; that of Russians to industrial-technical, socio-economic, and construction fields; and that of Jews to medical, construction, and socio-economic institutions. A similar distribution can be found also in professional schools:[39]

	Ukrainians	Russians	Jews	Poles	Germans	Belorussians	Moldavians	Bulgarians	Greeks	Czechs	Tatars	Others
Agric.	82.6	6.2	6.0	2.0	1.3	0.1	0.2	0.4	1.1	—	—	0.1
Ind-Tech.	56.4	13.0	27.2	1.4	1.0	0.3	0.1	0.1	0.3	—	—	0.2
Manuf. ..	63.1	10.1	25.1	0.5	0.2	0.1	0.1	—	0.7	—	—	0.1
Constr. ..	56.3	17.0	24.4	0.5	0.7	0.3	0.1	0.1	0.4	0.1	—	0.1
Transp. ..	74.2	20.7	1.8	1.3	0.2	1.4	0.2	—	—	—	—	0.2
Socio-Ec.	61.4	11.8	25.1	0.9	0.3	0.2	—	0.1	0.1	—	—	0.1
Medicine	57.4	13.9	24.8	0.9	1.9	0.3	—	0.1	0.4	—	0.2	0.1
Art	39.9	16.9	40.3	1.6	0.5	0.2	—	0.1	0.1	—	—	0.4
Average	65.1	11.1	20.2	1.4	0.9	0.2	0.1	0.2	0.6	0.0	0.0	0.2

The increased attendance of Ukrainians in the institutions of higher learning during the Ukranization period was also due to the policy of the Commissariat for Education of the UkSSR which, in many instances, made possible lectures in Ukrainian by inviting Ukrainian scholars from abroad for permanent or temporary periods. As a rule, the visiting scholars insisted on such a policy as one of the conditions for their services. This can be seen from a statement made by the well known Ukrainian historian, Professor M. Hrushevskyj, upon his return to the Ukraine in March, 1924. "The news of my return to the Ukraine," he said, "interested the Ukrainian emigration and the majority of it viewed my desire [to return] sympathetically. I think that this majority will follow very carefully the achievements of Ukrainization as well as the results of my scientific and cultural work. The achievement in this work will strengthen the growing tendency among the emigrants to return to the fatherland to work in cultural and economic fields." [40]

Alongside Ukrainization of schools went Ukrainization of periodicals and newspapers, and an increase in the publication of Ukrainian books. The scope of this process will be appreciated far better if we keep in mind that before the inauguration of Ukrainization, except for the *Visti VUTsVK,* almost all of the Ukrainian newspapers had suspended publication,[41] while in some cities Ukrainian titles were used to cover up the publication of Russian newspapers.[42] In the publication of books—from the quantitative rather than qualitative standpoint—the output as well as the ratio of Ukrainian books published in the UkSSR from 1917 to 1928, presents the following picture:[43]

Years	Ukr. percent of Total	Ukrainian	Russian	Others	Total
1917	54.4%	747	452	174	1,373
1918	64.4	1,084	386	56	1,526
1919	47.0	665	726	23	1,414
1920	53.1	457	369	34	860
1921	32.0	214	448	5	667
1922	29.3	385	927	—	1,312
1923-4	31.0	855	1,848	54	2,757
1924-5	40.2	1,813	2,535	160	4,508
1925-6	45.8	2,162	2,365	199	4,726
1926-7	48.6	2,445	2,427	156	5,028
1927-8	53.9	2,920	2,232	261	5,413

The above table indicates that with Ukrainization the volume of printed matter in Ukrainian began to increase steadily. According to one official Soviet spokesman, in 1924 alone, the total circulation of Ukrainian periodicals rose from 72,000 issues to 205,000. During the same period Russian periodical literature increased its circulation from 505,000 to 720,000.[44] There were instances, however, where the increase of Ukrainian printed matter brought a corresponding decline in Russian publications, especially newspapers. According to one report, between April 1, 1925 and April 1, 1927, the number of Ukrainian newspapers rose from 29 to 55, while that of Russian newspapers, during the same period, declined from 39 to 24.[45] Another report, made by the Trade Union Statistical Office of the UkSSR, arrived at the following conclusion on the circulation of Ukrainian and Russian newspapers as of January 1, 1927.[46]

District	Nat'l Comp. of Workers & Empl. in Percentage		Ukrainian Newspapers		Russian Newspapers	
	Ukrainian	Russian	Absolute No.	In %	Absolute No.	In %
Artemovsk	54.7	26.2	5,771	12.0	40,949	86.8
Dniepropetrovsk	46.3	34.9	16,512	21.6	58,965	77.3
Zaporozhie	56.6	24.7	6,631	38.7	10,006	58.4
Kiev	49.4	24.0	56,099	50.2	50,203	44.9
Krivoy Rog	64.0	30.2	6,991	64.5	3,575	32.9
Lugansk	38.0	55.9	3,588	10.5	30,547	89.0
Mariupol	41.9	40.8	2,619	16.0	9,911	70.0
Odessa	23.0	40.0	6,689	10.3	56,329	87.1
Stalino	29.5	62.7	3,796	7.3	48,304	92.3
Kharkov	47.5	34.4	30,851	21.4	112,905	78.0

By the end of 1928, newspaper circulation in the Ukraine had reached 1,100,000 issues, of which 56% was in Ukrainian.[47]

The Ukrainization period, and above all the economic recovery which the NEP brought in its wake, left a very heavy imprint on the cities of the Ukraine. The invasion of industrial centers by surplus village population, slowly but systematically, began to change the national composition of the working class in favor of Ukrainians, a process which, under normal conditions, sooner or later had to take place. The working force in the Ukraine increased from 252,000 in 1922-23 to 356,100 in 1924-25, to 574,800 in 1926-27.[48] In 1928-29, when the total working force of the Ukraine reached 1,071,856, the Ukrainians comprised 54.64%; the Russians 29.17%; the Jews 8.69%; and others 7.5%.[49] The significance of these changes lies in the fact that prior to the Ukrainization period, the industrial proletariat of the Ukraine, in its decisive majority, was composed of non-Ukrainian elements. Only among the railroad workers, especially in the territories on the Right Bank of the Dnepr River, and among the workers in industries connected with agriculture, were there to be found any sizeable influences of Ukrainian elements.[50] By 1929, however, official statistics re-

vealed the national composition of workers in the various industries
of the Ukraine to be as follows:[51]

	Agriculture	Factories	Crafts	Railroads
Ukrainians	81.33%	42.90%	41.53%	70.00%
Russians	9.57	41.02	13.59	23.53
Jews	1.06	7.89	38.42	1.10
Others	8.04	8.19	6.46	5.37

In addition to this natural process of changing the balance
of city proletariat in favor of Ukrainians, the government of the
UkSSR tried to accelerate it by artificial means. Some of
the non-Ukrainians, chiefly Jews, were removed from the cities
where they represented decisive majorities, to the countryside,
thereby weakening their influence in the cities, and at the same
time making their voice in the countryside almost nil. The transfer
of Jewish population from the cities to the countryside began in
1924, following official approval of such a policy by the Third
Session of the All-Ukrainian Central Executive Committee on October 11, 1924. On October 21, 1924, the Jews were granted 30,000
desiatins of land to accommodate about 3,000 families in the Odessa
and Ekaterinoslav Gubernias.[52] During 1924 and 1925, the Jews
received a total of 117,200 *desiatins* of land and by January 1,
1927, their farm population numbered 107,500.[53]

Thus, by virtue of natural processes and artifical manipulation
by the government, the national composition of the working force
in the cities of the Ukraine began to change in favor of Ukrainians.
Though the effects of this change became more vivid among the
rank-and-file workers, they also found some reflection in the Trade
Union, and the Comsomol as well as in the membership of the
Party. According to official reports, between April 1, 1922 and
January 10,1927, the membership of the CP(b)U rose from 54,818
members (of whom 27,490, or 53.6% were Russians; 11,920, or
23.3% Ukrainians; 6,981, or 13.6% Jews; 1,241, or 2.6% Poles;
and 3,604, or 7.1% others) [sic][54] to 168,087 members (of whom
the Ukrainians formed 87,185, or 52%; the Russians 46,156, or
27.5%; and other nationalities 34,746, or 20.5%).[55]

By virtue of all of these changes, the numerical strength of non-Ukrainians among workers and among Party members declined. This decline, however, did not affect key positions in the CP(b)U or the government of the UkSSR. The higher the post and the greater the power and authority, the less one could find Ukrainian personnel. Thus for example, as of January 1, 1924, there were in the Ukraine 27,628,000 people, of whom the Ukrainians formed 76.4%; the Russians 10.5%; the Jews 7.8%; the Germans 1.9%; and others 3.4%.[56] During the same period, a computation based on 463 persons representing the highest posts within the Party and the government revealed that the Russians had 44.7% of representation; the Jews 25.5%; the Ukrainians 20.9%; and others 8.9%. Thus, it has been said, a minority of 23.6% of the total population exercised 79.1% of the power.[57]

Ukrainian representation in the Soviet hierarchy was almost identical to that mentioned above. In 1924-5, for example, village soviets of the UkSSR numbered 240,947 members, of whom 211,503, or 87.8% were Ukrainians; among the 8,793 members of the *rayispolkoms* the Ukrainians had 6,955, or 79.1%; and among the 12,327 delegates to district soviets the Ukrainians had 9,457, or 76.8%.[58] At the IX All-Ukrainian Congress of Soviets in 1925, among 838 delegates the Ukrainians had 472, or 56.4%; the Russians 197, or 23.5%; the Jews 90, or 10.8%; the Poles 19, or 2.3%; and others 60, or 7%.[59] In the Central Executive Committee, which governed the country between sessions of the Congress of Soviets, Ukrainians were represented by 194 members, or 55.9%;[60] Russians by 96, or 27.4%; Jews by 21, or 6.03%; Germans by 3, or 0.8%; Poles by 9, or 2.6%; Moldavians by 9, or 2.6%; Belorussians by 5, or 1.4%; and Lithuanians by 5, or 1.4%. Among the People's Commissars (usually numbering 14 to 15), the Ukrainians had 1, or 2 members, or 1.2 to 1.8%.[61]

With only minute changes this ratio remained after the administrative reorganization of the Ukraine in the mid-1920's. Thus, for example, in the 1927 election to 10,518 village soviets in the Ukraine, peasants received 85.1% representation; workers 3.8%; service people (*sluzhashchie*) 10.0%; Red Army personnel 0.2%;

artisans 0.7%; and others 0.2%.[62] The percentage of peasants in the *rayon* soviets was 64.2%; that of workers 10.1%; and that of service people 23.2%.[63] Figures on the national composition for village or *rayon* soviets are unavailable. They are supplied, however, for the *okrug* soviets, which in 1927 had 69.8% Ukrainian representation.[64] At the X All-Ukrainian Congress of Soviets in 1927, the Ukrainians formed 60.3%; the Russians 22.6%; the Jews 8.6%; the Poles 2.9%; the Belorussians 1.5%; the Germans 1.3%; and the Moldavians 1.0%. Of those elected, 62% were for the first time; 13% for the second; 7.2% for the third time; and 0.8% had participated in all previous congresses.[65]

These changes, *i.e.*, the increase of Ukrainian participation in administering local affairs, greatly alarmed the non-Ukrainian officialdom in the Ukraine. Both the Party as well as the non-Party personnel, of the Right and of the Left orientation, as a ruling minority, feared the approaching end of its privileged position and monopoly of power in the Ukraine. Weak numerically, but spread throughout the Ukraine in key administrative posts, the non-Ukrainian officialdom had held, from the beginning, that Ukrainization meant yielding to peasant demands; hence that a higher culture was forced to yield to a lower one. "To place before oneself the task of *actively Ukrainizing the Party,* and also the working class," wrote D. Z. Lebed', a Secretary of the CC of the CP(b)U, "(and the Party cannot undertake this task without transferring this work on the working class), *will be a reactionary undertaking for the interests of the cultural movement.* To nationalize, that is, to impose artificially the Ukrainian language on the Party and on the working class with the present political, economic, and cultural relationship between the village and the city, would mean to place oneself at the point of view of *the lower culture of the village* as compared with the higher culture of the city." [66] Accordingly, the anti-Ukrainian elements within the CP(b)U insisted that, in place of Ukrainization, the Party undertake Russification and expel the peasants from its midst in order to achieve class purity.[67]

As the results of Ukrainization became more and more apparent, the anti-Ukrainian officialdom became more and more alarmed. It began to charge that Ukrainization had gone too far; that it had become too dangerous; and that instead of building up one common culture—proletarian—it had fostered Ukrainian nationalism. Speaking for the Left, V. A. Vaganian, who formulated his ideas in a book entitled *O natsionalnoi kulture,* argued that the task of communism excluded the existence of other national cultures within the USSR. These cultures, he stated, had to be replaced by Russian culture which, in his opinion, was the foremost and the most acceptable to all peoples. Since, in Vaganian's view, Russian culture had proletarian, revolutionary, and international features, he tried to deny the existence of local cultures and demanded their merger with Russian culture and acceptance of Russian language.[68]

Another spokesman of the anti-Ukrainization trend in the Ukraine, Iu. Larin, opposed Ukrainization on the grounds that it violated the rights of other national minorities in the Ukraine. These, he stated, formed about 25% of the total population, the percentage in the cities being somewhat higher.[69] Larin became especially bitter when on October 17, 1926, the People's Commissariat for Education of the UkSSR announced that 87.8% of the schools were Ukrainized. This, argued Larin, meant that almost half the non-Ukrainians were forced to use the Ukrainian language and were deprived of their native tongue.[70] He conceded that government officials, who served the people, should know the language of the people. But he opposed the government's orders which tended to force non-Ukrainians to use either Ukrainian or their own native tongue, denying them thereby the possibility of using the Russian language in their daily transactions with the government. To Larin, such Ukrainization was "Hebrewization," a policy which he violently opposed.[71]

Larin's opposition to Ukrainization, under the pretext that it violated the rights of national minorities, seems somewhat farfetched when one examines the possibilities and achievements other minorities were officially offered during this period. According to an official Ukrainian publication, in 1927, the non-Ukrainians comprised 5,757,729, or 18.9% of the total population of the UkSSR, of whom 9.2% were Russians; 5.8% Jews; 1.6% Poles; 1.3% Germans; and others less than 1%.[72] As of April 1, 1925, these minorities had 232 village soviets. By April 1, 1926, that number had risen to 648, and by April 1, 1927, it had increased to 872.[73] It was reported that between 1925 and 1927, the minority court system had increased its benches from 9 to 88.[74] A favorable and impressive report was likewise made concerning the minority school network, which, excluding Professional Schools and national departments at various Technicums, in 1925-6, totalled 1,500 schools with 4,000 teachers and 140,000 pupils.[75] In 1926-7, the number of non-Ukrainian schools rose to 2,600, with 357,591 pupils, and in the following year it was officially revealed that the number had increased to 2,948 schools with 393,000 pupils.[76]

These impressive figures, as well as the achievements of the entire policy of Ukrainization, might have been far greater had it not been for passive resistance to Ukrainization on the part of the anti-Ukrainian officialdom. Their distribution in key administrative positions was greatly responsible for the improper functioning of Ukrainization. The non-functioning of Ukrainization, along the lines which had been envisaged by the Party, forced the CC of the CP(b)U to reconsider some of the causes and obstacles that had prevented "the strengthening of the proletarian dictatorship and an alliance between the proletariat and the peasantry," in the Ukraine.[77] The result of this reconsideration was a lengthy resolution of the April, 1925 Plenum of the CC of the CP(b)U, in which past mistakes were explicitly acknowledged and future plans, which became the basis for the continuance of Ukrainization, were drawn.

This resolution reaffirmed the principles set forth in the decisions of the XII Congress of the RCP(b) in 1923. It stressed that the practical realization of these decisions would not only give the possibility for the proletariat and the Party to exercise their guidance over cultural and social life in the Ukraine, but would likewise serve as a very good weapon in the struggle with national chauvinism. The realization of the fundamental principles of the national policy in the Ukraine, the resolution went on, was easier than in other republics because the Ukraine 1) had some cadres of industrial proletariat of its own who had come from the peasantry; therefore were acquainted with village conditions and needs; 2) the CP(b)U itself had some Ukrainian cadres, while, in the Comsomol, Ukrainian membership comprised more than half; and 3) the Ukrainian language was closer to Russian than were the languages of other nationalities, and thus could be easily learned by Russian workers.

The resolution acknowledged that Ukrainization during the past two years (1923-5) had made some progress in the soviet and school apparatus on lower levels. It likewise acknowledged that the Ukrainization of the Party and Trade Union apparatus, as well as of over-all Soviet life had "met difficulties and in places passive opposition on the part of workers and members of the Party." This the resolution tried to justify by blaming Ukrainian nationalism, and especially its long stand against Bolshevism in the Ukraine. Resentment against everything Ukrainian, the resolution charged, prevented Party members from learning the Ukrainian language; hence from making the Ukrainian language a "weapon of Cummunist influence on peasant masses."

This resentment, the resolution stated, was a tragic thing, since economic improvement of peasant conditions under the NEP had increased their political interests as well as the interests of Ukrainian village intelligentsia—a process which was taking an independent road without proletarian participation or guidance. The Party, the resolution continued, had made a mistake by centering its attention exclusively on the Ukrainization of the Soviet apparatus alone. Such a process threatened a break between Party and Soviet apparatus—the more so since non-proletarian elements were to be found in the Soviet apparatus. It was necessary, therefore, that the Party use the Ukrainian language in presenting Ukrainian history and Marxian theory to the Ukrainian people so that these could be properly understood. Should this necessity be disregarded, the resolution warned, Ukrainian youth would be forced to rely upon the Ukrainian bourgeois interpretation of its past. Accordingly, the resolution called upon Party members to learn the Ukrainian language and to abandon their passiveness toward Ukrainization, in order to make possible the realization of the Party's nationality policy, thereby strengthening the proletarian dictatorship. "The Party," stated the resolution, "as the guide of the Ukrainian Soviet Republic, ought to explain to the working masses that Ukrainization is not and cannot be only an affair of Ukrainian workers, but that it is a task of the entire working class of the Ukraine."

To live up to this task, the resolution of the Plenum of the CC of the CP(b)U suggested the following actions to the Party: 1) Ukrainization of intra-Party work and a more active participation by the Party in the Ukrainian cultural process; 2) Selection, education, and placement of Ukrainian cadres from among Ukrainian peasants; 3) Organization of Party schools for *okrug* Party workers; 4) Learning of the Ukrainian language by all Party workers; 5) Translation into Ukrainian of important works; 6) Issuing of a Ukrainian Party organ (*i.e.*, publishing the theoretical Party magazine, *Kommunist* (Kharkov)), in Ukrainian; 7) Translating all decisions of the CC of the VKP(b) into Ukrainian; 8) Conducting in Ukrainian the business of the CC of the CP(b)U, as well as of all lower organs, by January 1, 1926; 9) Preparing all Party correspondence and official circulars in Ukrainian; 10) Transferring instruction in Party schools to the Ukrainian language; and 11) Stressing the importance of Ukrainization in the industrial areas of the Ukraine. The Politburo of the CC of the CP(b)U was directed to work out forms and methods of Ukrainization. All these actions were likewise to apply to the Comsomol and to the Pioneer organizations in the Ukraine.

For the Trade Union, this resolution of the April, 1925 Plenum of the CC of the CP(b)U proposed an intensified drive among its workers to study the Ukrainian language, and the issuing of a Trade Union organ as well as the publication of books in the Ukrainian language, in order to meet the growing demands. For Soviet institutions, the resolution proposed Ukrainization of the apparatus by January 1, 1926; changing the instruction in higher educational institutions to the Ukrainian language; and preparing future teach-

ers of Ukrainian. For the Red Army, the resolution decreed the
changing of its organ, *Krasnaia Armiia,* into the Ukrainian *Krasnaia Rota;* Ukrainizing some of its commanding personnel; and
supplying literature in Ukrainian. Finally, the resolution pleaded
with the CC of the VKP(b) to transfer Ukrainian officers from
other regions into the Ukraine.

In accordance with these instructions, the All-Ukrainian Central
Executive Committee and the Sovnarkom of the UkSSR, on May
20, 1925, issued the second Ukrainization decree, wherein they
acknowledged that the Ukrainization decree of August 1, 1923, was
working unsatisfactorily.[78] The May 20, 1925 decree placed the
blame for the improper functioning of Ukrainization on: 1) Difficult conditions which had been inherited from the past; 2) The
superiority of Russian culture over Ukrainian; 3) Lack of money;
4) The absence of cultural workers; 5) The disinterestedness of
Soviet workers toward the study of the Ukrainian language; and
6) Insufficient recruitment of Ukrainian elements into the Soviet
apparatus. The decree called upon all Soviet, Trade Union, and
public institutions and organizations to do their utmost in solving
the tasks set forth in the August 1, 1923 decree. It also provided
that all state institutions and state industrial enterprises should, by
January 1, 1926, transfer the conduct of their business into the
Ukrainian language. It likewise stipulated, in this respect departing from the August 1, 1923 decree, that All-Union economic organizations in their dealings with Ukrainian institutions should
employ the Ukrainian language.

The May 20, 1925 decree placed the responsibility for realization of Ukrainization of state institutions directly on the leadership
of the institutions concerned—a noted departure from the first
Ukrainization decree. The May 20, 1925 decree stipulated that
by January 1, 1926, all acts of a legal nature, advertising signs, etc.,
were to be in the Ukrainian language, or in Ukrainian and Russian,
or in Ukrainian and the language of a given minority. The Commissariat for Education of the UkSSR was asked to provide places
for the study of the Ukrainian language, an increase of books in
Ukrainian, distribution of Ukrainian literature, and general super-

vision over the Ukrainization process. It was also requested to try, in cooperation with the Ukrainian Academy of Sciences and the State Publishing Office, to issue a dictionary of the Ukrainian language, and a terminological dictionary as well.

The second Ukrainization decree ordered all central government institutions to establish Ukrainian clubs and libraries within their institutions for the purpose of Ukrainizing their personnel. Each institution was likewise to have a Commission for Ukrainization Affairs which was to be responsible for: 1) Condition and progress of Ukrainization; 2) Close supervision of Ukrainization; and 3) Power over the personnel as well as the management in accepting new employees who did not possess knowledge of the Ukrainian language. Ukrainization commissions were also to be established at the gubernia and the *okrug* institutions, as well as at the Sovnarkom of the UkSSR. These commissions were to be organized under the chairmanship of the respective heads of the central executive committees, and were charged with the guidance of the Ukrainization process under their jurisdiction. The organs of the People's Commissariat of the Workers and Peasant Inspection were charged with periodic examination of the progress of Ukrainization of the Soviet apparatus; checking on the recruitment of new personnel; testing the personnel's knowledge of the Ukrainian language; determining the personnel's attitude toward Ukrainization; and in unsatisfactory cases possessing the right to demand the dismissal of employees. The same rules and regulations which governed the Ukrainization process were also prescribed by the May 20, 1925 decree for the process of nationalization of other minorities in the Ukraine.

By virtue of the second Ukrainization decree the Ukrainian language was recognized as the official language of the UkSSR. However, this recognition was short-lived, thanks to the ill-fated last provision of the decree, which provided the anti-Ukrainian forces with an important legal loophole for their open sabotage of Ukrainization under the pretext that it violated the rights of other nationalities in the Ukraine. As time went on, the opposition along this point to Ukrainization became louder and louder, and the antagonism between the opposing groups greater and greater; each side accusing the other of violating the law.[79] The irreconcilability between the pro and anti-Ukrainian forces, in turn prevented the proper functioning, as well as the realization, of the tasks set forth in the Ukrainization decree.

Under the pretext that Ukrainization violated the rights of other national minorities, the anti-Ukrainization forces within the CP(b) U succeeded, at the April, 1927 Plenum of the CC of the CP(b)U, in forcing the adoption of a resolution, by virtue of which the Russian language regained its former position in the Ukraine. The resolution tried to justify this action by arguing that the Russian language was not only the language of the largest minority group in the Ukraine, but also that it was the language of the Russian proletariat; hence it had to receive special consideration and become the language of education as well as of government decrees alongside the Ukrainian language. The resolution likewise accused the pro-Ukrainian groups of violating the rights of other nationalities in the Ukraine, and accordingly stipulated that they be given complete protection by being served in either Russian or their own native language. As the national minorities in the Ukraine did not live in a compact mass, but were scattered throughout the territory of the UkSSR, the effect of this resolution was that the Russian language became the obligatory language in all institutions, enterprises, and schools throughout the Ukraine.[80]

The resolution of the April, 1927 Plenum of the CC of the CP(b)U, therefore, serves as an important mark in the official attitude of the CP(b)U as well as of the VKP(b) toward Ukrainization. It represented the abandonment of the old policy of cultural Ukrainization, which had been the source of constant troubles.[81] It also served as the first of a series of official acts intended to bring complete uniformity into every aspect of the Soviet system as a prerequisite to the forthcoming era of integral planning.

CHAPTER IV

National Deviations

In spite, or perhaps because, of its adherence to the philosophy of total regimentation of life, the history of the Bolshevik movement is filled with numerous deviations to the Right and to the Left in search of better ways and means for reaching the promised Utopia. The decade from 1920 to 1930, in particular, produced many suggestions, ready-made solutions and revolts against the unfulfilled promises. Since some of these revolts had strong undertones of national feeling or support behind them, they came to represent national deviations. In the Ukraine, among such deviations belong Khvylovism, Shumskyism and Volobuevism.

KHVYLOVISM

Khvylovism, from the name of its exponent, Mykola Khvylovyj, was one of the most important deviations within the CP(b)U against policies and practices of the Russian Bolsheviks in the Ukraine. The significance of Khvylovism lies not so much in its scope, though this will be dealt with later, but in its establishing of a precedent for other "deviations" to take place, and above all in its courage in exposing in total nakedness the incompatibility between the Russian Bolshevik theories and practices. However, to evaluate Khvylovism properly, it is necessary first to examine the personality of Khvylovyj himself.

Mykola Khvylovyj, real name Mykola Fitilov, was born in 1891. His father belonged to petty nobility; his mother was a school teacher in a village in the Kharkov Gubernia. Since the father left the family, Mykola and three other children were brought up by his mother, under whose aegis Khvylovyj received his education. As a student he was said to be quite capable, but extremely nervous, with inclinations toward rebellion on the one hand and fantasy on the other. Khvylovyj's rebellious and insubordinate personality was responsible for his dismissal from the 6th class of Gymnasium at Akhtyr. Upon his return home, he began hard work in the local *Prosvita* group, taking an active part in various theatrical performances, studying Ukrainian folklore, etc. In 1916, Khvylovyj was called into the Russian army. Army life, with all of its harshness, made a strong impression on him—impression which he described in numerous letters home. This was the beginning of Khvylovyj's literary activity.[1]

In 1917, Khvylovyj returned home. In the chaos of the revolution, his previous non-submissive and restless personality became cynically rebellious. In 1918, he opposed the rule of Skoropadsky; while in early 1919, he is reported to have joined peasant uprisings in the Ukraine against the second Bolshevik occupation of the Ukraine. The occupation of the Ukraine by General Denikin's forces in 1919 was the turning point in Khvylovyj's revolutionary development. Late in 1919, seeing the victory on the Bolshevik side, he joined the CP(b)U, and for a while was a political commissar in the Ukrainian Communist Army, from which post he was later transferred to the *CHEKA*.[1a]

His acquaintance with Russian Bolshevik propaganda and some of its literature, made while a political commissar, and especially the fanatical falling of his intellectually immature mind for the world revolutionary idea, internationalism and a vision of a universal Communist state, had a very strong and lasting effect on Khvylovyj. Accordingly, the abandonment of War Communism, the adoption of the NEP in 1921, and hence the relegation of world revolutionary concepts into the very distant future, and above all the incompatibility of Russian Bolshevik reality with their theories, was for Khvylovyj a great disappointment and disillusionment. For a while, he tried to utilize his restless energy in numerous activities—in literary organizations which he helped to establish, especially in the *VAPLITE* (the All-Ukrainian

Academy of Proletarian Literature). Then he was engulfed in conducting endless theoretical discussions among various groups on such problems as qualifications of writers; the understanding of the role and the significance of art; literary style and form; the problem of cultural revival; the place and significance of various literary schools in Ukrainian literature, etc. However, consideration of these problems only opened up new problems of wider scope and far more significance, such as the orientation of Ukrainian culture; Ukrainization of the proletariat; the role of Ukrainian intelligentsia in Ukrainian cultural construction; the theory of the struggle of two cultures; the problem of Ukrainian independence; Ukrainian relationship with Russia; etc.[2]

These arguments took a distinctive form and turn following Lenin's death in 1924. The bitter intra-Party struggle which Lenin's death created, the mysterious content of Lenin's testament, the appearance of "Left" and "Right" deviations, the search for the best ways to achieve Communism, etc., were also transferred in full force into the Ukraine, and into the CP(b)U, which for several years had been the scene of bitter strife between the adherents of Ukrainian National Communism and Russian Bolshevism. It was only natural that Khvylovyj, as a member of the CP(b)U, sooner or later would be drawn into this bitter struggle. The date came sooner than expected. Early in 1925, Khvylovyj, with the support of other Ukrainian Communists, began to publish a weekly pamphlet, *Kultura i Pobut,* as a supplement to the central newspaper *Visti VUTsVK.* Basing his arguments on the reality of life under the Russian Bolshevik rule on the one hand, and on the other hand on their theory and propaganda, Khvylovyj, in numerous articles which were later republished in book form—*Quo Vadis?* (1925); *Thoughts Against Currents* (1926); and *The Sociological Equivalent* (1927)—greatly deplored the fact that the Party did not break more completely with the Russian past, and especially with Russian literature which, in his opinion, was permeated with great-state chauvinism, messianism and pessimism. Comparing the prevailing opinion of his own surroundings with Vissarion Belinsky's article on Fonvizin, in which the former had expressed the opinion that

among all peoples the Russians were the only rightful heirs to the
world, Khvylovyj stated that "in the same spirit thinks the contemporary great-state [Russian] intellectual, and no matter how
much we shout that this view is old and does not express the demands of the present day, Moscow's messianism will live in the
minds of Moscow's intelligentsia, because even today the same
Belinsky is resurrected and studied." [3] Khvylovyj maintained that
Russian literature was "passive-pessimistic" with a tendency to educate "the cadres of 'superfluous' people, frankly speaking, parasites,
'dreamers,' people 'without definite occupation,' [and] 'sorrowful.' "
That literature had, in his opinion, "reached its limits and stopped
at the crossroads," hence it could neither be followed nor imitated.[4]
He deplored the Party's inability or unwillingness to break more
completely with the past in destroying Russian messianism, while
at the same time doing nothing for the new republics. Khvylovyj
argued that since theoretically the Ukraine was as independent as
Russia, it had the right, as an independent state, to pursue whatever literary trend it desired. However, he made it clear that
Ukrainian literature

> *ought never to follow Russian.* This is final and without any res-
> ervations. We cannot mix our political union with the literary.
> From Russian literature and from its style Ukrainian poetry should
> depart as fast as possible. The reason is that Russian literature
> has dominated us for centuries as the master of the situation and
> has turned our psychology to slavish imitations. Consequently, to
> let it influence our young art would mean to stop its development.
> We know the ideas of the proletariat without Moscow's art. More-
> over, we, as representaives of a young nation will grasp these ideas
> much faster and will faster produce necessary reflections. Our
> orientation must be toward West European art, its style, and its
> examples.[5]

At another place, Khvylovyj expressed his fundamental thoughts,
which later became the essence of his deviation, in these words:

> The ideas of the proletariat we all know without the guidance of
> Moscow. Only the young Ukrainian nation—the Ukrainian pro-

letariat and its communist intelligentsia—are the true bearers of
the great revolutionary socialist ideas and they must not orient
themselves on the centre of All-Union Philistinism: on the
Moscow sirens. They need to orient themselves on themselves and
Europe, but not on the Europe of Spengler, which is declining
and which we all hate, but on the Europe of great civilizations—
the Europe of Goethe, Darwin, Byron, Newton, Marx, etc.[6]

Khvylovyj's rebellion against Moscow, his favorable appraisal
of Europe, his attempt to interpret Marxism, his insistence on seeing the theory being put into practice, etc., caused considerable
excitement in the CP(b)U as well as in the VKP(b). The excitement ran higher when Khvylovyj's demands and theories as well
as his anti-Moscow stand were picked up and applauded by the
Ukrainian national press outside the UkSSR, since many of his
views coincided with their accepted ideas. It drew sharp, though
not public, criticism from Stalin, who was then reaching for the
heights of the Party's leadership. "Khvylovyj's demand," Stalin
wrote to Kaganovich, on April 26, 1926,

> to derussify the proletariat in the Ukraine immediately, his opin-
> ion that 'Ukrainian poetry must get away from Russian literature
> and its style as quickly as possible,' his assertion that 'the ideas of
> the proletariat are known to us without Moscow's art,' his en-
> thusiasm for a sort of Messianic role of the 'young' Ukrainian
> intelligentsia and his ludicrous and non-Marxist attempt to di-
> vorce culture from politics—all this and much like it, in the mouth
> of a Ukrainian Communist sounds more than strange. Whereas
> the proletarians of Western Europe and their Communist parties
> are full of sympathy for 'Moscow,' the citadel of the international
> revolutionary movement and of Leninism; whereas the proletarians
> of Western Europe turn with joy toward the banner waving over
> Moscow; the Ukrainian Communist Khvylovyj has nothing better
> to say for 'Moscow' than to appeal to Ukrainian public men to
> get away from 'Moscow as quickly as possible!' And this is called
> internationalism! What can we say of other Ukrainian intellectu-
> als, not belonging to the Communist camp, if Communists begin
> to talk in our Soviet press, in the language of Comrade Khvylovy?[7]

Khvylovyj's "Away from Moscow" concept was likewise bitterly denounced at the June, 1926 Plenum of the CC of the CP(b)U. In a resolution it stated that such "slogans may, under the conditions of the NEP, only serve the growing Ukrainian petty bourgeoisie which understands the resurrection of a nation as a bourgeois restoration, and under the orientation toward Europe it comprehends the inclination towards capitalist Europe and a separation from Moscow, the capital of the USSR, and the citadel of international revolution." [8] The July, 1927 Plenum of the CC of the CP(b)U, in its declaration to the Central Executive Committee of the Comintern, also denounced Khvylovism for its direct playing into

the hands of the forces hostile to the Soviet Ukraine. In the entire capitalist world at the present time there goes on a heated agitation against the USSR, 'against Moscow,' and everything possible is being done to inculcate the belief in the working masses of the capitalist states that in the USSR there is no socialism; that the Bolsheviks continue to conduct the imperialist foreign policy of the Tsars; that inside the country they are oppressing the non-Russian nationalities; that the entire Bolshevik national policy is an empty phrase, a deceit; that similarly as Bolshevik Moscow 'had subjugated' the Ukraine and Georgia it wants today to subjugate China. The slogan 'Away from Moscow,' in the international working movement, is the slogan of the Second International, is the slogan of Amsterdamites and of those ultra-left communists who took up the weapon of bourgeoisie and of social democracy . . . [It is evident that] the line of Ukrainian deviationists (even though their number is small) tries to discredit our Party and our national policy. They actually only pour water on the water wheel of national chauvinists the world over, and in the entire USSR; they help to spread doubts toward the VKP, the Comintern and the Leninist slogans about the solution of the national problem among the subjugated nationalities of the entire world.[9]

The opposition to, and the denunciation of Khvylovyj, and Khvylovism, by the pro-Russian members of the CP(b)U, their censuring of him, their open accusation of him for his "misunderstanding of the role of the proletariat in socialist revolution" and "in the national cultural construction," [10] as well as their forcing from him a formal letter of apology and self-accusation,[11] only increased Khvylovyj's cynical criticism of the leadership of the CP(b)U, as well as of the VKP(b), for their opportunism and for their abandonment of internationalist ideas and slogans. "Cannot the revolutionary slogans of today," he wrote in 1927, "become reactionary tomorrow? Do we not have many examples of it? And vice-versa: Did not slogans of a certain year, 1917, become pharisaic and material for speculation?" [12]

Khvylovyj's bitter attack on Russian Bolshevik opportunism reached a climax in 1927, in his description of a typical Party member.

> Here is the same Russian intelligent-internationalist, who willingly talks about the self-determination of nations . . . though not of those which form the Soviet Union; who sees throughout [the Ukraine] Petliurism but cannot see his own Ustrialovism; who even today thinks that Ukrainian culture exists . . . as an Austrian intrigue; who, by pointing out to Europe the achievements of the Russian genius, leads into the arena as an interesting 'Zoo' other peoples of the Union who have been harmed by Russian Tsarism. In other words, he is the same internationalist who, behind his cosmopolitanism, preserves his own zoological nationalism.[13]

This stubborn anti-Russian stand created among some Ukrainian nationalist writers a tendency to eulogize Khvylovyj as a national hero and as a convinced nationalist.[14] This is far from reality, for a closer examination of Khvylovyj's writings and his activity shows that he was, and to the very end of his life, which he himself ended, remained a convinced revolutionary internationalist—greatly disillusioned to be sure.[15] Khvylovyj's anti-Russianism was not a product of his nationalism, but of his internationalism. As an undeviating believer in world revolution, Khvylovyj despised the advocates of Russian supremacy, of alleged Russian hegemony of language, literature, culture, etc., then quite prevalent in the circles of the CP(b)U. In such advocacy he saw the re-establishment of the very same Russian colonialism against which war and revolution had been waged. As an orthodox member of the CP(b)U, Khvylovyj was alarmed by the Party's inability and unwillingness to prevent the spread of these dangerous views. He believed this would in the end result in a clash between the Russian and the Ukrainian, and between the Russian and other colonial peoples who, having once experienced independent status, would never succumb to their former subjugated position and to their former colonial status. "Ukrainian society," Khvylovyj wrote,

> once strengthened, will never agree with its actual, if not *de jure* decreed hegemon, the Russian competitor. Consequently, one cannot go far with empty phrases. Our task is to prevent this conflict. In other words: we ought to side immediately with the active young Ukrainian society which represents not only the peasant but also the workman, and thus we should end once and for all the counter-revolutionary idea of building up Russian culture in the Ukraine. All the talk about the equality of languages is nothing but a concealed desire to cultivate that which will never be resurrected. In other words, we ourselves, make barriers in socialist construction. We must reject this as soon as possible. By doing so we will accelerate within the Ukrainian society a complete ideological break toward our side.[16]

Khvylovyj's advocacy of the Party's taking a decisive stand, not only in theory but also in practice, brought upon him severe criticism for his attempt to make the Party "nationalistic," and for his inability to comprehend the theoretical significance of the October Revolution which, by placing into power the dictatorship of the proletariat, made "impossible" any struggle between cultures.[17]

Khvylovyj's anti-Russian stand, in addition to his internationalism, was strongly motivated by his personal disappointment and disillusionment with the events which followed the revolution. It has been suggested, and perhaps rightly so, that having accepted Bolshevik slogans at their face value, Khvylovyj, as well as many of his co-thinkers, hoped to become the masters and self-styled leaders of the Ukrainian people.[18] However, the opposite was the result. Having been fully utilized by the Russian Bolsheviks in their attempts to pacify the Ukrainian population, Khvylovyj and his co-thinkers were relegated from the heights of glory and power to secondary positions of importance—the dominant posts going to Russian Party members. For Khvylovyj, this degradation was a great disappointment. This disappointment runs through all of his writings, and can be narrowed down to these fundamental points: 1) The October Revolution had not fulfilled the hopes which the proletariat, and especially the Ukrainian working class, had placed in it; 2) The leadership of the Party and of the Soviet state had changed radically, decomposed morally, become bourgeois, and was utilizing its position for personal advantages; 3) Moscow had failed to become the center of world revolution and a real progressive stimulus for other peoples, especially for the Ukrainians, and instead had become a retrogressive, reactionary force which prevented the development of world revolution and the victory of Communism; and 4) Since Western civilization was likewise decaying, there was need for a new revolution in order to create all necessary prerequisites for a Communist society—a revolution in which Khvylovyj's personal prestige could rise again to its previous heights.[19]

As long as the outcome of the struggle for power inside the VKP(b) was uncertain, Khvylovyj's views, with some limitations, were allowed to circulate. With the emergence of Stalin in firm control of the Party, and with the inauguration of the era of integral planning, Khvylovyj's non-conformism became intolerable. On February 29, 1928, in a letter of confessioin, Khvylovyj for the second time placed his mistakes on the scale of judgment, "at the mercy of my Communist Party and its Central Committee." "My fundamental mistake," he wrote, "was that I resurrected the old theory of the struggle of two cultures." The second mistake, Khvylovyj admitted, was his advocacy of the Party's abandonment of its "role of corrector and judge," and of taking a definite pro-Ukrainian stand in the struggle. In doing so, Khvylovyj declared, *"I tried to bring an attempt on the purity of Communist ideology.* . . . [and] I came, against my will, to play a part in supporting

Ukrainian nationalism." [20] After stating that all the other of his mistakes were nothing but logical by-products of this fundamental misconception, Khvylovyj publicly asked all of his

> fellow and literary thinkers to reject all of those forms of struggle
> on the literary front against the vulgarities in which, up to now,
> the struggle has been conducted, because such a struggle . . . is
> being used by the Ukrainian counter-revolution in its class inter-
> ests . . . to aid in the formation of a united front against bourgeois
> culturists . . . not to believe that my proclamation is a proclama-
> tion written under pressure . . . [and] forgiveness (even condi-
> tional) from those friends with whom I carried on a heated strug-
> gle for several years.[21]

For all practical purposes, this confession brought an end of Khvylovism as a deviation. To appraise this "deviation" is not an easy task. Appearing at the time when the Party atmosphere was filled with numerous ready-made solutions for the attainment of the Communist Utopia, it may be argued and rightly so, that Khvylovism, with its advocacy of the return to early revolutionary meth-ods, was only one of them. Though it had some following, its influence is quite disputed,[22] and can never measure up in importance, in scope, or in force, to either the Right or the Left deviations within the Party. Its danger was not so much in its following as in its advocacy of national Communism, which if adopted by other Communist parties of the Soviet Union, would have created a grave problem. Moreover, Khvylovism's danger lay in its setting up a precedent for other national deviations to follow. It was mainly for these reasons that Khvylovism received quick attention and was immediately suppressed without its spread beyond Party circles.

SHUMSKYISM

Alongside Khvylovism there developed in the CP(b)U a far more dangerous movement known as Shumskyism, from the name of its chief spokesman, Oleksander Shumskyj, former Ukrainian Socialist Revolutionary, a member of the Ukrainian Central Rada, one of the leaders of the *Borot'bisty* and the chief advocate of its

merger with the CP(b)U, one time Plenipotentiary of the UkSSR
to Poland, then the Head of the Agitation and Propaganda Department of the CC of the CP(b)U, a member of the Politburo of the
CC of the CP(b)U, and finally, a Commissar of Education of the
UkSSR. Like Khvylovism, Shumskyism was a centrifugal and a
national Communist movement. Unlike Khvylovism, which with
its naïveté attempted to glorify the revolutionary past and advocated the return to revolutionary methods in order to achieve universal Communist society, Shumskyism, being a revival of the spirit
of *Borot'bism* and taking advantage of the weakness of the center
during the struggle for power following Lenin's death, centered its
efforts on the present and tried to gain the impossible—the possession of political power in the Ukraine. As a result of this, Shumskyism represented a far greater danger to the centralism of the Party
than did Khvylovism.

To appreciate Shumskyism more fully and to evaluate it properly, it is necessary to examine some of the underlying causes that
contributed to its appearance. Having been absorbed by the
CP(b)U and then subtly placed into obscurity or eliminated,[23]
many of the *Borot'bisty*—especially those who, in the game of revolutionary opportunism and in their gamble with the Bolsheviks, had
visualized themselves as the leaders of a new Ukrainian state—
became greatly embittered. Their sudden plunge from the political
heights into nothingness was greatly degrading. To many of the
Borot'bisty, this decline of prestige and hope seemed the end of
everything. There was, however, a single factor which reversed the
entire trend. That factor was the total bankruptcy of the Bolshevik
nationality policy, as was so vividly pointed up at the XII Congress
of the RCP(b) in 1923. The renewed pledge by high Party spokesmen to fulfill numerous empty promises made to various nationalities—a pledge which in the Ukraine took the form of Ukrainization
—revived the prestige and hope of the *Borot'bisty*. Many of them,
because of their knowledge of customs and conditions were brought
from obscurity and exile back into the Ukraine to divert the anti-
Bolshevik movement of the peasantry along a road favorable to
Bolshevism, a task which they had performed in 1919. Accord-

ingly, many of them were restored to their previous high government, and even Party, posts. In the process of this restoration, Shumskyj at first became the head of the Agitation and Propaganda Department of the CC of the CP(b)U, then a member of the Politburo of the CC of the CP(b)U, and, in addition, a Commissar of Education of the UkSSR.

However, these changes, important as they may have been, were not strong enough either to reverse the incompatibility of Bolshevik theory and practice, or to change the incurable anti-Ukrainian feelings among Party, Soviet, and Trade Union officials in the Ukraine. Ukrainization, whose fundamental aim was to divert the strong anti-Bolshevik movement among Ukrainian peasants along lines which would, in the end, produce favorable results for the Party, had, according to the resolution of the April, 1925 Plenum of the CC of the CP(b)U, "encountered difficulties and, in places, passive opposition on the part of workers and members of the Party." [24] These hindrances dissatisfied many *Borot'bisty*. But from their previous experiences, they were aware—and among those also belonged Shumskyj—that to accomplish their objective they would have to reach, if not for complete political power within the Party, at least for the right of appointment of high Party officials, in order to eliminate all future barriers. And while Lenin's death and the ensuing struggle for power in the CC of the VKP(b) presented a good opportunity for such a demand, Khvylovyj's call for "Away from Moscow" encouraged such thinking.

These demands of some of the *Borot'bisty*, which became known as Shumskyism, were quite clearly formulated and presented by Shumskyj to Stalin himself in a long conversation in April, 1926. According to Stalin's own account—the only one in existence— Shumskyj charged that Ukrainization was progressing "far too slowly" and that it was "looked upon as an imposed obligation" and was, therefore, "carried out reluctantly and very haltingly." Since Shumskyj held that Ukrainian culture and intelligentsia were growing at a rapid pace, he believed that Ukrainization, in order not to bypass the CP(b)U, should have been headed by people who believed in Ukrainian culture, who wanted to become acquainted with it, and who were supporting it. Because the top leadership of the Party and of the Trade Unions in the Ukraine was basically non-Ukrainian in its composition, and anti-Ukrainian in its feelings, Shumskyj expressed to Stalin dissatisfaction not only with its conduct and hindrances of Ukrainization, but also with its inability to "draw Communists who are directly linked with Ukrainian culture into the direction of Party and Trade Union work." Shumskyj especially voiced great dissatisfaction with "the organizational pressure," and the high-handed methods of Stalin's own protege in the Ukraine, the General Secretary of the CC of the CP(b)U, Lazar Kaganovich. To remove all the shortcomings and to reestablish normal conditions in the Ukraine, Shumskyj suggested to Stalin a change in the composition of the top Party and Soviet leadership. He proposed that H. F. Hrynko, former *Borot'bist*, Deputy Chairman of the Sovnarkom of the UkSSR, "be appointed to the post of Chairman of the Council of People's Commissars [of the UkSSR] and [Vlas Ya.] Chubar to the post of Political Secretary of the CC of the CP(b)U; that the composition of the Secretariat and the Political Bureau should be improved; and so forth." [25]

Stalin sympathized with Shumskyj's dissatisfaction and fears. He agreed especially that "under no circumstances" should Ukrainization be allowed "to fall into the hands of elements hostile to us"; that many Party members "do not realize the meaning and importance of that movement and are therefore taking no steps to gain control of it"; that "a change of sentiment must be brought among our Party and Soviet cadres who are still imbued with an ironical and skeptical attitude towards Ukrainization, and Ukrainian culture and Ukrainian public life"; and that the Party "must painstakingly select and build up cadres capable of gaining control of the new movement in the Ukraine." However, Stalin charged Shumskyj with committing errors in tempo. He accused Shumskyj of confusing Ukrainization of the Party apparatus with Ukrainization of the proletariat. While the former, he said, could and should be Ukrainized, Ukrainization of the latter was impossible, for it would mean compulsion to abandon its Russian culture. Hence it "would be contrary to the principle of the free development of nationalities," and could create "anti-Ukrainian chauvinism among the non-Ukrainian sections of the proletariat in the Ukraine." Stalin also cited Shumskyj for failing to see that "in view of the weakness of the indigenous Communist cadres in the Ukraine . . . [Ukrainization], which is very frequently led by non-Communist intellectuals, may here and there assume the character of the struggle to alienate Ukrainian culture and public life from general Soviet culture and public life; the character of the struggle against 'Moscow' in general; against Russians in general; against Russian culture and its highest achievement—Leninism." [26]

Stalin's reaction to Shumskyj's proposals was almost identical to his reaction to Shumskyj's complaints. He agreed with Shumskyj that the top leadership of the CP(b)U as well as the top Soviet bodies and Trade Unions should be "reinforced with Ukrainian elements." However, he accused Shumskyj of forgetting that there were "not enough purely Ukrainian Marxist cadres for this as yet"; of not realizing that such cadres "cannot be created artificially"; and of not taking into account the effect such a change might have on the Party in general and on the Party cadres in particular. [27]

In spite of this rebuff from Stalin, early in June, 1926, Shumskyj's charges were brought for consideration before a special Plenum of the CC of the CP(b)U. It is interesting to observe that neither in its deliberation nor in the resolution which the Plenum adopted, is there anything which would tend to suggest that Shumskyj's charges were untrue. The contrary is the case. "The fundamental question," read a joint statement of Kaganovich and Chubar, "is how to eliminate such occurrences." The statement proceeded to make the following suggestions: 1) A correct conduct of national policy; 2) Further firm execution of Ukrainization; 3) The Party's capture of commanding heights in the fields of culture, ideology, press and literature; 4) Steeling up of real Leninist cadres from among the Ukrainian workers; 5) Serious work among the Ukrainian youth; and 6) A "decisive struggle in the midst of our Party against petty bourgeois and chauvinism." [28] In accordance with these suggestions, and after analyzing the pro and con arguments on Ukrainization which resulted from Shumskyj's charges, the

Plenum of the CC of the CP(b)U set before the Party the following tasks: 1) Continuation of Ukrainization policy of the Party and a vigorous struggle against Russianism which was responsible for Ukrainian national deviation; 2) Explanation to proletarian masses of the essence and the significance of Ukrainization (especially to the Trade Union and the Comsomol); 3) Struggle against the theory of "two cultures"; 4) Uncovering of deviations; 5) Increased attention to Ukrainian press and literature; 6) Increased attention to Ukrainian higher schools; their curriculum; their teaching personnel and its qualification and recruitment; 7) "Bringing into the work of the Party apparatus and into the leading Soviet work, Ukrainian Communists, trying at the same time to preserve the old, fundamental, Leninist cadres"; and 8) Turning attention to the problem of bringing into the Soviet apparatus the non-Party Ukrainian intelligentsia. Finally, in its resolution, the June, 1926 Plenum of the CC of the CP(b)U recommended to the Politburo of the CC of the CP(b)U, the studying of all violations of the Constitution of the USSR by the All-Union Commissariats and other central organs. It also proposed "to conduct further work on the problem of uniting within the borders of the UkSSR all neighboring territories wherein the majority of the population is Ukrainian . . . " [29]

In the absence of first hand information it is difficult to state with any degree of precision the effects these recommendations to the Party by the Plenum of the CC of the CP(b)U, for which he was personally responsible, had on Shumskyj. His activity seems to point out that he considered it as a great triumph. As a member of the CC of the CP(b)U Shumskyj, against great odds, began to defend Khvylovyj's presentation of his grievances.[30] At the same time there was to be noticed in Shumskyj's speeches and pronouncements, increased resentment against Russian Bolsheviks and great contempt for those Ukrainian Communists who, in his opinion, gave up their pride for a servile status. "In the Party," he declared openly at the Session of the Politburo of the CC of the CP(b)U on May 12, 1927,

the Russian Communist governs with suspicion and unfriendli-
ness . . . He rules by receiving support from a contemptible Little
Russian who, throughout all historical epochs has been basically
hypocritical, servilely deceitful and treacherously underhanded.
Now he sings his faulty internationalism, defies with his indifferent attitude everything that is Ukrainian and is ever-ready to spit
at it (sometimes even in Ukrainian) if this only would give him
a possibility of being recommended or of obtaining a better
position.[31]

Being reminded of his past associations and especially of his
connections with Ukrainian Central Rada and the *Borot'bisty,*
Shumskyj not only did not attempt to hide his past associations,
but declared that he was proud of his background.

Except for the class struggle and national emancipation of the
working class and the peasantry, I had no other traditions. From
this, throughout my revolutionary activity, beginning with 1919,
I did not deviate a single iota. I do not repudiate anything in my
past and consider that I fought as a Bolshevik-Leninist under the
conditions of Ukrainian reality, even though at the time I did
not belong as yet to the Party of Lenin. I do not reject that
[past]—but, on the contrary, I am proud of my past.[32]

Shumskyj's pride, as well as his usage of strong language in
indicting his close associates of blind servility to Russian Bolshevism
—an accusation not very appealing to Bolshevik ears—caused Shumskyj's reprimand by the CP(b)U. From the standpoint of the unity
of the Party and blind obedience, his accusations became dangerous.
This was not only because they were well received by the anti-
Bolshevik groups who, in their press re-echoed Shumskyj's theme
of "contemptible traitor," [33] but also because these accusations
threatened the possibility of spreading throughout the entire Party
apparatus. In the final analysis, it was fear of the latter that made
Shumskyism a very dangerous deviation. This was frankly admitted
by Skrypnyk at the June, 1927 Plenum of the CC of the CP(b)U,
which met to consider Shumskyism. Characterizing Shumskyj,
Skrypnyk stated that "not having found ground on Ukrainian ter-

ritory among the rank-and-file membership of our Party, Comrade Shumskyj attempted to find for himself ground and support beyond the borders of our Party, in the midst of another Communist organization, the KPZU [the Communist Party of Western Ukraine]." [34]

The degree of importance attached to Shumskyism is evident from the fact that a special Plenum of the CC of the CP(b)U was called in 1927 to consider Shumskyj's case. In a lengthy resolution, which the Plenum prepared and dispatched to the Executive Committee of the Comintern for its consideration,[35] the Plenum of the CC of the CP(b)U, in addition to condemning Shumskyism, officially unveiled—to be sure not for the first time—the total bankruptcy of the Party's nationality policy as well as the Party's utter inability to cope with the national problem. The resolution began with an attempt to minimize the Shumskyj episode by declaring that it was not important in the Ukraine proper, since it had no support. At the same time the resolution stressed that Shumskyj's case was very vital outside the UkSSR, where it was being fully exploited by the Ukrainian press. Following these remarks there came a lengthy presentation of various causes which, in the opinion of the Plenum of the CC of the CP(b)U, were responsible for the appearance of Shumskyism. In its nationality policy, it was stated, the Party followed faithfully the fundamental line worked out by Lenin; namely that a proper solution of the national problem could be found only under the leadership of the proletariat. In the Ukraine, the resolution went on to complain, the following of this principle was difficult, because the majority of the proletariat was non-Ukrainian in language. This factor had at first led to an improper evaluation of the national problem in the Ukraine, and then was greatly responsible for a bitter struggle between centralism and local nationalism. Since the introduction of the NEP, the resolution continued, this struggle, in view of the partial stability of life in cities and in villages, had begun to intensify, and had been transferred from the bourgeoisie to the peasantry and workers, and finally to the Party. The resolution acknowledged that the anti-Ukrainian sentiment found many adherents among Russian bourgeoisie, city inhabitants, military men, various specialists, Russian population outside the UkSSR, and above all among the workers of the Soviet apparatus on the All-Union level. They, contrary to the Party line, tried "to utilize the indispensable centralization of the Soviet power in the struggle with the economic and cultural development of national republics." In view of this, the resolution went on, it was necessary to assume that this anti-Ukrainian group of Russian chauvinists put great pressure on the Party, for the purpose of preserving for itself, and for Russian culture, a privileged status in the Ukraine. The resolution noted that within the Party there were to be found the following forms of Russian chauvinism: 1) Ignoring or not evaluating sufficiently the significance of the Ukraine as a part of the USSR; 2) Attempting to explain the creation of the USSR as actual liquidation of national republics; 3) Spreading of rumors of a neutral attitude of the Party toward Ukrainian culture, and treating the latter as a culture of peasantry in contrast to Russian proletarian culture; 4) Attempting to preserve the Russian language in state, cultural, and social life in the Ukraine; 5) Repeating "chauvinist views" that the Ukrainian literary language was a Galician dialect unknown to the Ukrainian peasantry; 6) Cultivating these views inside the Party; and 7) Attempting to limit Ukrainization to villages, an action intended to weaken and undermine the relation of the Party with the toiling masses and thereby cause a break between the peasantry and the workers.

Alongside the growth of Great Russian chauvinism in the Ukraine, the resolution of the July, 1927 Plenum of the CC of the CP(b)U presented dangers stemming from Ukrainian nationalism. Under the NEP, ran the argument, the more well-to-do peasantry began to revive rapidly. In view of the unsatisfactory material conditions of the village intelligentsia, the peasantry began to exercise a considerable control over the latter. The NEP likewise strengthened numerically the Ukrainian city bourgeoisie by a considerable shift of the population from the villages into the cities. It was to be assumed, the resolution stated, that, because of its connections, the Ukrainian intelligentsia had tried not only to influence

but also to capture cultural processes and impose its not very clearly
formulated ideology on the Ukrainian workers in the state and
Party apparatus, among whom there were to be found many newcomers, and that it had tried to divert Ukrainian economy along
the lines of capitalist development, and contrary to the interest of
other union republics. The mistakes of this group, whose members
had entered the Party since the revolution, were said to be the following: 1) Non-appreciation and misunderstanding of the role of
the working class and of the Communist Party in solving the national
problem in the Ukraine; 2) Bureaucratic approach to the tempo
and form of Ukrainization of the non-Ukrainian workers; 3) Maintaining defeatist views regarding the perspective of socialist construction; 4) Disbelief in the Party's capability to carry out the
national policy in the Ukraine; 5) Attempts to undermine faith in
the non-Ukrainian Party workers; 6) Presenting the Party as the
carrier of Russian chauvinism which had subjugated the Ukraine;
7) Smearing those Ukrainian Communists who faithfully followed
Party orders; and 8) Supporting Ukrainian cultural orientation
toward Europe rather than toward Moscow.

It is interesting to note that in all of these "crimes" committed
by the Ukrainian side, not only was the name of the Party fully
involved but also its "righteousness" and capability were questioned.
In the "crimes" committed by the anti-Ukrainian side, the Party's
weaknesses were conspicuously absent. This becomes quite significant when we proceed to the second part of the resolution of the
Plenum of the CC of the CP(b)U, which accused Shumskyj of his
crimes and justified, before the Executive Committee of the Comintern, his proposed expulsion from the CP(b)U. This part of the
resolution accused Shumskyj and his followers of inability to understand Lenin's teaching on the national problem, the leading role
of the Party, and close friendship between the Ukrainian and Russian workers. In addition, Shumskyj was charged with maintaining
the view, even in 1920, that the CP(b)U was a Party of occupants.
He was accused of working for the destruction of the dictatorship
of the proletariat, and was condemned for his inability and unwillingness to repudiate his past—a sign which, stated the accusation,
suggested that Shumskyj fully approved his previous struggle and

affiliations. The resolution further accused Shumskyj of being guilty of insubordination; of holding dangerous views in charging that there was Russian domination within the Party; of resisting the Politburo and the Central Committee of the Party by parliamentary tactics; and of using his high Party and government positions to influence others to think along similar lines.

Passing final judgment on Shumskyism, the resolution of the July, 1927 Plenum of the CC of the CP(b)U stated that, as a national opposition within the Party, Shumskyism was very dangerous in that it tried to decompose, weaken, demoralize, and, above all, tried to spread its danger beyond Party circles—a factor which led to "the undermining and decomposition of our Party and to the undermining of the proletarian dictatorship." Moreover, according to the resolution, Shumskyism, as a deviation played into the hands of the enemies of the USSR the world over, who were doing everything possible to inculcate into the minds of the working class that there was no socialism in the USSR; that the Bolsheviks continued the imperialist foreign policies of Tsarism; that inside the country they oppressed non-Russian nationalities; and that they planned to subjugate China, similarly as they had done with the Ukraine, Georgia, etc. The resolution concluded that Shumskyism, and the slogan "Away from Moscow," were only part of this general campaign which was trying to spread disbelief in the Party, the Comintern, and Lenin's slogans of the existence of a possibility of solving the national problem throughout the entire world.

There is no doubt that, in the opinion of the CC of the CP(b)U, these were sufficient reasons to cause Shumskyj's expulsion from the Party. The chief reason for all the publicity and lengthy arguments was that his expulsion alone could not insure the suppression of Shumskyism as a deviation which, as has been pointed out, had spread beyond the borders of the Ukraine. Shumskyism found considerable support in the KPZU, which was a branch of the Polish Communist Party (PCP), and it was especially warmly defended by a candidate to the CC of the KPZU, Karlo Maksymovych. Maksymovych, who was present at the Plenum of the CC of the CP(b)U, which considered Shumskyj's case, took the stand that expulsion and possible exile of Shumskyj from the Ukraine would greatly strengthen anti-Bolshevik forces in the Western Ukraine, and accordingly would completely annul the insignificant following and influence the KPZU possessed. This stand not only placed Maksymovych in Shumskyj's camp, but also created an uproar at the Plenum and drew a strong protest from the CC of the PCP which, in a special resolution, branded Maksymovych's stand as "a political demonstration against the national policy of the CC of the CP(b)U and the CC of the VKP(b)." This mistake, declared the resolution of the CC of the PCP, was very dangerous because under "present conditions in Poland it works in favor of Pilsudski's Government and its national policy in the Western Ukraine, which is dictated in full force against the USSR and which covers up the preparation for war against the Soviet Union under the flag of a real 'independent' Ukraine." [36]

The news of Maksymovych's support of Shumskyj likewise drew a protest from a special session of the CC of the KPZU which met in the presence of a delegate from the Comintern to appraise what had then become known as the Shumskyj-Maksymovych deviation. A majority of the CC of the KPZU fully endorsed the Shumskyj-Maksymovych stand. However, a declaration of the minority of four members[37] announced its "complete solidarity with the national policy of the CP(b)U." Following the example of the CP(b)U, it condemned Shumskyj for his deviation of a "nationalist nature," and also for his support of Khvylovyj; for his hatred "of the co-operation" between the Russian and the Ukrainian proletariat; for his condemnation of those Ukrainians who co-operated with the Russians; etc. Accordingly, the minority declaration of the CC of the KPZU considered Maksymovych's defense of Shumskyj's mistake an attempt to cover up Shumskyj's deviation, and an attempt to give the impression of the existence of differences between the CP(b)U and the KPZU on the question of national policy, thus playing directly into the hands of the Ukrainian petty bourgeoisie. The minority declaration likewise branded the pro-Shumskyj stand taken by the majority of the CC of the KPZU as a "grave nationalistic error"; as a sign of conflict with

the line of the Comintern and that of the CC of the CP(b)U; as
a disorientation of the entire Party; and as a paralyzing blow to
its struggle with the UNDO [Ukrainian National Democratic
Union] and the Polish Government.[38]

The split within the KPZU, for which Shumskyj was held indirectly responsible, created considerable excitement among the members of the CC of the CP(b)U. In part, this excitement was a
product of complete ignorance of the Communist movement in the
Western Ukraine, of its strength, and of its following among the
masses.[39] Also this excitement was due, in part to the satisfactory
and joyful accounts of Bolshevik trouble in the Ukraine by the anti-
Bolshevik press in the Western Ukraine. The latter tried to interpret Shumskyj's deviations as a well-planned Ukrainian nationalist
conspiracy aimed at protecting Ukrainian cultural and national
interest and at propagating in the midst of the CP(b)U "the idea
of Ukrainian statehood, even though of Communist nature." [40] The
excitement about the split in the KPZU and the rise of anti-
Ukrainian feeling among the members of the CC of the CP(b)U
was likewise due to the open call by Ukrainian Social Democratic
spokesmen abroad demanding that it was "the duty of socialists
(and Communists if they are honest)" to unveil "the atrocity of
Moscow over the toilers of the Ukraine . . . before the world proletariat in its complete moral nakedness." Finally, it was due to
the Ukrainian Social Democratic appeal to all Ukrainian elements
to give Shumskyism their support in its effort to defeat Leninism
with Leninism, "a paradox [that] should be understood by all those
who want to destroy Moscow's dictatorship." [41]

It is impossible to make any definite statement on the effect
this call had on European Socialists, for the Ukrainian issue had
been considered on previous occasions by Socialist bodies.[42] In
1927, at the peak of the Shumskyj affair, a German Social Democrat, Emil Strauss, called upon European Socialism to give the
Ukraine its moral support in the struggle for freedom against
Russian Bolshevik oppression. "European Socialism," Strauss declared, "has all grounds to support morally the struggle of the
Ukrainian people for their freedom. It has become the best social-

ist tradition since Marx, to struggle against any social and national oppression. The solution of the Ukrainian problem is the prerequisite for peace in the East and also for peace in the world." [43]

These pro-Ukrainian pronouncements abroad, which directly and indirectly endorsed Shumskyism, were greatly responsible for the excitement which Shumskyism and the split in the KPZU had created among the members of the CC of the CP(b)U. The excitement can be appreciated far better when we take into consideration the role world revolutionary strategy had assigned to the Western Ukraine in general and its Communist Party in particular. Ever since its organization in 1920, the KPZU, though forming a part of the PCP, had maintained very close relations with the CP(b)U, or as Skrypnyk, the founder and staunchest supporter of the KPZU, put it, "Our task has always been to help our brothers, at first the Communist Party of Eastern Galicia and then of Western Ukraine, in their acquaintance with and acceptance of the indispensable knowledge of Leninism in the sphere of theoretical, organizational, and tactical problems." [44] In return for this aid and in accordance with the tactical scheme worked out by Lenin during World War I, whereby the proletariat of the dominant nation was to call for the right of self-determination and the proletariat of the oppressed nation for unity,[45] the KPZU and the CP(b)U, in spite of the Soviet official rejection of the claim on the Ukrainian territory beyond the borders established by the Treaty of Riga in March, 1921,[46] had constantly advocated the unification of the Western Ukraine with the UkSSR. This advocacy, which the PCP began to support following its second congress, found warm approval from an official spokesman of the RCP(b), D. Z. Manuilsky, at the Fifth Congress of the Comintern in 1924.[47] In accordance with his assertion of the righteousness of the tactics pursued by the KPZU and the PCP, and following the arguments presented to the Congress by the representative of the KPZU, Vasilkov,[48] the Fifth Congress of the Comintern adopted a resolution which declared the Ukrainian problem to be "one of the most important national problems of Central Europe . . . [whose] solution is dictated by the interests of the proletarian revolution in Poland, Czecho-Slovakia [sic], and Rou-

mania, as well as in those countries adjoining." [49]   Consequently
all Communist Parties concerned were ordered "to launch the general slogan of separation of the Ukrainian lands from Poland,
Czecho-Slovakia [sic], and Roumania and their union with Soviet
Ukraine and through it, with the Union of Soviet Socialist Republics." [50]   In 1926, at the Session of the Enlarged Executive Committee of the Comintern, on the initiative of Skrypnyk, who was a
very strong advocate of this policy, the Western Ukrainian problem
again received considerable attention and assurances of the un-
changeability of the principles declared by the Fifth Congress in
1924.[51] In a word, the Western Ukraine, by virtue of its linguistic,
racial, and cultural ties with the UkSSR, and also thanks to its
peculiar geographic location, became, in the strategy of world revolution, a starting point—a *Platzdarm*—for Communist expansion
into the Central Danube region and into Central Europe. Thanks
to Shumskyism and the subsequent split in the KPZU, this grand
scheme collapsed like a house of cards, forcing a complete revision
of the Comintern's strategy, and turning the Western Ukraine
from a springboard of World Revolution into a *Platzdarm* "wherefrom world imperialism concentrates the preparation of war against
the USSR." [52]

The importance which the Comintern attached to the Western
Ukraine and to Shumskyism, which was responsible for the break
in the ranks of the membership of the KPZU, is evident from the
Comintern's efforts to prevent the break. In February, 1928, two
long resolutions on the problem were published—one by the Executive Committee of the Comintern and another by the Plenum of
the Executive Committee of the Comintern.[53] At the same time an
appeal by the Comintern to all the members and organizations of
the KPZU, which pleaded for unity, was made public.[54] In March,
1928, a special Plenum of the CC of the CP(b)U was held to
consider the problem of the break in the KPZU,[55] and, in June,
1928, the CC of the CP(b)U made a declaration to the Central
Executive Committee of the Comintern on the same issue.[56] In
addition to these formal declarations, on the initiative of the Political Secretariat of the International Control Commission of the

Comintern, a Commission composed of the members of the Central Executive Committee of the Comintern and of the CC of the VKP(b) was organized to study the Shumskyj-Maksymovych case and the break within the KPZU. Because the spokesmen of the break considered Shumskyj and Maksymovych their ideological leaders, Shumskyj and Maksymovych were asked by the Commission to reject the deviationists. Although in April, 1928, a statement to that effect was obtained, the Commission felt that it was insufficient, for in this document neither Shumskyj nor Maksymovych mentioned the correctness of the line of the CC of the CP(b)U on the national problem.[57] On March 18, 1929, Shumskyj and Maksymovych signed another declaration, which was later published in *Pravda,* wherein they condemned the split in the KPZU "not only as an organizational but also as an ideological break with the Comintern, a treason to the principles of Communism and the adoption of the position of bourgeois nationalism." They protested against the using of their names by the KPZU to justify the break. At the same time, however, they asserted that they themselves were being accused unjustly of national deviation, since their views in the national problem did not deviate from the line pursued by the CP(b)U.[58] The Commission felt that the second declaration was also unsatisfactory in that it tried to place blame for the break on the CP(b)U. As a result, Shumskyj was strongly reprimanded while Maksymovych was expelled from the Comintern and from the KPZU.[59]

On April 28, 1930, Shumskyj signed his final confession, wherein he assumed the entire blame. He declared that he had taken the wrong position in the problem of Ukrainization and in the struggle with Ukrainian nationalism. "Until now," Shumskyj stated,

> I considered that my position was a correct one, and that I, and not the CC of the CP(b)U, was right. I considered the criticism of my position and its treatment as a national deviation as a political mistake of the CC of the CP(b)U . . .
>
> But reality has demonstrated that the CC of the CP(b)U, and not I was right, which follows that my position was incorrect, and the position of the CC of the CP(b)U was a correct one.[60]

He announced that his fundamental mistake was that he had over-estimated the difficulties confronting the Party and had under-estimated the capabilities of the Party and of the working class of the Ukraine. Shumskyj also declared that his insistence on increasing the tempo of Ukrainization of the working class had been erroneous and without consideration of the effects of such a policy—especially of its harm to the working class, its weakening of relations between the Russian and the Ukrainian workers, its undermining of the international spirit; and its strengthening of the position of Ukrainian nationalism. He repudiated his declaration on, and definition of "Little Russian"; took most of the blame for Khvylovism and Khvylovyj's defense; the break in the KPZU; and repeated that his position had been always wrong, whereas that of the CP(b)U and of the Comintern had been always right.[61]

With this confession, the political career of Shumskyj ended. In 1933 he was arrested, and was last seen in June, 1934, on Popov Island in the Solovetsky Islands Forced Labor Camp.[62] As a deviation, Shumskyism represents an interesting chapter in the history of the Russian Bolshevik nationality policy in the Ukraine by its exposing, in total nakedness, the incompatibility between the Bolshevik nationality theory and practices. The danger of Shumskyism lay in its efforts to wrest from Moscow political control; control of appointment of high Party officials from the center; and in the fact that it spread beyond the borders of the UkSSR. In doing so, it upset in part the world revolutionary scheme on the eve of the Russian Bolshevik plunge into economic experimentation—the era of integral planning. Finally, Shumskyism represents an interesting chapter in the history of Ukrainian leftist intelligentsia which, while capable of finding a solution for the exclusion of all political groups to the right of their beliefs, was unable to do the same justice to the leftist extreme at whose hands it finally perished.

VOLOBUEVISM

The third major deviation within the CP(b)U was that known as Volobuevism, from the name of its exponent, Mykhailo Volobuev, a member of the CP(b)U and a lecturer in the Institute of Economics in Kharkov. Like Khvylovism in literature, and Shumskyism in politics, Volobuevism tried to point out the incompatibility between Russian Bolshevik theories and their practices in the sphere of economics. Unlike Khvylovism or Shumskyism, whose early appearance made it possible for them to exist, with various interruptions, for several years, thus producing considerable literature, Volobuevism, arising after the forces under Stalin's command were fully entrenched in power, was liquidated as soon as it made its appearance. The fundamental importance of Volobuevism, therefore, centers primarily in its courage in placing on record the economic exploitation of the border regions by Moscow, under the cover of internationalism, and in the name of the dictatorship of the proletariat.

Volobuev presented his views in two articles, which he published in the early part of 1928 in *Bilshovyk Ukrainy,* the official journal of the CC of the CP(b)U. In the first article, basing himself on the works of some Ukrainian and Russian historians and economists, and treating the Ukraine as an economic whole, and as Russia's equal, Volobuev surveyed the economic relations between the Ukraine and pre-Revolutionary Russia. In his presentation he showed that, contrary to the prevailing belief of many Russian observers, and especially those who adhered to the principle of concentration, Russian economy was not one uniform, single unit, but a combination of several economic complexes—of which the Ukraine was one. These complexes, Volobuev argued further, were not only capable of being economically independent of Russia, but, according to him, they also demonstrated a desire to enter the world economic system not through the Russian economy but independently of Russia. In his treatment, Volobuev also pointed out various methods of Russian economic exploitation of the Ukraine, Russian policy of concentrating important industries and enterprises in Russia proper, rather than in the Ukraine, etc., and came to the conclusion that the Ukraine, deprived of economic and political independence, was nothing but a colony of Russia. However, he maintained that, being Russia's equal culturally and possessing a capitalist system of economy, the Ukraine was a European type colony, *i.e.*, a semi-colony.[63]

In accordance with this conclusion, Volobuev maintained that had the revolution occurred throughout the world simultaneously, the Ukraine, as a semi-colony, would have entered the world economic complex on an equal basis with its former political and economic master, Russia. In his opinion, the more backward regions of Russia, such as Turkestan, would have entered future communist society through Russia and not independently. Since, however, the simultaneous universal revolution had failed to materialize, the Ukraine, Volobuev stated, had entered the Union with the economic and political hegemony passing to Russia. Theoretically, therefore, he argued, the Ukraine had gained nothing from the revolution; while in practice, Volobuev complained, citing increasing Ukrainian contribution to the economy of the USSR without adequate compensations, the Ukraine was becoming more and more a colony of the RSFSR, similarly as it had been under the Tsarist system. To strengthen his arguments, that the Ukraine was economically a colony of the RSFSR, Volobuev charged that the Ukraine was so treated by the Party as well as by Soviet officialdom in words as well as in deeds. He complained that the term "Ukraine" was being intentionally avoided. To remove this—what he labelled a colonial mask left by Tsardom—Volobuev proposed that the Ukraine be treated as an equal; that a different industrial policy be adopted toward the Ukraine than that appplied toward Turkestan; that the proposed Five Year Plan give more attention to the development of producing-type industry in the Ukraine, and not simply utilize Ukrainian natural resources for the purpose of building other industrial centers; and that the Party, in reality as well as in resolutions, give the Ukrainian national problem appropriate attention.[64]

Volobuev's conclusions, charges, and demands, which became the foundation of Volobuevism, drew bitter replies and denunciations, though, at the time, some of his critics agreed with his charges. Condemnation of Volobuev assumed additional bitterness because many of Volobuev's conclusions were the same as those advanced or maintained by Ukrainian spokesmen abroad.[65] Speaking at the XVI Congress of the VKP(b) in 1930, Skrypnyk defined Volobuevism as "an economic formulation of Ukrainian nationalist deviation whereby the Ukrainian economy is being set against that of the Union and is looked upon as being completely independent and without any connections with the economy of the rest of the Union." [66]

One of Volobuev's critics, while disagreeing with his assertion that the Ukrainian problem did not receive sufficient treatment by the authoritative bodies of the Party or of the government,[67] indirectly came to Volobuev's defense by arguing that Great Russian chauvinism and the Russian hatred of everything Ukrainian was mainly responsible for the appearance of Volobuevism. "In practically every issue of Russian economic journals," wrote Andrij Richytskyj, "[and] in practically every book dealing with the *rayonization*, there is a tendency to exclude the name 'Ukraine' and to substitute 'South Russia,' 'Southern *okrug*,' 'Southern USSR,' [or] 'Southern part of European USSR'." [68] It was in these remnants of former subjugation of the Ukraine, argued Richytskyj, that the answer to Volobuevism must be sought.[69] He also agreed with that part of Volobuev's demand which called for the construction of industries for finished products in the Ukraine— especially industries which from the economic standpoint were fully justified, as for example the building of a sugar refinery in the Ukraine rather than in Moscow. Richytskyj complained that as long as Moscow pursued this uneconomic policy, the Ukraine could never hope to develop a proletarian force of its own, but would always remain subject to Russian control.[70]

Hirchak, who acted as another critic of Volobuev's views, proved to be far more damaging to him than did Richytskyj. Hirchak accused Volobuev of an unjustified comparison of conditions in pre-revolutionary and post-revolutionary Ukraine. He branded as completely erroneous Volobuev's assertion that the revolution had not realized its slogans for the oppressed nationalities of Russia in general, and of the Ukraine in particular. Hirchak likewise assailed Volobuev's statement of the independence of

Ukrainian economy from Russian economy as a counter-revolutionary view. In addition, he denounced him for inciting animosity
between Russian and Ukrainian workers; for maintaining Trotsky's
view on the problem of the construction of socialism;[71] for rejecting
the existence of Ukrainian proletarian statehood; for misunderstanding the real nature of the USSR; and for his narrow, selfish,
chauvinism revealed by his insistence on full protection and toleration of the Ukraine, but inability to practice the same policy toward
other republics.[72]

Hirchak attacked very strongly Volobuev's complaint that the
Party paid very little attention to the Ukraine, and declared that

> This is not a criticism of separate 'mistakes' or violations, but it
> is the non-recognition of a great work done by the Party, by the
> Soviet Government, and by the working class in the Ukraine, in
> the matter of construction of a proletarian state, its economic,
> political, and cultural consolidation. This is the non-recognition
> of great achievements in the sphere of economic, cultural and
> national construction in the Ukraine. This is a slander and ac-
> cusation of our national policy in the Ukraine. This is what is
> now being done by the Undovites, Petliurists, [etc.] . . . [73]

As a result of this unfavorable criticism, Volobuev was forced,
in view of its alleged unfitness in the proletarian system, to withdraw his charge that the Ukraine was becoming a colony of the
RSFRS. First, in two separate articles, he confessed all of his errors,[74]
and then he repeated the same confession of errors in a letter to
the Editors of *Bilshovyk Ukrainy*. "The first and principal mistake I made," he admitted,

> [was] that I considered [only] isolated facts of violations of the
> correct Party line in the national problem; I never considered
> this cardinal problem: are these violations the mistakes of indi-
> vidual persons or of the system? These separate facts, which I
> had at my disposal, led me to an erroneous impression, and based
> on this incorrect set [of facts], which was the result of alien ideo-
> logical influences, I made incorrect deductions, viewing these
> facts not as exceptions but as a rule. I never thought, and do

not think, that the USSR conducts toward the Ukraine a colonial policy, and I consider such views as being nationalist and anti-Soviet . . .

Secondly, I declare that the line of the Party in the national problem . . . is without doubt the correct one and the only possible one. I condemn and repudiate all nationalist deviations and influences.

Thirdly, I consider it wrongful, that in differentiating separate types of colonial dependencies, I mentioned only two types of colonies at the time when talk could have been in the difference in the branches of unity . . .

Fourthly, I believe to be wrong my assertion that the Party, in its resolutions on the matter of the national problem, had only in mind backward nations and not the Ukraine . . . From such an assertion of the problem there results a distortion of the national theory of Leninism as a theory of 'backward nations.'

Fifthly, I believe also that in connection with the above stated main mistakes, my concept in essence and in form received the appearance of the 'economic foundation of the theory of the struggle of two cultures.' Even though I did not intend to give such a conclusion, not being an adherent to this anti-Leninist theory; nevertheless I must take all the responsibility for such deductions which stem directly from my article . . .

Sixthly, . . . I especially underline that I consider as very erroneous the stand on the manner of distribution of positions in Ukrainian factories, because it [such a stand] causes a break of international solidarity.[75]

Following this confession, Volobuev disappeared from public life, and with him vanished Volobuevism, because, like Khvylovism and Shumskyism, it had tried to point out various contradictions between Russian Bolshevik theory and practice in the Ukraine.

CHAPTER V

Integral Standardization

One of the most outstanding characteristics of the Russian Bolshevik nationality policy in the Ukraine during the 1920's was the inability of the ruling Party to bring about a reconciliation between the centrifugal and the centripetal forces, and to satisfy the needs and demands of Ukrainian and Great Russian nationalisms. As time went on, this failure, which was fundamentally a product of the incompatibility between Russian Bolshevik theory and practices, increased, and the antagonism between the opposing forces intensified. Since, for obvious reasons, the Party could not afford to alienate those forces which were hostile to each other, it chose a very vague middle course—that of fighting both Great Russian and Ukrainian nationalism, blaming, however, the former for the appearance of the latter.

The decision to adopt a policy of integral planning, and the subsequent launching of industrialization and collectivization of the country introduced a new chapter in the Russian Bolshevik nationality policy in the USSR in general, and in the Ukraine in particular. Industrialization of the country signalized the development of new factories, of new plants, and of new industries. It meant, therefore, the appearance of hundreds of thousands of new workers, whose peasant origin and Ukrainian background was bound to bring important changes to the national composition of the working class of the Ukraine, as well as of the city population. Collectivization of the countryside, aside from its social and economic implications, likewise meant the appearance of hundreds of thousands of new workers. Thus, both the industrialization and collectivization aimed at fundamental shifts of population in the Ukraine, as well as the reconstruction of the entire life of the country; the integration of all economic regions of the USSR into one economic whole; the solidification of the state and the standardization of its political and cultural life; and the creation of a new goal—SOVIETISM—a new concept which would form a basis for unity of all the peoples of the USSR.

Since industrialization and collectivization became not only the determining factors of every aspect of life in the USSR, but also policies upon which the Party placed all hopes for finding the ultimate solutions to every problem, all problems, including the national, were subordinated to the needs of industrialization and collectivization. "The period of socialist construction," wrote Popov at the end of 1929,

> . . . does not diminish in any way the tasks set forth by *the XII Congress.* On the contrary, now we have entered the period of *the fundamental and complete solution of these tasks,* the period of actual elimination of national inequality and of all of its economic consequences. *The problem of cultural revolution* with respect to the national republics is unbreakably tied with the complete realization of uprooting (*korenizatsii*); it signifies not the prevention, but the *furthering of great development of national-cultural construction.* Without such a development we shall be unable to destroy the roots of capitalism and precapitalist barbarism in the national Republics.[1]

Speaking before the delegates of the proletarian students in 1930, Skrypnyk argued along the same lines as had Popov, when he underlined that

> *Cultural construction today, during the construction period, takes a different meaning from the one it had in the preceding period. Instead of being a separate third front, alongside of the cultural front, cultural construction becomes an inseparable part of the entire socialist construction, an inseparable component part of the reconstruction of our entire socialist country, being at the same time not only a component part of our constructive work, but also its prerequisite.*[2]

These expectations and hopes for the solution of the national problem, which the architects of integral planning placed in the industrialization and collectivization, being based on an erroneous assumption that the tensions between the centripetal and the centrifugal forces—between Russian and Ukrainian nationalisms—would be solved as soon as the announcement of the Plan was made, were short lived. Industrialization and collectivization, with all of its intensity, only increased these tensions, multiplied the tactlessness, strengthened the inflexibility, and increased the distrust within and outside the Party. A typical example was the picture of existing tensions and the reign of chaos in the Marx-Lenin Institute in Kharkov. There, according to the December 7, 1929 resolution of the Kharkov *Obkom* Bureau of the CP(b)U, some Party members, in their search for a solution to the national problem, attempted to present Great Russian chauvinism as the Left deviation, and Ukrainian nationalism as the Right deviation. Others did exactly the opposite. Still others neglected Great Russian chauvinism altogether, and saw the danger in Ukrainian nationalism. There were some who held that every member of the Party ought to fight the chauvinism of his own nationality. The followers of this view maintained that since the majority of the membership of the CP(b)U was Ukrainian, the struggle had to be waged first against Ukrainian nationalism, and once that danger was eliminated the Party would then be free to turn its attention to Great Russiann chauvinism.[3]

High Party spokesmen maintained that the tasks of socialist construction, to be successful, demanded from every participant the adoption of a definite, and not a vague position, of "an active, and not a cold, warm, or neutral attitude."[4] Therefore, the resolution of the Kharkov *Obkom* Bureau condemned all of these interpretations and deviations as hampering reconstruction, hindering Ukrainization, and blocking the development of Ukrainian proletarian culture. At the present moment, stated the resolution, "all deviations, waverings, or vagueness in the ranks of the Party on the problem of national policy are dangerous."[5] The resolution acknowledged that because of the rapid growth of Ukrainian cultural construction, which the Party was forced to support, and because of the Party's attempt to keep up with that growth by Ukrainizing Soviet, Trade Union, Comsomol, and Party apparatus, the Great Russian chauvinists had inaugurated a campaign directed against the Party's national policy. The resolution stressed that this factor should in no way weaken the Party's struggle with Ukrainian nationalism. However, it declared that in conditions of Ukrainian reality, where the position of Great Russian chauvinism was especially strong, "the struggle with Great Russian chauvinism and its various forms in the Party not only should remain as of old, first on the agenda, but that it also should be intensified, continued, and be resolute." [6] This, the resolution stated, was necessary because of the yet incomplete results of Ukrainization of Soviet, Economic, Trade Union, Comsomol, and Party apparatus; because of maintenance in the state apparatus of old official elements; and because of the insufficient recruitment of Ukrainian cadres for leading work.

The tensions between Russian and Ukrainian nationalisms, as exposed in the resolution of the Kharkov Party *Obkom* Bureau, were not the exclusive attribute or the privilege of the Kharkov area, or of the Marx-Lenin Institute. These tensions existed throughout Ukrainian territory and could be found in Kiev, Dniepropetrovsk, and all other places where the villiage population, thanks to intensified industrialization, had begun to challenge the numerical, political, and cultural influence of alien cities. The existence of wide-spread tensions between Ukrainian and Russian nationalisms—between the city and the village—was formally and officially acknowledged in a decision of the CC of the CP(b)U on December 23, 1929, regarding the continuation of Ukrainization. [7]

This lengthy document began with the general assertion that in spite of various difficulties, there was to be noticed, because of socialist construction, the correct line of the Party in the national policy, and the growing support for that policy among Party members, a considerable achievement "in the development of Ukrainian Soviet culture and in the strengthening of Ukrainian proletarian statehood." However, the decision of the CC of the

CP(b)U went on to declare that there were many organizations of the Party which still failed to appreciate the significance of the policy of Ukrainization; that many resolutions and decisions of the Party on the Ukrainization problem were looked upon with disgust; that the entire work had still a campaign character; and that Ukrainization was suffering from the absence of a systematic check. The decision complained that many Party organizations failed to give sufficient consideration to the recruitment of Ukrainian cadres into the Party in order to promote Ukrainization. Because of the absence of Ukrainian personnel in strategic positions, the decision deplored that the attitude of many party organizations toward Ukrainization was formal; that the fulfillment of directives of the CC of the CP(b)U was unsatisfactory; that educational work among various organizations and clubs was unproductive; and that the explanatory work on the significance of the nationality policy and the tasks of the proletariat in the construction of Ukrainian Soviet culture had a casual character.

The Comsomol, the Trade Union, and the Party's lower organs came under particular blame and criticism in the decision of the CC of the CP(b)U. They were charged with open sabotage and unwillingness to work in the development of Ukrainian Soviet culture at the time when there was a growing tendency and a demand for Ukrainian books, literature, pamphlets, newspapers, etc., among the new workers who had just arrived from the village. The decision of the CC of the CP(b)U strongly reprimanded Trade Union organizations. It accused them of utter failure to conduct educational work on Ukrainization among technical personnel, economic specialists, engineers, etc., who, in their decisive majority, were anti-Ukrainian, chauvinistically inclined, and who, by virtue of their position and influence, transferred to the Party their feeling of hatred toward everything Ukrainian. At the same time, the decision of the CC of the CP(b)U admitted that this sentiment had not received the required repudiation from the Party, the Trade Union, or the Soviet organs.

In view of all these unsatisfactory performances in the field of Ukrainization by the organs of the Party, the CC of the CP(b)U announced that henceforth the following points were obligatory throughout the Ukraine for all Party, Comsomol, and Trade Union organizations: 1) A systematic development of broad educational work on the problem of national cultural construction; 2) Struggle with the formal attitude towards the directives of the Party on the problem of Ukrainization; 3) Adoption of measures for practical realization of Ukrainization of the cadres; 4) Acceptance of more Ukrainians into the Party; 5) Periodic check on Ukrainization; 6) Punishment of violators or those who ignored Ukrainization; 7) Transfer of Party educational schools in the cities to the Ukrainian language of instruction; 8) Development of Ukrainization in workers' clubs, Houses of Culture, etc.; and 9) Increase of publication of news bulletins in the Ukrainian language in all factories. In addition to these obligations, the CC of the CP(b)U directed the Central Committee of the Trade Unions in the Ukraine to Ukrainize its leading personnel by May 1, 1930. The People's Commissariat for Education of the UkSSR was ordered to provide for the industrial areas teachers capable of speaking the Ukrainian language; to develop in the industrial areas Ukrainian schools, theaters, etc.; and to work out ways and means on how to satisfy best the Ukrainian readers with Ukrainian books. Finally, to give an example of its own desire to aid Ukrainization, the CC of the CP(b)U promised to transfer 30 Ukrainian members into the industrial areas in place of non-Ukrainians.

These intensified efforts by high organs of the Party to foster Ukrainization were basically the product of their fear of being by-passed by the effects of industrialization. Growth of industry, of cities, and of entirely new industrial centers, introduced a large number of basically Ukrainian surplus population from the villages. As time went on, the change in the national composition of the working force and of the city population began to shift in the Ukrainian favor. Among industrial and construction workers, this change amounted to an increase from 41% in 1926, to 53% in 1932. The overall increase among manual and white collar workers for the said period is reported to have been from 49.9% to 59%.[8] This shift of population was more vivid in the national composition of city inhabitants. Between 1926 and 1932-33, for example, the Ukrainian population of Kharkov rose from 160,000 to 330,000; that of Zaporozhie from 26,500, or 47% of the total, to 60,000 or 56%; that of Lugansk from 31,200, or 43%, to 71,000 or 60%; and that of Dniepropetrovsk from 83,000 or 36%, to 185,000 or 48%.[9] In all of these, and in many other cases, the Ukrainian peasant brought with him his peasant habits, his peasant psychology, and the Ukrainian language. To prevent him from using that language would have meant to alienate him, a gamble which the architects of integral planning were unwilling to take. At the same time, to deny him the learning in his own language of how best to utilize modern equipment connected with industrialization, would have meant slowing the tempo of industrialization. Accordingly, to prevent materialization of these possibilities, and at the same time to make every participant in industrialization conscious of his duty, it was necessary to make him literate alphabetically, technically, and also politically. This meant not only the liquidation of illiteracy and spread of the school network, but also intensified continuation of Ukrainization.[10]

In the field of education, the continuation of Ukrainization meant a rather sizeable increase of Ukrainian schools. Already on the eve of the planning era, the Ukrainian Planning Commission had recommended that between 1928 and 1932 there should be opened, in every *rayon*, an economic school to raise the understanding and qualification of peasant youth for rural economy. It also suggested that 150 trade schools be opened, and proposed that the number of seven-year schools in industrial areas be brought up from 119 to 300.[11] Between December 1, 1928 and January 1, 1930, the reported actual increase of elementary schools in the Ukraine was from 20,032 to 20,764—of which 14,430 were Ukrainian, 1,504 Russian, 291 Jewish, 302 Polish, and the remainder divided among other nationalities.[12] In the field of journalism, the continuation of Ukrainization meant an increase of Ukrainian language newspaper circulation. The overall increase of circulation of these newspapers between 1928 and 1929 was from 2,635,246 to 4,220,363. The circulation of some individual

Ukrainian language newspapers between 1928 and 1930, is reported to have represented the following change: *Kommunist* from 28,000 to 122,000; *Visti* from 46,000 to 90,000; *Proletar* from 11,000 to 79,000; and *Radianske Selo* from 172,000 to 600,000. Lesser increases were reported in factory newsbulletins in the Ukrainian language, which, percentagewise, rose from 43.6% to 63% between 1928 and 1930. The publication of journals in the Ukrainian language during the same period climbed from 71.2% to 84.8%; while the publication of books in Ukrainian rose from 54% to 70%.[13]

These increases during the period of intensified Ukrainization would undoubtedly have been greater had it not been for intentional sabotage of, and negative attitude toward, Ukrainization by Party and government officialdom. Within that body many persons still maintained that Ukrainian literary language was "a Galician" dialect alien to the Ukrainian peasantry and forced upon them by the Ukrainian intelligentsia.[14] A large majority of that officialdom, according to Kosior, took a negative stand toward Ukrainization. Others entertained the Russifying attitude, while still others practiced subtle sabotage of Ukrainization. Finally, there was a great number, especially in the Party, whose attitude toward the nationality policy was indifferent.[15] Yet all of these officials held high and responsible positions. In the Soviet apparatus, for example, following the 1929 election, the non-Ukrainian members on the Republic level possessed 2,312 posts, or 63.8% of membership out of a total of 3,624, while the remainder of 1,312 posts, or 36.2%, were held by Ukrainians. In the *oblast'* apparatus, out of 339, the Ukrainians had 91 members, or 26.84%; whereas non-Ukrainians possessed 248, or 73.16%. In the *okrug* apparatus of the Soviets, Ukrainian membership had climbed to 13,980, or 53.46% of a total of 26,151 members, and on the *rayon* level, Ukrainian membership had risen to 10,903 or 75.9%, while the non-Ukrainians held 3,461, or 24.1%.[16] As can be seen from this official data, the lower the authority the more Ukrainian membership was to be found, and *vice-versa*. It was this disproportionate distribution of authority that prevented smooth functioning of official Ukrainization in spite of the intensified drive.

However, at the very same time that intensified Ukrainization was being undertaken, when a drive for Ukrainian teachers was at its peak, and when everything seemed to have been said by the highest Party spokesmen in favor of Ukrainization, there took place an important de-Ukrainization process. This process was the trial of 45 members of the *Spilka Vyzvolennia Ukrainy* (SVU), held in Kharkov from March 9, to April 19, 1930. This show trial, with all its pomp, press and radio coverage, display of documents, etc., was in many respects a forerunner of the big trials of the later 1930's. The main object of this burlesque was the elimination of Ukrainian cultural and scientific institutions and their foremost leaders; *i.e.*, of Ukrainian intelligentsia as the possible leader of the growing anti-Bolshevik sentiment among the Ukrainian peasantry. It also aimed at discrediting in the eyes of pro-Bolshevik groups, both inside and outside the USSR, the Ukrainian intelligentsia by picturing it as a warmonger and a conspirator against the "peaceful" USSR, and by trying to implicate it in sabotage aimed at breaking up the state of "noble experiment."

The trial attempted to show through the magnifying glass of the GPU the growth of Ukrainian opposition to Bolshevik rule and Ukrainian intimacy of contact with political emigration. However, a careful scrutiny of the testimony at the trial does tend to convince one that the Ukrainian intelligentsia had attempted to continue the struggle where politicians and armies had failed—by working, organizing, and preparing the Ukrainian peasant masses to assume their rights at some future date. This prime objective of the accused seemed to have been centered in the cultural field. It was intended to awaken the peasantry's national consciousness; to place Ukrainians in responsible positions; to educate Ukrainian youth; to work toward increased publication of Ukrainian books; etc.—in a word, it aimed at giving the mistreated and forgotten Ukrainian peasantry an education, a feeling of security, and self-confidence. Accordingly, these were doubtless the utmost objectives and activity of the SVU. Other charges brought against the 45 teachers (such

as attempts to separate the Ukraine from the USSR, organize
terroristic acts, attempts to assassinate Stalin, Voroshilov, and other
Party leaders, restore the capitalist system of economy in the
Ukraine, etc.) were but pure hoaxes. Because many of these accusations were too fantastic to be true, the trial, from a political
standpoint, acted as a boomerang. Instead of winning over adherents to the Bolshevik cause among emigre groups and Ukrainians
in Galicia, the trial created a wave of protest, antagonized a large
portion of the Ukrainian population and pushed them toward the
extreme Right.[17] The trial revealed again, quite vividly and publicly, the inability of the Party and of the Soviet Government to
solve the national problem.

The inability to find a solution to the national question in the
Ukraine, and the entire national problem, came under discussion
at the XVI Congress of the VKP(b) in 1930. The national problem was introduced as part of a deviation within the Party, against
which Stalin declared an all-out war. Although Stalin tried to
minimize its significance, it nevertheless was an official admission
that, in spite of repeated assurances of complete solution of the
national problem in the USSR, it not only had not been solved,
but also it had grown out of proportion. On the one hand Stalin
admitted that there was Great Russian chauvinism—the principal
danger to the Party and to the USSR. He defined it as a threat
which tried to ignore national differences in language, culture,
and mode of life; which tried to prepare liquidation of national
republics and regions; which tried to undermine the prinicple of
national equality; and which tried to force amalgamation of nations under the cover of socialism and internationalism by misinterpretation of Lenin's teachings, while in reality it prepared for
the domination of Great Russian nationalism. These attempts,
said Stalin, were deliberate distortions of Leninism. He maintained
that Lenin had never held that with the establishment of socialism,
even on a universal scale, national differences would disappear.
The demand for abolition of national republics and regions at the
present time, Stalin declared, was a reactionary one directed against
the interests of the proletarian dictatorship. It aimed at depriving

millions of people of the USSR of the opportunity of being educated in their native language, and of having their courts, schools,
administration, public, and other organizations, conducted in their
native language. It aimed, therefore, at depriving them of the
possibility of taking an active part in socialist construction.

On the other hand, Stalin pointed out that there was a danger
of deviation toward local nationalism. This, he said, tried to draw
peoples of the USSR apart; tried to isolate them; tried to smooth
over class differences; tried to unify them against Great Russian
chauvinism; tried to turn them away from the general current of
socialist construction; and tried to emphasize that which divides
the nations and not that which unites. "The danger of this deviation," he said, "lies in the fact that it cultivates bourgeois nationalism, weakens the unity of the toiling peoples of the USSR, and plays
into the hands of the interventionists." [18]

In a discussion inaugurated by Stalin's treatment of the national
problem, Skrypnyk, in a lengthy speech, while pledging himself to
persecute without mercy all elements with national feelings, blamed
the Russians for the rebirth of Ukrainian nationalism. He complained that the declaration of the right of nations was for many
Russians only a screen behind which they had hidden a plan for
further oppression. For many Russians, Skrypnyk stressed, this
declaration was only a tactical maneuver, while for non-Russians,
he said, it was the most important of all documents. He charged
that some Party members viewed this important declaration as
valid only prior to the October Revolution, and considered it
counter-revolutionary thereafter. He stressed categorically that
there could be no discussion of a revision of Lenin's national policy,
and still less of liquidation of national republics. To act contrary,
he said, would mean to force Ukrainian nationalists underground.[19]

As the discussion of Stalin's treatment of the national problem
proceeded aimlessly and created a considerable amount of confusion and bitterness, several delegates requested Stalin to offer
further explanation on the national policy of the VKP(b). In his
answer, Stalin repeated that attempts to amalgamate all nationalities
of the USSR, to assimilate them, and to create one Great Russian

nation, was a reactionary thing, founded on chauvinism, and contrary to the principles of Marxism-Leninism. Only after the revolution and victory of socialism on a universal scale, he said, could the replacement of national languages by one new language be thinkable. He reminded all the delegates to the XVI Congress of the VKP(b) to pay attention, in their approach to the solution of the national problem, to the fact that there was one Ukraine in the USSR, but that there was also another Ukraine outside the USSR; and that similar conditions existed in the case of Belorussia and several Asiatic Republics. These factors, Stalin declared, not only could not be neglected, but also they served as indicators that the problem of national cultures and languages could not be resolved within the framework of the USSR alone.[20]

While these theoretical arguments on the national problem were being re-emphasized, and while it was officially admitted that the solution of the national problem would have to be postponed until the victory of Communism on a universal scale, in the Ukraine the national problem, in actuality, was being transferred from a purely literary sphere, from political discussions and theoretical arguments into the economic field and into the struggle for existence. This transfer was the product of a series of events. The program of industrialization of the economically backward country—the type of factories, their strategic allocation, etc.—had as its fundamental objective the preparation of the USSR for the realization of world revolution through military strength. Collectivization of the countryside was not only a logical outcome but also an indispensable result of this program. This was especially true when it became apparent that the realization of industrialization would be impossible without requisitioning of food supplies from the peasants in order to finance the industrialization program—and without obtaining from them cheap labor, gaining complete control over them, and transforming them into robots of the Party.

Though, originally, the First Five Year Plan had foreseen only loose collectivization of about 20% of peasant holdings, an intensified drive for complete collectivization was undertaken because of fear of the peasantry and because of improper functioning of industrialization. In the Ukraine, the scope of this intensified drive can be seen from the fact that between January 1, 1928 and June 1, 1932, the number of collective farms rose from 9,734 embracing 2.9% of the total sowing area, to 25,300 embracing 80.5% of the total sowing area.[21] On the All-Union scale that drive, according to Kaganovich, meant that between 1929 and 1933, there were created, on the average, 120 collective farms, 2 MTS's and 4 Soviet farms every day. However, since things progressed unevenly, there were days when "not 120 but 500 and more collective farms were organized." [22]

As a means of disapproval of the collectivization scheme, which, especially in the Ukraine, was totally alien to peasant traditions and psychology, the Ukrainian peasantry slaughtered its livestock, destroyed its implements of production, and put up, in places, an unorganized armed resistance. Above all, the peasants decreased the sowing area, thereby threatening the disruption of the entire Plan. Though the harvest of 1930 was good, it was reported that the projected deliveries of 464,000,000 puds of grain to the state were barely fulfilled.[23] In spite of this resistance, the collectivization of peasant holdings continued. In 1931 collectivization was reported to have embraced 68% of all peasant holdings; and by 1932 it reached 73%. During the same time, the total sowing area decreased by 20%.[24] From this struggle between the peasantry and the government there resulted a disruption in Ukrainian agriculture. This disruption was vividly reflected even in the government's expectation of grain for the year 1932, which was lowered from 464,000,000 puds to 355,000,000 puds.[25] To obtain that minimum as well as to force the peasantry into submission, the government, on August 7, 1932, and the Party, issued a decree which established the death penalty without right of amnesty for any violation or damage of the property of collective farms.[26] At the same time, a policy of full scale requisitioning was adopted toward individual owners. In answer to this scheme of the Party and of the government, the peasantry replied with silent sabotage by leaving the grain in the fields thereby causing, according to Kosior's calculations, a loss of about 200,000,000 puds of grain.[27]

These actions on the part of the Ukrainian peasantry not only endangered the entire policy of integral planning, but also disrupted the already not-too-smooth functioning of the First Five Year Plan. Frightened by peasant opposition, the CC of the CP(b)U and the Sovnarkom of the UkSSR, on December 6, 1932, issued a joint decree in which they directed local Party and administrative organs to exterminate organized sabotage both in and out of the Party. "It is necessary," stated the decree, "to liquidate the opposition on the part of the Communists who have become the actual leaders of sabotage, and to liquidate the passive attitude of some Party organs towards the sabotage." [28] On December 14, 1932, the CC of the VKP(b) and the Sovnarkom of the USSR, in a joint decree, ordered the CC of the CP(b)U and the Sovnarkom of the UkSSR to "turn serious attention to proper execution of Ukrainization; remove its mechanical conduct; disperse Petliurists and other bourgeois nationalist elements from the Party and Soviet organizations; carefully select and educate Ukrainian Bolshevik cadres; and safeguard systematic Party leadership and control over the execution of Ukrainization." [29] Finally, on January 24, 1933, the CC of the VKP(b), after Stalin's denunciation of the situation in the Ukraine and of the leadership of the CP(b)U, issued a no-confidence resolution. It assailed the CP(b)U for failure to fulfill the recommendations of the VKP(b) on the organization of bread deliveries to the state, which had been greatly reduced.[30]

On the basis and in pursuance of these decrees there was inaugurated in the Ukraine a reign of terror against the Ukrainian peasantry, the Ukrainian intelligentsia, Ukrainian institutions, and Ukrainian members of the CP(b)U. It was conducted by members of Political Departments that were organized for that purpose, and the entire operation was supervised by P. P. Postyshev. By November, 1933, there had been established in the Ukraine 3,800 Political Departments which were staffed by 17,000 steeled and faithful career-seeking Party men. Each department was headed by a chief whose selection and qualification for the position was checked from among 25,000 eligibles.[31] Officially the duties and the role of these Political Departments were said to have centered on strengthening

the MTS's and Soviet farms by improving their political role and
influence in the village; by elevating to proper heights the political
and economic work of central organs of the Party; and by serving
as the "Party's eyes and control in all branches of work of the MTS
as well as of the collective farms supervised by the MTS's." [32]

In practice, members of these Political Departments seem to
have been a law unto themselves. Being brought from other regions
of the USSR into the Ukraine, and being completely ignorant of
Ukrainian conditions and situation, members of the Political Department met with resentment on the part of local Party officials.
This was revealed by Postyshev at the June, 1933 Plenum of the
CC of the CP(b)U, when he complained that there were

> various *raykom* secretaries who, up to the present time, cannot
> understand the great role of the Political Departments of the
> MTS's and the Soviet farms. There we have, it seems, secretaries
> of the *raykoms* who give preference to small, trivial matters in-
> stead of Bolshevik, united work, and comradely struggle along-
> side of the Political Departments for the solution of our socialist
> tasks in the village.
>
> In the latest period we have encountered a few unsatisfactory
> factors when the leading *rayon* comrades instead of giving help
> to the Political Departments, ignore them by all means, avoid
> them, and even discredit the workers of the Political Departments
> before the members of the collective farms. Some *rayon* secre-
> taries look upon the workers of the Political Departments as the
> 'pretenders for power' in the *rayon*.[33]

Though the activity of the Political Departments centered fundamentally in the countryside, being thus the most responsible organs for bringing about the man-made famine[34] which took a toll
of from three to seven million lives, the Political Departments were
also charged with other activities. By virtue of general tasks, as
set forth in a joint decree of the CC of the VKP(b) and the Sovnarkom of the USSR, on December 14, 1932,[35] and by virtue of
the objectives set before the CP(b)U by Kosior at the July, 1933
Plenum of the Kharkov Party organization, Political Departments
were also responsible for: 1) Uncovering of all theory and practice

which, either directly or indirectly, aimed at the breaking up of international solidarity of the USSR; 2) Purging the ranks of the CP(b)U of nationalist elements; 3) Carrying out Bolshevik Ukrainization; 4) Selecting and carefully placing Bolshevik cadres at all strategic points of life; 5) Checking, to the very foundation, the work of the Ukrainian Academy of Sciences, and of all educational institutions of the UkSSR; 6) Strengthening these institutions with Bolshevik cadres; and 7) Improving the guidance of the CP(b)U over the Ukrainian press, literature, theater, criticism and self-criticism.[36] Political Departments thus were charged with the conduct of a general purge in the Ukraine.

The scope of this purge outside the Party is unknown. It is a safe assumption, however, that it ran into the tens of thousands. In the CP(b)U, the purge of 1933, according to Postyshev's own testimony before the November, 1933 Plenum of the CC of the CP(b)U, took a toll, between January and October, 1933, of 27,000, or 21.6% of the total membership of the CP(b)U, who were labelled as "class enemies and unstable and demoralized elements."[37] Though the purge took most of its victims from among the rank and file membership of the CP(b)U, among its prey were many leaders of the CP(b)U. Indirectly, the events of 1933 were responsible for the death of Skrypnyk who, on July 7, 1933, committed suicide.

A correct appraisal of Skrypnyk and of his activity is very much wanting. The son of a railroad official, Mykola A. Skrypnyk was born in 1872. He attended, but failed to complete, the St. Petersburg Technological Institute. His revolutionary activity, for which he was sentenced several times to exile wherefrom he managed each time to escape, began in 1901. It was during this period that he made personal acquaintance with Lenin and became his ardent follower. During the revolution, Skrypnyk took an active part in numerous events. He was a member of the Military Revolutionary Committee in Petrograd and later played a vital role in organizing Soviet rule in the Ukraine, serving first as Commissar of Labor of the UkSSR, then of Trade and Industry. In 1918, Skrypnyk became the Chairman of the People's Commissars of the UkSSR, and, in addition, he also headed the Commissariat for Foreign Affairs. During the 1920's he occupied numerous posts in the government of the UkSSR. For some time he was head of the Commissariat of Workers and Peasant Inspection; then of the CHEKA, of Justice, of Education and of the Ukrainian State Planning Commission. He was also the co-author of the 1924 Constitution of the USSR, and for some time served as Chairman of the Council of Nationalities. Skrypnyk likewise held important positions in the Party apparatus. He was one of the original founders of the CP(b)U and of the KPZU. For a number of years he was a member of the CC of the VKP(b), as well as a high ranking official in the hierarchy of the Comintern where he was one of the strongest spokesmen on the Ukrainian problem. Skrypnyk was also one of the staunchest defendants of the policy of Ukrainization. Many of his speeches on the problems of Ukrainization were adopted verbatim as resolutions of various Plenums of the CC of the CP(b)U. Last, but not least, Skrypnyk was the author of a number of pamphlets on Communist theory of the national problem. He was an able writer and critic, as well as an inspirer and leader of a pro-Soviet trend among Ukrainians abroad.

In view of his numerous high positions in the government and in the Party, and because of his authority, his personal prestige, and his activity, Skrypnyk's suicide in many respects was a turning point in the Russian Bolshevik policy toward, and treatment of, the Ukraine. The new policy, as well as justification and results of the purge, was very vividly presented at the November, 1933 Plenum of the CC of the CP(b)U. The principal speaker at the Plenum was Kosior, who declared that the summary of achievements in the Ukraine was necessary in view of the international situation; because of international designs on the Ukraine; increased activity of Ukrainian nationalism; and the national deviation within the CP(b)U.[38]

Following this introduction, Kosior went on to declare that, thanks to the efforts of the Party, the aid of the Russian proletariat, and as a result of industrialization and collectivization, the Ukraine had been able to abolish "the late colonial position," and to become a country of heavy industry, socialized agriculture, and socialist culture. He cited various percentage figures; making numerous comparisons between the pre and post-revolutionary outputs of Ukrainian industry, as well as between Ukrainian and European industries. He drew a picture of the extent of the proletarization of Ukrainian cities; showing the degree of progress of collectivization of the rural areas, and mechanization of agriculture. Thus, Kosior attempted to refute contentions of the Ukrainians abroad that the Ukraine was being made a colony of the RSFSR. On the contrary, he argued, these achievements demonstrated independent creativeness of the Ukrainian people. Thanks to these efforts, he said, the Ukraine had begun to create a Soviet culture. The Ukrainian language had become the language of the state apparatus. Ukrainian attendance in schools had increased; illiteracy had declined; Ukrainian publications had spread; and higher educational opportunities and chances for participation in the government had presented themselves. All of these achievements, Kosior stressed, had been impossible for Ukrainians before the revolution.

All of these gains, Kosior went on to assert, had been made possible thanks to the hard work of the Party and the aid of the Russian proletariat, and would have been greater had it not been for the mistakes committed by the CP(b)U, and, above all, for its lack of vigilance. As a result of this grave mistake, Kosior declared, there arose a possibility for the Ukrainian nationalists, who were allegedly in the service of foreign capital, to penetrate the apparatus of the Party. They had entrenched themselves, he said, in several branches of educational institutions (Commissariats of Education, Justice, Ukrainian Academy of Sciences, Institute of Marxism-Leninism, Agricultural Academy, The Shevchenko Institute, etc.) and in economic institutions (Commissariat of Agriculture, Industry, in collective farms, MTS's, etc.). From these institutions, Kosior charged, the Ukrainians carried on their anti-Bolshevik activity from within by inciting the peasant, by distorting Ukrainian history, by sabotage, by spreading national prejudices, enmity and discord, by trying to restore the pre-revolutionary order, by trying to hinder the consolidation of revolutionary forces, and by trying to break up the unity of the USSR—unity which he declared was the highest achievement of the revolution, and the highest achievement of mutual cooperation. Ukrainian danger, he underscored, thus had become the most important danger.

The significance of the Ukrainian danger, Kosior proceeded, could not be underestimated, because the Ukraine occupied "the foremost position" in the USSR in relation to capitalist encirclement. This factor, he declared, made it incumbent upon all members of the CP(b)U to be particularly vigilant and prepared to repel any attack against the USSR from the outside, or subversion from within on the part of the Ukrainian nationalists. He held the latter responsible for the total bankruptcy of the Russian Bolshevik nationality policy, and he ordered the CP(b)U to "discover and unmask [them] before the toilers of the Ukraine" as "foul and despicable traitors of the Ukrainian people."

The discovery of Ukrainian nationalists, Kosior continued, was also important in view of Skrypnyk's lack of vigilance, his pride, his inability to see changes, his egotism, which led him, in his defense of Ukrainian Communists, to belittle Stalin, and led to his own nationalist degeneration which the CC of the CP(b)U had failed to uncover in time. Kosior charged that under Skrypnyk's protection Ukrainian nationalists had been able to penetrate the Party apparatus, and that many of them had been welcomed with open arms either as persecuted members of the KPZU, or as converted emigres. He accordingly accused all the major participants of "Petliurization" in the Ukrainian policy of trying to reinforce Ukrainian nationalist culture and, under the direction of Poland and Germany, of preparing an armed uprising. He expressed satisfaction that many Ukrainians had already confessed their part in the conspiracy. He went on, however, to warn all the members of the CP(b)U not to be satisfied with these confessions alone, and directed them to: 1) Educate the masses in the spirit of internationalism; 2) Strengthen the militant revolutionary unity of the peoples of the USSR; 3) Prepare Ukrainian Bolshevik cadres; 4) Select and place loyal persons, true to the cause of socialism, in all the main sections of socialist construction; 5) Direct the press and mass political work; 6) Strengthen the departments of the Commissariat of Education and of the scientific institutions; 7) Pay serious attention to the theoretical front—history, political economy, agrarian policy, etc.; 8) Guide the development of Ukrainian literature and arts; and 9) Work among national minorities of the Ukraine.

Following Kosior's stress on the danger of the Ukrainian national problem, and his placing the entire blame for the incompatibility between the Russian Bolshevik theory and practices on Ukrainian nationalism, other speakers at the November, 1933 Plenum of the CC of the CP(b)U devoted much attention to that aspect. In his report to the Plenum, Postyshev put the entire blame for the improper functioning of industrialization and collectivization, as well as for the violent peasant opposition to various administratively applied economic pressures, on the Ukrainian emigration and the Ukrainian "counter-revolution." [39] He charged both groups with trying to prevent, and with sabotaging, the rule of the workers; with attempting to bring about a disunity between the other peoples of the USSR and the Ukrainian people; and with consciously attempting to separate the Ukraine from the USSR with foreign aid, being aware of the damage such a separation would create for the rest of the USSR in view of the Ukraine's economic importance. To discredit still further the Ukrainian opposition in the eyes of domestic, and above all foreign, observers, and at the same time to cover up the inability of the Party to cope with the peasantry, as well as to justify the famine whose creation he had supervised, Postyshev accused the Ukrainian opposition of intentional sabotage of the harvest at a time when "the Party was worrying about the well being of the peasantry." He likewise charged them with sabotaging Ukrainization and with inciting hatred between the Ukrainian and other peoples of the USSR—cf. the Russians.

Like Kosior, Postyshev charged that the penetration of institutions and sabotage of work had been possible because of the lack of vigilance of Skrypnyk, behind whose authority all nationalists had taken refuge. Skrypnyk, Postyshev stated, had made several mistakes in the past, but it was not until the decision to liquidate the peasantry as a class that Skrypnyk's mistakes had become a deviation. From then on, Postyshev charged, Skrypnyk opposed everything that was Russian as well as everything coming from the CC of the VKP(b). It was mainly because of Skrypnyk's opposition, he said, that collectivization had met with so much difficulty in the Ukraine. Postyshev also accused Skrypnyk of sabotaging various measures of the Party in the field of Ukrainization; of distorting the nationality policy of the Party by supplying his own interpretation; and of viewing the Union as a loose, rather than a strong, organization, implying thereby that his views were closely tied with those who favored separation of the Ukraine.

At the close of his speech, Postyshev read a part of the projected resolution of the Plenum, which stated in essence that Great Russian chauvinism remained the principal danger on the All-Union scale and for the entire VKP(b), but that in the Ukraine, at the moment, Ukrainian nationalism was the fundamental danger because of its alliance with foreign intervention. Postyshev acknowledged that this was a new formulation, but he tried to justify it by arguing that it was dictated by the intensification of the struggle against the USSR; by foreign designs on the Ukraine; by the intensification of collectivization; and by the deviation of Skrypnyk. He tried, at the same time, to assure members of the Plenum that the new formulation in no way tended to diminish the danger of Great Russian chauvinism.

Another speaker at the November, 1933 Plenum of the CC of the CP(b)U, Popov, fully endorsed Postyshev's formulation. He warned his listeners that Ukrainian nationalism sought all possible support from international imperialism. He argued that since the ultimate objective of Ukrainian nationalism, and of all Ukrainian political parties, irrespective of their platform, lay in the separation of the Ukraine from the rest of the USSR, it would be a grave mistake to think that because of the recent setbacks the Ukrainians would stop their anti-Bolshevik activity.[40] The same charge was also made by Panas P. Liubchenko, Chairman of the Sovnarkom of the UkSSR who, in addition, accused all Ukrainians of non-

Bolshevik orientation, of trying to separate the Ukraine from the rest of the USSR; of working not for independence or sovereignty of the Ukraine but trying to betray the Ukraine to foreign imperialism.[41]

At the end of all the debates and speeches, the November, 1933 Plenum of the CC of the CP(b)U adopted a lengthy resolution on the results and immediate tasks of the national policy in the Ukraine.[42] The resolution confirmed many assertions made at the Plenum by the principal speakers. It announced that, thanks to the policy of industrialization, the Ukraine had undergone important changes not only with respect to industrial self-development but also as regards the creation of its own urban population. The resolution stated that by virtue of collectivization, the Ukraine, in addition to technical improvement in agriculture, had begun "the abolishment of the antithesis between town and country." Industrialization and collectivization, the resolution went on, had created "a base for the further improvement of the welfare of the toiling masses, and for the powerful growth of Ukrainian Soviet culture"— national in form, and socialist in content. All of these achievements, the resolution argued, had been made possible only by the Party's pursuing of the Leninist national policy—by "crushing" Russian chauvinists, who had opposed Ukrainization, and by "smashing" Ukrainian nationalists who utilized Ukrainization "for the purpose of strengthening the position of the Ukrainian bourgeoisie and of separating the Ukraine from the Soviet Union, which, if achieved, would have meant the restoration of capitalism."

The resolution acknowledged that "the policy of mass collectivization and the liquidation of the kulaks as a class," had encountered "desperate resistance" among the peasantry and also within the CP(b)U itself. Having failed to prevent the realization of the collectivization policy, the Ukrainians, applying "the method of deception, duplicity, and camouflage," had penetrated into factories, government offices, Soviet farms, MTS's, collective farms, and even Party organizations in order to disrupt them from within. The resolution accused all anti-Bolshevik Ukrainian forces abroad of connivance with foreign governments (Polish, German, and British). At the same time it condemned the deposed leaders of the CP(b)U for their relaxation, lack of vigilance, and for allowing Ukrainian nationalists to penetrate into Bolshevik institutions where, under the cover of Ukrainization, they had instigated national hatred.

The resolution particularly attacked the CC of the CP(b)U for its relaxation of "Bolshevik vigilance," and especially for its overlooking the nationalist deviation headed by Skrypnyk. The resolution accused Skrypnyk of yielding to the pressure of Ukrainian nationalist elements as early as 1923, by opposing "the creation of a single Soviet state with a single foreign policy." It condemned him for maintaining that the main danger which had to be fought was Great Russian chauvinism. Skrypnyk was also branded for his association with Ukrainians abroad—associations which, the resolution stated, implied his agreement with their main objective, namely the separation of the Ukraine from the USSR. The resolution assailed Skrypnyk for his abandonment of Leninism and for his slipping "into the position of the Ukrainian nationalists," a change which led him to support the policy of relaxation of economic, political, and cultural ties between the Ukraine and the other Soviet Republics; the weakening of the USSR; of maximum separation of the Ukrainian language from the Russian language; of forceful Ukrainization of schools, etc. Accordingly, the resolution condemned Skrypnyk "and the trend that he led" for: 1) His facilitation of "the work of the Ukrainian nationalists that was directed towards separating the Ukraine from the Soviet Union and towards converting it into a colony of Polish fascism or German imperialism"; and 2) His facilitation of "the work of the Russian whiteguards and foreign interventionists who are also striving to separate the Ukraine from the Soviet Union and thereby to strike a blow at the economic and political power of the Soviet Union, the international centre of the proletarian revolution."

The resolution called upon all members of the CP(b)U to wage a determined struggle against the remnants of Skrypnyk's deviation in order to achieve "real Bolshevik Ukrainization, the real international education of the masses, and the further growth of Ukrainian Soviet culture." Accordingly, the November, 1933 Plenum of the CC of the CP(b)U, in its resolution, decreed that the CP(b)U, in the sphere of national policy, should further Bolshevik Ukrainization on the basis of international education of the masses, and the struggle against Great Russian chauvinism and Ukrainian nationalism. It labelled Great Russian chauvinism as the principal danger confronting the whole of the USSR, and of the VKP(b). But, at the same time, it stated that in the Ukraine local Ukrainian nationalism presented the principal danger because of its alliance with various interventionist camps, which were trying to separate the Ukraine from the USSR, to weaken the position of the USSR, and to convert the Ukraine into a colony of foreign capital. The resolution ordered the Party to: 1) Train and educate Bolshevik Ukrainian cadres in the collective farms, Soviet farms, MTS's, factories, universities, and technical institutes, "from among the youth and the socialist intellectuals who are loyal to the cause of socialist construction"; and 2) Select and promote real Ukrainian cadres, both Party and non-Party, to Soviet work on the Republic, regional, and district levels in the Party apparatus and educational institutions. The resolution also instructed all organizations of the Party "to assure proper Bolshevik guidance of Party educational and Party mass work"; and combat any underestimation of that work; and to secure an improvement in the quality of the press and in the mass explanatory work. The resolution of the November, 1933 Plenum of the CC of the CP(b)U likewise directed the Party to reinforce the school network "with tried Party forces," fully endorsed the purging of the personnel of educational institutions, and ordered the publication of the fundamental works of Marx, Engels, Lenin, and Stalin in the Ukrainian language. It called for exercising "real every-day Bolshevik leadership on the front of literature and art" and condemned Ukrainian orientation on "the bourgeois capitalist West," rather than on the "proletarian culture of the Russian working class." Accordingly, it gave the Party the responsibility of intensifying "the struggle against those nationalist tendencies which are hostile to the proletarian revolution, of strengthening the cultural ties of Ukrainian Soviet literature and art with the literature and art of other nations of the Soviet Union, of the fraternal interchange of experience, of improving the work of training and developing Ukrainian Soviet writers, [and] of enlarging and improving the publication of artistic literature in the Ukrainian language." The resolution likewise called the attention of the Party organizations to the existence of "relaxation of Bolshevik vigilance" in the institutions of national minorities (collective farms, schools, clubs, institutes, etc.) and directed that "necessary measures be taken to purge these organizations of hostile elements, to reinforce them with Bolshevik cadres in order to assure that Bolshevik work will be carried on among the national minorities."

The resolution thrust aside arguments which were circulating abroad that the events of 1933 in the Ukraine had signalized "a revision of the national policy." It labelled such views as being "slanderous and provocative" and called for "the most ruthless resistance" against their spread. The resolution likewise called for the "utter defeat of Ukrainian nationalism and the exposure of the nationalist hypocrites who have penetrated into the Party," as a prerequisite for further Bolshevik Ukrainization. Simultaneously, it promised to continue "the most ruthless struggle against Great Russian chauvinism," labelling it an ally, and the partial source, of Ukrainian nationalism. Finally, the resolution pledged to crush any attempts "on the part of Great Russian chauvinists" either to wreck or hinder "the further development of Bolshevik Ukrainization," or of those who "under the cover of Leftist phrases" maintained that the national question was obsolete and that the national republics were unnecessary because such views meant the revision of the Party's decision on the national problem and the weakening of the "dictatorship of the proletariat."

Though the resolution of the November, 1933 Plenum of the CC of the CP(b) U attempted to discard rumors that a new interpretation of the national problem had occurred, the November Plenum, in its words and in its deeds, marked officially the turning point in the Russian Bolshevik nationality policy in the Ukraine in particular, and in the USSR in general. Prior to that time, in all of its major resolutions and pronouncements on the national problem, the Party had considered Great Russian chauvinism as the fundamental danger. Local nationalism had always been viewed as a secondary danger which came as a reaction to Great Russian chauvinism. By reversing the position of these two dangers, an entirely new interpretation—and hence an entirely new national policy—was inaugurated. That it was a new formulation was officially acknowledged by Postyshev himself in his speech before the November Plenum.

The decisions adopted at the November, 1933 Plenum of the CC of the CP(b)U not only were re-echoed several weeks later at the XII Congress of the CP(b)U, but were also formally approved by the Congress and thus became the official policy of the CP(b)U. The pattern for the Congress' proceedings was provided by Kosior's keynote address.[43] Speaking as the representative of the CC of the VKP(b), he dwelt at great length on the crisis of capitalism, wherein, he said, existed unemployment, growing chauvinism, fascism, intensification and growth of contradictions among capitalist states and the preparation for war against the USSR. In contrast he pointed to the Soviet Union, which, he said, externally conducted a peace policy, non-aggression agreements, and attempted to bring about normal conditions in international relations. On the home front, he declared it conducted creative work, industrialization, collectivization, material improvement of the toiling people, liquidation of the kulaks, creation of "a classless, socialist society," development of industrial centers in Union Republics in order to eliminate the remnants of colonialism, growth of cultural achievements, and the spread of education. All of these achievements, Kosior argued, had been made possible by the correct line of the Party—in spite of nationalist opposition and deviation which had been headed by Skrypnyk, whose unmasking, he complained, had come with considerable delay. Kosior stressed heavily the new formulation of the danger of nationalist deviation as had been adopted at the November Plenum of the CC of the CP(b)U. He danger of nationalist deviation," especially since that danger worked warned his listeners "not to understimate the significance of the in complete harmony with foreign intervention. Accordingly, he reiterated the correctness and righteousness of the formula, which stated that, while Great Russian chauvinism was the main danger for the entire USSR and the VKP(b), at the moment in the Ukraine the fundamental danger was Ukrainian nationalism.

Kosior's line of argument was developed in much greater detail, at much greater length, and with greater criticism, by Postyshev in his political report to the XII Congress of the CP(b)U on the work of the Party's Central Committee.[44] Though he acknowledged that Ukrainian conditions differed in several respects from the conditions in other republics, Postyshev maintained that, being an important organization, the CP(b)U had important responsibilities to perform. However, in this case, he said, the CP(b)U had failed to live up to its responsibilities. He denounced the deposed leadership of the CP(b)U for its mistakes in the guidance of rural economy and industry, and asserted that only after the liquidation of that leadership had visible progress in these fields been made. The Ukraine, he said, thanks to "creative enthusiasm of the masses and Bolshevik leadership" had been transformed into a country of foremost socialist industry and of socialist mechanized agriculture. These achievements, Postyshev argued, citing numerous statistics, meant also material improvement for the Ukrainian people.

Postyshev became much more critical of the leadership of the CP(b)U when he turned to the question of the nationality policy of that organization. He attacked the deposed leadership for failure to increase its Bolshevik vigilance; to check the cadres and purge undesirable elements from all branches of socialist construction; to intensify the struggle against Great Russian chauvinism and Ukrainian nationalism; to develop international education among the toilers; and to unmask Ukrainian nationalists and their organizations, showing their connections with foreign interventionists. Postyshev particularly assailed Skrypnyk, and, after comparing him with Shumskyj, denounced him for working toward the separation of the Ukraine from the USSR. Though he cited numerous figures taken during Skrypnyk's period on the progress of Ukrainian schools; on the increase of Ukrainian newspapers, books, periodicals; on the attendance of Ukrainians at the institutions of higher

learning; on the decline of illiteracy in the Ukraine; on the increase
of the Ukrainian working class; on Ukrainian participation in government, etc.; Postyshev declared that all these achievements had
been possible only thanks to the elimination of Skrypnyk and his
group. To maintain, as well as to improve, these achievements,
Postyshev repeated before the XII Congress of the CP(b)U the
tasks that had been set forth at the November, 1933 Plenum of the
CC of the CP(b)U—namely intensified Bolshevik vigilance, unmasking of nationalist deviation, international education, and the
development of Ukrainian Soviet literature.

It was both logical and inevitable that the new formulation of
national danger would find the approval of the highest authority,
and would henceforth become not only the official policy but also
part of the Russian Bolshevik theory on the national problem.
Speaking before the XVII Congress of the VKP(b) in January,
1934, and without making any change in the theoretical formula-
tions on the national danger that had been adopted at the X and
at the XII Congresses, Stalin fully endorsed the new formulation.
Both deviation toward Great Russian chauvinism and toward local
nationalism, he said, had one common source—the departure from
Leninist internationalism. Accordingly, he declared that it would
be purposeless to argue which of the deviations was more dangerous. "It would be absurd," he announced,

> to attempt to give ready-made recipes for the major and minor
> danger that would be suitable for all times and for all conditions.
> Such recipes do not exist. The major danger is the deviation
> against which we have ceased to fight and thereby enabled it to
> grow into a danger to the state.
>
> Only very recently, in the Ukraine, the deviation towards
> Ukrainian nationalism did not represent the major danger; but
> when we ceased to fight against it and enabled it to grow to the
> extent that it joined with the interventionists, this deviation be-
> came the major danger. The question as to which is the major
> danger in the sphere of the national question is determined, not
> by futile and formal controversies, but by a Marxian analysis of
> the situation at the given moment, and by the study of the mis-
> takes that have been committed in this sphere.[45]

To avoid mistakes and to eliminate future deviations, Stalin called for: 1) The raising up of the theoretical level of the Party; 2) Intensification of ideological work in all Party organizations; 3) Conducting of unceasing propaganda of Leninism in the ranks of the Party; 4) Training in the spirit of Leninist internationalism all Party organizations and the non-Party *activ*; 5) Criticism of deviations of the members of the Party; and 6) Systematic exposure of the ideology and remnants of trends hostile to Leninism.[46]

Stalin's endorsement of the new formulation of the national danger, which the XVII Congress of the VKP(b) unanimously approved, officially ended the old, and introduced the new era in the theoretical as well as in the practical treament of the national problem in the USSR. Basically, this new formulation was the logical and the inevitable outcome of industrialization and collectivization. It was likewise a product of the policy of integral planning, of intensified centralization, and of total regimentation of all aspects of life in the USSR.

CHAPTER VI

Total Regimentation

The XVII Congress of the VKP(b), from the standpoint of theory as well as practice, was a very significant milestone in the history of the Russian Bolshevik nationality policy in the USSR in general, and in the Ukraine, in particular. It marked the end of an old, and symbolized the beginning of a new era. It also signalized complete victory of the centripetal over the centrifugal forces. Accordingly, it inaugurated a period of increased toleration of Great Russian nationalism because of the latter's support of the Party's centralism, uniformity, and territorial unity of the USSR. By the same token, it introduced a period of increased hostility towards all forces which, in one way or another, hindered the effective perfection of centralism.

Because of the Ukraine's strategic location and economic importance to the success of industrialization and collectivization, the effects of the formal adoption of the new interpretation of the national danger by the XVII Congress of the VKP(b) were felt more strongly in the Ukraine than in any other union republic or national region of the USSR. On the one hand, the new interpretation meant an increased drive for glorification of the achievements of the planning era and of its leaders, while on the other hand it heralded an intensified and well-organized anti-Ukrainian trend. Detailed directives on the course of the new policy were provided by Postyshev. Addressing the Party organization at the All-Ukrainian Association of Marxist-Leninist Institutes, the VUAM-LIN, in Kharkov, in January, 1934, he told the assembled future Party theoreticians "to show the role of Stalin in the further devel-

opment and elaboration of the philosophical heritage of Marx-
Lenin . . . [and] to present all the greatness of this major theoretician
of the international Communist movement." He also directed them
"to develop the problem of the birth of a new man, of new psychology, [and] of new attitude toward the work on the basis of
socialist revolution," and commanded them to study and assimilate
all the achievements of "socialist construction." Postyshev likewise
suggested that they elaborate the problem of the dictatorship of
the proletariat, and especially "the problem of the strengthening of
the proletarian state as a prerequisite towards its withering away
and complete disappearance." At the same time, Postyshev ordered
them "to clean the philosophical front of the Ukraine of everything
that has been brought there by . . . the philosophers of Ukrainian
national fascism." Since, politically and organizationally, he declared, Ukrainian national forces had been destroyed, the task
remaining was "to uproot the deeply entrenched remnants of their
subversive work in the scientific field and in the sphere of education." He suggested that the same formula be followed in the economic, agricultural, national, and other spheres of activity.[1]

An identical proposal was also made by Kosior, at the XIII
Session of the All-Ukrainian Congress of Soviets in January, 1935,
when he declared that the discovery and destruction of Bolshevik
enemies was the main prerequisite to further progress in all branches
of socialist construction. "It is necessary to expel these enemies
from wherever they can be found . . . It is necessary to throw them
out from all dark places wherein they hide—and there are such
hide-outs." [2]

In accordance with Postyshev's and Kosior's directives and suggestions, especially those dealing with the problem of uprooting
Ukrainian intelligentsia, there appeared in Soviet journals numerous articles on that issue. The aim of these articles seems to have
been on the one hand to approve the *fait accompli; i.e.,* to justify
the liquidation of the semi-independent existence of some Ukrainian
institutions and their spokesmen prior to the XVII Congress of the
VKP(b). On the other hand, these articles were intended, through
criticism, to pave the way for annihiliation of the remaining edu-

cational institutions and organizations as well as their associates. Under particular attack came the work and program of the All-Ukrainian Academy of Sciences, the VUAN, in Kiev. "Through the VUAN," declared one Soviet writer, ". . . they [Ukrainian national intelligentsia] spread nationalist poison, . . . organized sabotage in industry, transport, rural economy, etc., . . . strove to upset the economy of the Ukraine, to create famine, and to prepare a counter-revolutionary uprising." [3] Identical charges were leveled at the Ukrainian Academy of Rural Economy and all of its research institutes; the Institute of the History of Ukrainian Culture; the Shevchenko Institute; and the VUAMLIN.[4] As a result, some of these institutions became branches of the corresponding All-Union organs. Others, with their personnel, which was accused of maintaining petty bourgeois views, disappeared. Ukrainian institutions and Ukrainian intelligentsia thus became scapegoats for the improper functioning of industrialization and collectivization, and accordingly they fell victims to the Party's self-created fear.

In addition to charges of subversion from within, Ukrainian intelligentsia was assailed for allegedly conniving with foreign powers to separate the Ukraine from the USSR. An analysis of the charges leveled against the Ukrainians shows that the authors of these charges had, in advance, set opinions on foreign plans irrespective of the existing facts or situation. Ukrainian intelligentsia was accused of conspiring with Polish, German, and British intelligence staffs. The latter allegedly were to utilize, in their anti-Soviet crusade, slogans of "the 'freeing' of the Ukraine, Georgia and perhaps Central Asia as a cover-up for Ukrainian, Georgian, and other plans of imperialism connected with Soviet oil, coal, [and] iron." [5] Ukrainian intelligentsia was likewise accused of collaborating with the Nazis, whose aims included the separation of the Ukraine from the USSR and the establishment of a German-Ukrainian economic and military alliance.[6] The Ukrainian intelligentsia was, in addition, denounced for its opposition to, and demonstration against, the Soviet Union's entry into the League of Nations.[7] It was also charged with alleged adherence to, and spread of, anti-Semitism among the Ukrainian people. Finally, the Ukrainian intelligentsia was blamed for all acts of economic disruption of integral planning.[8]

Alongside of these accusations, condemnations, and denunciations of Ukrainian intelligentsia before both domestic and foreign audiences, there was launched a greatly intensified campaign aimed at showing all kinds of achievements the Ukrainian people had made in various spheres of activity. These highly publicized achievements, for example, revealed that in the field of public education there were in 1934-5 in the Ukraine 4,685,000 students in 21,941 schools—an increase of 3,021,000 students and 2,601 schools since the year 1915. Of the 21,941 schools, 17,327 were said to be Ukrainian (there were no Ukrainian schools in 1915); 1,394 Russian; 432 Jewish; 627 German; 238 Polish; 186 Moldavian; etc.[9] By 1936-7, the number of schools with Ukrainian as the language of instruction was reported to have climbed to 17,336, or an increase of 9 schools, while during the same period the total number of students reached 5,564,000, or an increase of 879,000.[10]

In the field of general raising of the cultural level of the population, the highly praised achievements revealed that in 1935 the Ukraine had 97 theatres, of which only 28 were non-Ukrainian, 2,622 movies and a drop of illiteracy to 4% of the total population.[11] Of the total newspapers and bulletins, which numbered 2,454, the Ukrainians had 1,960, or 79.8%; the Russians 405, or 16.5%; the Germans, 21 or 0.9%; the Jews 19, or 0.8%; etc.[12] Periodical literature was reported to have the following distribution: Ukrainian 134, or 56.1%; Russian 92, or 38.4%; Jewish 5, or 2.1%; etc.;[13] while the printing of books was divided as follows: Ukrainian 50,683,000; Russian 8,970,000; and other languages 1,932,-000.[14] By 1936-7, the reported cultural progress and achievements in the Ukraine included among others 13,767 libraries; 16,000 clubs; 439,000 radio sets; 5,501 movies; 1,160 sound movies; 88 theatres (a decline of 9); 1,830 newspapers, of which 1,402 were Ukrainian (a noticeable decline); 177 journals; and 69,104,000 books published in the Ukrainian language.[15]

However remarkable and self-satisfying these reports of achievements in the cultural sphere in the Ukraine may have been, they failed utterly to affect the political field. This is vividly demon-

strated in the national composition of the executive organs of the
Soviet hierarchy in the Ukraine in 1934-5.[16]

CEC of the	Ukrainians	Russians	Moldavians	Germans	Jews	Poles	Others
UkSSR	50.3%	25.4%	1.4%	1.1%	14.7%	1.4%	5.7%
Oblast' EC	43.7	20.6	4.9	1.5	20.4	1.1	7.8
Rayon EC	68.8	13.6	0.8	1.5	10.0	1.5	3.8
City EC	56.1	23.2	0.2	0.5	15.2	0.9	3.9
Village EC	86.1	5.7	1.0	1.7	2.2	1.9	1.4

As can be seen from the above table, the lower the authority and
power, the more one could find the presence of Ukrainians, and
vice-versa. One outstanding characteristic of this composition is
that, when compared with the same distribution during the mid-
1920's, it shows a considerable, and unexplained, decline of Ukrainian representation at all levels of the Soviet structure.[17]

In spite, or perhaps because, of this disproportionate representation, the Russian Bolsheviks conducted a dual propaganda campaign. On the one hand they presented the achievements of their
nationality policy, and on the other hand they attempted to conceal
numerous failures, for which the blame was placed on potential
or imaginary enemies. This campaign reached a high mark immediately before and after the adoption of the new constitution of
the USSR in late 1936. Speaking at the Extraordinary VIII All-
Union Congress of Soviets which approved the new constitution,
Liubchenko, "in the name of the Ukrainian people" welcomed the
new constitution. On the one hand, in accordance with the prevailing spirit, he assailed Ukrainian nationalists, accusing them of
connivance with foreign and domestic enemies. He attacked them
for continuing the struggle against Ukrainian workers and peasants.
He charged them with conspiracy and betrayal of the Ukraine to
foreign capital. On the other hand, he glorified the work of the
Communist Party, which in his opinion had not only created "a
truly independent sovereign Ukraine," but had also safeguarded

the development of the Ukrainian people. Thanks to that care, he said, the Ukraine had become "a mighty country, inseparable part of the great Soviet Union, a country of coal, machine building, a republic of Soviet and collective farms, [and] a republic of new people." Citing statistics on the increased industrial production, on the growth of the Ukrainian working class, on the development of different branches of industry, on the growth of technical education, on the increase of schools, etc., Liubchenko declared that these achievements represented a great cultural creation by the Ukrainian people. It was because of these achievements, he stated, that the rest of the world tried to upset the march of progress. He warned, however, that "physical annihilation" of any intruder would result from any attempt to try to separate the Ukraine from the rest of the USSR.[18]

Kosior, as another speaker for the Ukraine at the VIII Congress of Soviets, reiterated all of Liubchenko's contentions, laying heavy stress on the changes which had occurred in the Ukraine under the leadership of the Party, on the growth of socialism, on the elimination of illiteracy, and on the development of a new culture—a culture of workers and peasants. Like Liubchenko, Kosior assailed Ukrainian nationalists who, he charged, had betrayed the Ukrainian people to foreign capitalists, and warned that the Ukrainian people would destroy all "traitors" who, through terror, subversion, spy networks, etc., tried to destroy the rule of the dictatorship of the proletariat.[19]

Kosior developed his achievement and condemnation theme at greater length during the XIII Congress of the CP(b)U in 1937. In his report to the Congress, he began by presenting economic achievements the Ukraine had made from 1934 to 1937. He cited progress in industry, agriculture, transport, and the material well-being of the people. Industrialization, he argued, had brought important changes, both social and national, into the Ukraine. Many Ukrainians, he said, had become city inhabitants—a change which had found reflection in the composition of the Party as well as of the government apparatus. The state apparatus, he argued, had become close to the Ukrainian people, not only in national composition but also in language. He noted that these changes had affected the student body, teachers, and leaders in all branches of science. Kosior stressed heavily that during the period from 1934 to 1937, Ukrainians had made considerable progress in literature and art. As an example, he cited the fact that many "outstanding works" of Lenin and Stalin had been translated into the Ukrainian language. All this, he said, had been made possible only thanks to the elimination of Ukrainian nationalism. He warned, however, that to continue to make progress along the lines he had indicated, the CP(b)U had to be vigilant and not forget that a nationalism against which they stopped fighting was the most dangerous one.

Kosior then declared that all these achievements which the Ukrainian people had made in the economic and in the cultural field would have been far greater had it not been for nationalist subversion, and nationalist infiltration of the Party apparatus. He accused Ukrainian nationalists, as well as the Trotsky-Bukharinites, of blocking progress in all spheres of activity. With Postyshev in disgrace, he singled out the Kiev Party organization which Postyshev previously had headed.[20] He accused Postyshev of protecting the "subversive elements" who had promoted themselves, co-opted their own members, selected members for the Party by anti-Party methods, had not listened to criticism from below or to directives from above, etc. Kosior acknowledged that, though many harmdoers had been excluded from the Party, their infiltration into the ideological front, into the Party propaganda, into the Marx-Lenin Institute, etc., called for vigilance and intensified search for them.[21]

Kosior's line of reasoning, as well as the arguments and charges brought by other spokesmen of the CP(b)U at its XIII Congress, found full reflection in a resolution which the Congress adopted. The resolution noted with satisfaction increased industrial production, the growth of industrial centers, the building up of factories, and the overall fulfillment of the Second Five Year Plan. It likewise underscored the growth of the new technical cadres and of the new working class. The resolution took notice of the scope of collectivization and of the general improvement of the material well-being of the people as was evidenced by the increase of pay and social security.

The resolution acknowledged, however, that there were many failures "in cultural construction in the Ukraine"—especially in the quality of school work, in the slow reorganization of higher institutions of learning, and in the mass cultural work. This did not, however, prevent the resolution from making the assertion that cultural achievements in the Ukraine were great, as could be seen from the newly adopted constitution, which created "the unbreakable brotherly union" of the peoples of the USSR. Cultural achievement, the resolution stated, could also be seen from the growth of Ukrainian cities, of the Ukrainian working class, and of the technical intelligentsia. The resolution acknowledged that many organizations of the CP(b)U had failed to appreciate the importance of the national problem and had lessened their attention to the question of the nationality policy of the Party. The resolution tried to explain that this occurrence was due "to the insufficient Ukrainization of the Party, the Soviet, and especially the Trade Union and the Comsomol organizations [and] to insufficient elevation of Ukrainian Bolshevik cadres to leading Party, Soviet, economic, and Trade Union work."

Following these self-congratulatory appraisals, the resolution went on to declare that all these achievements, in the economic and cultural field, would have been far greater had it not been for the sabotage and subversion from within, which took place in the entire CP(b)U because of the lack of vigilance on the part of its Central Committee. The resolution especially singled out Postyshev for his misguidance of the Kiev Party apparatus,[22] and for his allowing the Central Committee to be infiltrated by nationalists and Trotskyites. It accused him of power-drunkenness, which, in turn, resulted in the use of high-handed tactics, and the absence of criticism and self-criticism. The resolution likewise acknowledged that there had been many violations of Party statutes and of democratic centralism—violations which weakened the Party and its relations with the masses. The resolution subjected to particular attack the ideological work of the CC of the CP(b)U in higher institutions of learning, as well as in the entire press.

To prevent future occurrences of sabotage, of the spread of misleading theories, etc., the resolution of the XIII Congress of the CP(b)U obligated all Party organizations to: 1) Reconstruct the Party's entire political and economic work on the basis of Stalin's directives at the March, 1937 Plenum of the CC of the VKP(b); 2) Develop extensive criticism and self-criticism; 3) Increase the revolutionary vigilance; 4) Improve the Party's work; 5) Fulfill the assignment of the Second Five Year Plan; 6) Improve economic, political, and cultural conditions in the Donbass, where slowdowns were reported to be at a dangerous level; 7) Give increased attention to the lag in light industry of the UkSSR; 8) Improve material and cultural conditions in the collective farms; 9) Improve political and economic work in rural areas; 10) Increase Ukrainian membership in leading positions in the Party, the Soviet, the Trade Union, and the Comsomol; and 11) Intensify international education. The resolution likewise obligated the CC of the CP(b)U to improve its ideological propaganda and instructor staff, and called for a collection of material on the history of the CP(b)U. It directed the CC to exert all of its efforts and use all media of communication to try to liquidate the last remnants of illiteracy in the Ukraine, and warned that care should be exercised in selecting Party members and Party secretaries for responsible positions. Finally, the resolution called upon the Trade Union and the Comsomol organizations to aid in carrying out all of these tasks, and likewise suggested increasing the vigilance of the entire Party apparatus—especially Party organizations in the Red Army, in view of the danger of foreign intervention.[23]

The self-created fear of foreign intervention, and the anxiety that the Ukrainian issue might be used by other powers in their attack against the USSR, figured very prominently in the Moscow trials of "old Bolsheviks" in 1937-8. It also played an important part in the less publicized, though victim-wise as effective, trials of the remainder of "old" Ukrainian intelligentsia, which was eliminated for its alleged efforts toward the separation of the Ukraine from the USSR; for treason to the state, and for trying to betray the Ukraine to Polish nobility, German fascism, and other foreign capitalists. The scope of this elimination is unknown, but it is a safe assumption that it reached into the tens of thousands during 1937-8. In part, the extent of this elimination of Ukrainian intelligentsia can be seen from a statement made by Nikita S. Khrushchev, at the IV Party Conference of the Kiev *oblast'*, in his first major pronouncement as the Secretary of the CC of the CP(b)U. "We have," he declared, "destroyed a considerable number of enemies, but not all . . . [for] as long as there exists capitalist encirclement, they [the outside world] will send to us spies and saboteurs." [24] For that reason, he called upon all members of the CP(b)U to maintain their vigilance, to work hard and to undo the harm that had been done. Above all, he urged them to give all of their efforts and forces for the purpose of strengthening "the brotherly union of the Ukrainian people with the people of our great Soviet Union, and, in the first place, with the Russian people," who, he said, had come on all occasions to the aid of the Ukraine against foreign invasions.[25]

The call for increased vigilance against the wreckers of socialist construction; for total mobilization to repair the damage in all phases of that construction; for the fulfillment of the state plans; for education of new cadres; for the strengthening of Russo-Ukrainian unity, etc., was also the theme of an editorial in *Pravda,* on the eve of the XIV Congress of the CP(b)U in 1938.[26] The same theme was also pursued by Khrushchev in his report to the XIV Congress of the CP(b)U in June, 1938. On the one hand, he assailed all "enemies"—dead and alive—for their alleged sabotage of agricultural and industrial construction, and for their misguidance and misinterpretation in the cultural sphere. Accordingly, he accused them of intentionally working with Germany and Poland towards the separation of the Ukraine from the USSR. He also held them fully responsible for the slaughter of livestock, and charged them with provoking and inciting the peasantry against the Soviet government. In addition, he condemned them for all actions which, in one way or another, aimed at the weakening of the Soviet rule.

To cover up many of these "wreckings," which in reality seem to have been inevitable and logical results of regimentation and centralism, Khrushchev cited in contrast numerous statistics which pointed to the achievements the Ukrainians had made. He singled out the progress made in various branches of industry, in agriculture, and in housing construction. He likewise dwelt at great length on the achievements the Ukraine had made in the cultural field. Under Soviet rule, he said, there had been constructed in the Ukraine 5,653 new schools; illiteracy among the people had been reduced to 2.3%; and the attendance in schools had increased tremendously, reaching 5,143,783 students in 1938, among whom Ukrainians predominated.

Following the presentation of these impressive figures on cultural progress the Ukrainians had made under Soviet rule, Khrushchev expressed great disturbance over the fact that the Russian language—"the language of Leninism-Stalinism"—had received no preferential treatment in Ukrainian schools. He placed the entire blame for this situation on the deposed Ukrainian intelligentsia, and cited this state of affairs as another example of their effort to exclude intentionally the influence of Russian culture on the Ukraine and to separate the Ukraine from the USSR. The Russian language, Khrushchev argued, was the language of the revolutionary teachings of Marx and Engels, as developed and elaborated by Lenin and Stalin. To exclude, therefore, the Russian language from wide usage and employment in schools, he said, meant to renounce the revolutionary method. The exclusion of obligatory teaching of the Russian language in Ukrainian schools, he complained, was the more appalling since people the world over were increasingly studying the Russian language in order to master the revolutionary teachings. "Enemies of the people—," he declared,

> bourgeois nationalists, knew the force and influence of the Russian language and of Russian culture. They knew that this was the influence of Bolshevism, the influence of Lenin-Stalin on the

minds of the Ukrainian people, of the Ukrainian workers and peasants. Therefore, they pushed the Russian language from the schools.

In many Ukrainian schools they taught German, French, Polish, and other languages, but not the Russian. The enemies tried by all means to separate the culture of the Ukrainian people from Russian culture. In Kiev, for example, there was not a single newspaper in the Russian language.[27]

A resolution, which the XIV Congress of the CP(b)U adopted, not only followed very closely all of Khrushchev's arguments but in many instances employed his vocabulary. It fully endorsed the policy of liquidating Party and non-Party members as well from all Government institutions. It also enjoined all members of the CP(b)U to remember that, as long as there existed the danger of capitalist encirclement, "spy networks" would have to be fought and unmasked. This long-range policy, the resolution declared, was especially true with regard to the Ukraine which, as "the outpost of the country of socialism in the West," was the prime object of foreign intervention. It was for that reason, the resolution went on, that the Bolsheviks in the Ukraine had to be extremely vigilant; had the duty of liquidating subversion from within and attacks from without; and had to fulfill all the Plan assignments.

The resolution pointed also to the achievements in various branches of industry and agriculture, and devoted considerable space to the progress that had been made in the cultural field. Although it cited various figures on the growth of the school network in the Ukraine during the Soviet rule, and pointed to the sizeable increase of Ukrainian attendance in the institutions of higher learning, it admitted that progress in the cultural field was the most feeble. The resolution tried to blame this lag on the work of the deposed Ukrainian intelligentsia, and stressed that because of this fact, extreme vigilance was necessary for a long time to come.

The resolution likewise heavily underscored the importance of the study of the Russian language in Ukrainian schools, and strongly condemned its previous lack of attention. Following Khrushchev's style of attack, the resolution placed the entire blame for the existence of such conditions on the deposed opposition. It charged them with trying to separate the Ukrainian people "from brotherly union with the Great Russian people," and with the separation of the Soviet Ukraine from the USSR. Accordingly, the resolution called upon all members of the CP(b)U to increase their vigilance; to intensify the unmasking of enemies; to improve criticism and self-criticism; to improve the quality of the press; and to strengthen their connections with the Armed Forces of the USSR.[28]

While calls for increased vigilance were being made, while liquidation of the remnants of the old Ukrainian intelligentsia was in full swing, and while, under the pretext that it was the language of Leninism-Stalinism, the Russian language was being forcefully introduced into Ukrainian schools and other government and Party institutions—the whole Ukrainian problem suddenly became an active issue in European diplomacy. Thanks primarily to Franco-British irresoluteness and consistent blunders between 1933 and 1938, the Nazis had executed a series of *faits accompli*. In September, 1938, their successes were crowned by the Munich settlement. As a result of this classic example of appeasement, Czechoslovakia—once a strong and unified state, one of the keys to the French security system, a key to the whole Danube Basin as well as to Central Europe, and the first line of defense of the Balkans—was reduced territorially, and broken up internally into a loose Czecho-Slovakian-Ukrainian Federation. Czechoslovakia's weakening as an effective political and military power lowered the resistance of all the other Danubian states. Not only were Hungary, Yugoslavia, and Rumania endangered, but Poland in the North, and Greece and Turkey in the Southeast, were threatened. In other words, with Czechoslovakia's destruction, the doors of the whole Danube region and of the neighboring areas were thrown open to the expansionist Third Reich.

However far-reaching were the external repercussions of Czechoslovakia's dismemberment, its breakup into a loose three-state federation was also of great significance to the neighboring states. This particularly was true with respect to the creation of an autonomous Carpatho-Ukrainian State. Among Ukrainians, especially those living in Poland and among political emigres, this act produced an unprecedented wave of national enthusiasm. Almost overnight, a territory whose population had been the least nationally conscious became, in the eyes of many Ukrainians, a Piedmont and a Mecca of the Great Ukrainian ideal. Both legally, and illegally, Ukrainians of all political groupings began to make their way to the Carpatho-Ukraine to participate in the formation of what they believed to be the nucleus of a future Ukrainian state, which would include all territories inhabited by Ukrainians.

The developments in the Carpatho-Ukraine received serious and immediate attention from the Polish government. The latter, although unable to solve the national problem at home, was ambitious for territorial expansion, and was quite eager to suppress the Carpatho-Ukrainian state as well as the national sentiment among the large Ukrainian population in Poland. A desire for territorial aggrandizement at the expense of the Carpatho-Ukraine played also an important part in Hungarian attempts to see the elimination of the Carpatho-Ukraine. Finally, the wave of Ukrainian national sentiment and the enthusiasm for creation of a Greater Ukraine which would include all territories inhabited by Ukrainians, received very serious attention from Bolshevik leaders who demonstrated anxiety and eagerness for the liquidation of the Carpatho-Ukraine.

Polish ambition, Hungarian desire, and Bolshevik anxiety to see the Ukrainian problem removed from European politics, played into the hands of the Nazis. In the negotiations which followed the Munich settlement, the Nazis were able to exploit successfully the anti-Ukrainian opposition. Thanks mainly to Nazi agreement to the persistent Hungarian demands for occupation of the Carpatho-Ukraine, Hungary not only fell completely within the Nazi orbit, but even became an active member of the Anti-Comintern Pact. Polish unwillingness to follow the same path proved disasterous, and paved the way for a Nazi-Soviet understanding, which on August 23, 1939, culminated in a Non-Aggression Pact.[29]

Although there were many factors which contributed to the bringing of this most irrational agreement, in the initial Nazi-

Soviet negotiations the Ukrainian problem played an important part—a much greater part then many observers are willing to attribute. The importance of the Ukrainian problem in initiating Nazi-Soviet negotiations can be sensed from Stalin's own statement. Speaking at the XVIII Congress of the VKP(b) on March 10, 1939, he assailed bitterly the press of the Western powers for spreading what he called "vociferous lies" about "the weakness of the Russian Army," "the demoralization of the Russian Air Force," the "riots" within the USSR, and German invasion of the USSR. "The gentlemen of the press there" [Britain, France, and the U.S.]

> shouted until they were hoarse that the Germans were marching on the Soviet Union, that they now had what is called Carpatho-Ukraine with a population of some 700,000, and that not later than this spring the Germans would annex the Soviet Ukraine, which has a population of over 30,000,000 to this so-called Carpatho-Ukraine. It looks as if the object of this suspicious hullabaloo was to incense the Soviet Union against Germany, to poison the atmosphere and to provoke a conflict with Germany without any visible grounds.[30]

Though Stalin acknowledged that there might be some "madmen" in Germany who thought of annexing the Ukraine, he argued that if one were to ignore these "madmen" and turn to normal people, it would be clear that it was "ridiculous and stupid to talk seriously of annexing the Soviet Ukraine to the so-called Carpatho-Ukraine."[31]

Several other speakers at the XVIII Congress of the VKP(b) elaborated on Stalin's statement. Speaking for the CP(b)U, Khrushchev warned that any external or internal attempt to upset socialist construction in the Ukraine would meet with disaster. As an example, he cited the recent liquidation of Ukrainian intelligentsia, and also recalled some unsuccessful foreign invasions of the Ukraine in the past. Having disposed of this matter, Khrushchev then proceeded to outline the progress of Ukrainian industry and agriculture. He cited numerous figures, compared its production with the pre-war level as well as with that of neighboring countries, and stressed time and again that, because of material riches, possibilities for improved production were unlimited in the Ukraine. He also pointed out the progress the Ukraine had made under Soviet rule in the cultural field. As an example, he cited the growth of the school budget, increased pay of the teaching personnel, increased attendance of Ukrainian students in higher educational institutions, and the growth of Ukrainian Soviet intelligentsia. All this, he declared, had been made possible only thanks to the Bolshevik revolution and proper national policy of the Party. Because of these achievements, he argued, any attempt to upset socialist construction would be disasterous to the invader. Accordingly, he warned the spokesmen of the Carpatho-Ukraine that the Soviet Ukrainian people, together with the Russian people, were ready to repel any armed attack.[32]

Other delegates of the CP(b)U to the XVIII Congress of the VKP(b) voiced the same warnings almost verbatim. Mykola P. Bazhan, a Soviet Ukrainian literary figure, after recalling numerous misfortunes of foreign invasions in the past and the progress made in the economic and cultural fields under Soviet rule, declared that the "Ukrainian people, the guard of the Western border of socialist construction," were watching vigilantly the events around them, and no would-be attacker would succeed in upsetting their way of life.[33] M. A. Burmistrenko, Chairman of the Supreme Soviet of the UkSSR, Secretary of the CC of the CP(b)U, and a member of the CC of the VKP(b), in his speech likewise emphasized the material and cultural progress the Ukraine had made under the Soviet rule. He gave, in addition, various figures on the changes that had taken place in the national composition of several cities, and on the growth of the Ukrainian new intelligentsia. He ridiculed any idea of the Carpatho-Ukraine's trying to annex the Soviet Ukraine. At that same time he warned that any attempt to invade the Ukraine would be repelled with disaster to the would-be aggressor.[34] Warnings directed toward Germany, Poland, and the Carpatho-Ukraine, that the UkSSR was not an object for aggression, but an inseparable part of the USSR, were also sounded by L. R. Korniets, Deputy Chairman of the

Sovnarkom of the UkSSR, and a member of the CC of the VKP(b);[35] by Z. T. Serdiuk, Kiev Party Secretary and a Candidate of the CC of the VKP(b);[36] and by Ya. A. Khomenko, Secretary of the Ukrainian Comsomol.[37]

Whatever other motives or objectives these and numerous other pronouncements might have had, the manner in which they were formulated and presented reveals beyond any shadow of a doubt that, from Stalin down, Bolshevik leaders were quite disturbed about the danger of the national problem in general, and in particular about the enthusiasm for a Greater "bourgeois" Ukraine. Though given little credit or emphasis in the literature on Nazi-Soviet negotiations, Stalin's anxiety about the national problem played an important part in bringing about the Nazi-Soviet Pact of August 23, 1939. By virtue of this most illogical coalition, Hitler, in return for an assured *status quo* in the East while he was engaged in the West, gave Stalin about half of Poland's territory which was inhabited in the main by Ukrainian and Belorussian population. In addition, Germany expressed its disinterest in the fate of Bessarabia and Bukovina, which also had large Ukrainian populations.

German invasion and swift penetration of Poland permitted Soviet occupation of their share on September 17, 1939. Though undertaken in the name of national liberation from Polish oppression, the occupation of these territories met with little real enthusiasm on the part of the victims. It was perhaps because of this passive reception that, immediately following the occupation, an intensified "Ukrainization" of the territory was undertaken. For that purpose, a huge propaganda network was established, and hasty, but elaborate, preparations were made throughout the country for election of a National Assembly. On October 22, 1939, elections were held, and of the 4,776,275 eligible voters, 4,433,997, or 92.83%, approved the selected list of candidates.[38] On October 26, 1939, the newly-elected National Assembly of 1,484 members convened in Lvov, elected members of the Politburo of the CC of the VKP(b) as its honorary presiding committee, and on the following day issued a declaration which established Soviet rule in the Western Ukraine.[39] On the same day, the National Assembly adopted another declaration which asked the Supreme Soviet of the USSR to accept the Western Ukraine into the UkSSR, *"in order to unite Ukrainian people in one state and thus end the centuries-old division of Ukrainian people."* [40] On the following day, two additional declarations were made. By virtue of the first, all movable and immovable property of the nobility's estates, monasteries, and state officials was confiscated without payment.[41] The next declaration nationalized all banks and industrial enterprises.[42] On November 1, 1939, with great pomp, fanfare, and publicity, the Supreme Soviet of the USSR accepted the Western Ukraine into the Soviet Union,[43] and two weeks later the same formality was replayed in the Supreme Soviet of the UkSSR.[44] In less than a month and a half, the Western Ukraine thus became an integral part of the USSR, a change which found full reflection in the Constitution of the USSR. As a result of these developments, one of the objectives laid by the V Congress of the Comintern, in 1924, was thus achieved.

The changes that took place in Western Ukraine had important economic and strategic value for the USSR. As a result, the revolutionary base of Communism, without any difficulty, had expanded Westward by about 76,500 square miles, while its population had increased by about 13,000,000. This point was strongly emphasized by V. M. Molotov, in his report on the foreign policy of the USSR at a session of the Supreme Soviet of the USSR on October 31, 1939.[45] Incorporation of these territories likewise had significant political value. It united the Belorussian people, and almost all of the Ukrainian people under one rule, thereby eliminating any possibility that rival republics might be created by Soviet opponents, either to compete with or to attract Soviet republics.[46]

The achievement of Ukrainian territorial and ethnic unity under Soviet rule—under the guidance of the Party and with the help of the Russian people—from that time on began to play an important part in Soviet propaganda as well as in reality. For, once the formalities of incorporation were ended, there was introduced a period of firm centralization of the new territories. Administratively, West Ukrainian territory was divided into six *oblasti*. Economically, there was inaugurated a strong campaign for the creation of collective and Soviet farms, as well as MTS's.[47] Finally, there was begun an accelerated process toward cultural uniformity, *i.e.*, the elimination of some old institutions, subordination of others to existing similar organizations, and the introduction of many new ones.

The achievement of Ukrainian territorial and ethnic unity during Soviet rule—under the guidance of the Party and with the aid of the Russian people—figured very prominently at the meeting of the XV Congress of the CP(b)U in May, 1940. On the eve of the Congress, *Pravda* editorially emphasized that the centuries-old aims of the Ukraine—the unity of Ukrainian people—not only had been realized, but that many Ukrainians now had the possibility of building up their own new life, speaking their language, having their newspapers, theaters, schools, universities, and developing their own culture, "national in form and socialist in content." The editorial also paid respect to the Ukraine's economic potentials and its strategic value, calling it "a mighty, indestructible outpost of the country of socialism in the West," and "a republic of coal, iron, and many other precious mineral resources, a republic of widely developed metallurgy and machine building."[48]

In his report to the XV Congress of the CP(b)U, Khrushchev heavily underscored the achievement of territorial unity of the Ukraine. He repeatedly asserted that this achievement, which opened up for many Ukrainians new possibilities in using their own language, publishing their newspapers, and having their own schools, had been made possible thanks to the proper policy of the Party under Stalin's direction. Though he expressed satisfaction at the progress that had been made thus far in the economic field, in the organization of new schools, and in the spread of libraries and other educational institutions in the Western Ukraine, Khrushchev acknowledged that "one must put much more work there in order to create real Bolshevik Soviet conditions."

Most of Khrushchev's report, however, was devoted to economic problems of the Ukraine—the problems of production of iron,

steel, and coal. He pleaded for increased output of these materials
in order to meet the demands of the Red Army, and further industrialization of the country. To meet these demands, he argued,
it was imperative not only to fulfill, but to overfulfill, the assigned
quotas. He assailed the bureaucratic approach to production, and
stressed time and again that every ton of coal and metal, every
new machine, and every ton of finished product, meant the
strengthening of the socialist fatherland; the strengthening of the
state and of Communism. Khrushchev likewise dwelt at great
length on the problems of agriculture, citing the degree of collectivization, mechanization, and increased production. Although
he painted a somewhat rosy picture, he called upon all Party
members to increase their attention to collective farms, and pointed
out that there were only 8,609 leading Party workers in rural
districts of the Ukraine, or one worker per three collective farms.

Toward the end of his report, Khrushchev turned his attention
to various other problems facing the CP(b)U. He called for a
careful approach to Party membership, and also demanded improvement of the quality of articles in newspapers and magazines.
He likewise called for defense preparedness and military strengthening of the country. In addition, he voiced satisfaction that under
the Party's leadership, the Ukrainians were developing a culture,
"national in form and socialist in content"; that the school network
was expanding; that school attendance was on the increase; that
the number of other educational institutions was on the rise; and
that the new Ukrainian Soviet intelligentsia was assuming its
proper role in all branches of socialist construction.[49]

The theme of unity of territories inhabited by Ukrainians, which
figured quite prominently during the XV Congress of the CP(b)U,
was further strengthened by the events which took place at the end
of May and in June of 1940. On June 26, 1940, Molotov de-
livered a note to the Rumanian ambassador in Moscow, demanding the return of Bessarabia to the USSR, and at the same time
requesting that Bukovina, whose population "by virtue of history,
language, and national composition," was tied with the Ukraine,
be ceded to the Soviet Union.[50] On June 27, 1940, Molotov's

note was followed by an ultimatum, and on the following day, Soviet forces began the occupation of both territories.[51] Similarly as in the Western Ukraine, the occupation of this area was undertaken in the name of national liberation, and served to expand the revolutionary base of Communism in a southwesterly direction by about 50,000 square kilometers, and about 3,000,000 population, a point which Molotov again strongly emphasized in his report to the Supreme Soviet of the USSR.[52] With the settlement of this problem, the second objective laid down by the V Congress of the Comintern, in 1924—the destruction of Rumania—was realized.

The territorial gains which the USSR made while in alliance with Germany—gains which responsible government and Party officials defended and justified on the basis of ethnic affiliation—were offset by German invasion of the USSR in June, 1941. The astonishing swiftness with which German armies advanced all along the front, the welcoming receptions they received from the native population, the massive surrender of Soviet forces, and many other factors, were strong signs that the unity which Bolshevik spokesmen had, on all occasions, so persistently emphasized was very much absent. Although these factors of dissatisfaction were products of numerous causes (economic, personal, logistical, etc.), they had also strong national undertones. German inability and unwillingness to take these factors into consideration; evaluation of their victories as manifestations of their might and infallibility; mistreatment of the population; utter disregard of peasant wishes and interests; suppression of national forces; granting of Ukrainian territories to Rumania, etc., began to change rapidly the opinion of the population and, together with climatic conditions, were greatly responsible for the outcome of the war.[52a]

The population's disillusionment with the Germans, which began to set in by the fall of 1941, was skillfully exploited by the Bolsheviks in all of their publications, in their radio and press appeals, and in their propaganda leaflets. On November 26, 1941, for example, a group of the evacuated Soviet Ukrainian intelligentsia held a meeting in Saratov, during which they composed an appeal to the Ukrainian people. In it they pictured the horror of war and the destruction which it had brought to Ukrainian cities, villages, factories, and educational institutions, holding the Germans fully responsible for everything. In this appeal, they argued, too, that the aim of Germany was to turn the Ukraine into a German colony—to exploit Ukrainian natural resources and to make the Ukrainian people German slaves. Apparently to strengthen the power of resistance of the Ukrainians, the appeal cited the heroism of Soviet forces and stressed very heavily the material aid England and the United States were giving the USSR. The appeal also cited certain heroes from Ukrainian history who had resisted foreign domination.[53]

On January 17, 1942, the Government of the UkSSR, then in exile in Ufa, in the Ural Mountains, issued an appeal to the Ukrainian people, fully exploiting German mistreatment of the Ukrainian people, which by then was in full swing. Like the previous appeal, this government request contended that the aim of the Germans in the Ukraine was to re-establish the rule of the nobility, to restore Tsarism, to destroy national culture and national statehood of the Ukraine and of all other peoples of the USSR, and to turn them into German slaves. The appeal of the government also argued that "in this just war" a fundamental question of the Soviet Ukraine was being decided: Whether the Ukraine be free, its people having the right to work, speak their native tongue and be masters of their own destiny, or whether the Ukraine be turned into a German colony, its wealth exploited and its people perishing in concentration camps. Accordingly, the government called upon all the people to disobey German orders, to aid Soviet Armies and guerrillas, to sabotage German war materiel and communications, to kill German personnel, etc. To stiffen Ukrainian resistance, the appeal pointed out the various small victories of Soviet Armies, and heavily emphasized the fact that Great Britain, the United States, and many other countries of the world were fighting on the same side as the Soviet Union.[54]

On April 1, 1942, Soviet Ukrainian academicians, professors, composers, and writers signed their appeal to the Ukrainian people,[55] and on September 30, another plea was made by the group of Ukrainian Soviet intelligentsia in Saratov.[56] Both of these requests exploited to the utmost German mistreatment of the Ukrainian population, arrests of Ukrainians, German plundering, their colonization scheme, etc. Both appeals likewise took full advantage of the peasantry's disappointment with the Germans for not granting them the land they had hoped to receive. "The Germans," stated the appeal, "did not come to the Ukraine to give lands to the Ukrainian peasants," but to colonize. Both requests also underscored the unity of the Ukrainian territories, and both called upon the people to resist the German occupation and to struggle actively.

These and similar appeals by the Party and by the government, were forthcoming until complete German withdrawal from the Ukraine. These appeals, in turn, were supplemented by various "concessions." In 1943, for example, there was established a high military decoration for Ukrainians—the Order of Bohdan Khmelnytskyj. At the end of that year, the Southern Fronts were designated Ukrainian Fronts, and the Armies which operated there were accordingly renamed Ukrainian Armies. Identical changes were introduced in the Central and Northern sections of the front, where Belorussian names were adopted. Along with this trend of "concessions," in February, 1944, the constitution of the USSR was even amended to give each union republic the right to have its own Commissariat of Armed Forces and Commissariat for Foreign Affairs—a privilege which only the UkSSR and the Belorussian SSR were allowed to put into practice. In 1944, too, a poem expressing love for the Ukraine won Stalin's Prize.[57]

All of these appeals and concessions have several distinctive features. First, none of them either retreated from centralism or rejected total regimentation of life. The preservation of these fundamentals, which were emphasized again and again alongside the would-be concessions, made these concessions totally unworkable.[58] Second, though directed at the Ukrainians, these appeals and concessions were also aimed at the foreign audience. They served as important factors in extracting Western agreements for the UkSSR and the Belorussian SSR to have seats in the new world organization—the United Nations.[59] Third, these concessions acted as important factors in Bolshevik demands and justification for the possession of Western Ukrainian territories which the USSR had acquired while in alliance with Germany.[60] Finally, the artificial stimulation of Ukrainian nationalism acted also as a vital force in the USSR's expansion of its territorial base beyond the Carpathian Mountains, by claiming and acquiring the Carpatho-Ukraine from Czechoslovakia,[61] thereby fulfilling the third objective laid down by the V Congress of the Comintern in 1924.

The employment of what seemed to have been a pro-Ukrainian trend and sentiment began to decrease as soon as the objectives, for which the feeling was artificially stimulated, were achieved. With the reoccupation of Ukrainian territories, the pro-Ukrainian sentiment was sharply curtailed. This change of attitude and an embryonic preview of the Party's post-war policies in the Ukraine, were revealed by Khrushchev in his report to the Sixth Session of the Supreme Soviet of the UkSSR, on March 1, 1944. In it, he reviewed at some length various accomplishments the Ukraine had made under Soviet rule. He gave numerous figures on economic achievements, especially on the scope of industrialization and collectivization, and he also pointed out cultural gains, citing the elimination of illiteracy, the expanded school network, the increased school attendance, etc. Khrushchev also underscored the attainment of Ukrainian territorial unity under Soviet rule, and declared that this unity would remain, irrespective of Polish dislike. In his report, too, he paid tribute to Ukrainian war efforts and sacrifices, and warmly applauded the accomplishments of Ukrainian Bolshevik guerrillas.

Though a large portion of Khrushchev's account dealt with the scope of destruction of Ukrainian economy and the problem of its reconstruction, he also devoted considerable time to attacking Ukrainian armed resistance against the Bolsheviks. He branded the Ukrainian national forces "traitors to the Ukrainian people," "fascists," etc. He said that under the cover of national slogans, they were trying to break the unity among the Soviet peoples, separate the Ukraine from the USSR, place it at the disposal of

Germany, and thereby weaken the Soviet Union. Accordingly Khrushchev viewed Ukrainian nationalist resistance against the Germans as a maneuver to deceive the Ukrainian people further. He acknowledged, however, that the forces of the Ukrainian Insurgent Army were large, and declared that he hoped, that since the Presidium of the Supreme Soviet of the UkSSR and the Sovnarkom of the UkSSR had issued appeals to the Insurgents calling upon them to surrender, their number might decrease. For those unwilling to lay down their arms, Khrushchev promised death.[62]

In his report, Khrushchev also devoted some time to the problems of cultural reconstruction of the Ukraine. He applauded the participation of Ukrainian Soviet intelligentsia in war efforts, and, at the same time, directed it to take as active a part in the reestablishment of schools, in the organization of teaching personnel, and in the strengthening of discipline in schools. He also called upon them to produce in the near future literary works that would reflect upon the struggle of the Ukrainian people against the Germans and against the Ukrainian nationalists, as well as works that would portray the accomplishments of Bolshevik guerrillas, efforts of post-war reconstruction, and "the great friendship among the peoples of the Soviet Union." Though, at the end of his report, Khrushchev again applauded Ukrainian war efforts, sacrifices, and Ukrainian Soviet patriotism, he asserted that without the aid of other peoples of the USSR, and especially without "the aid of the elder brother—the Great Russian people" the liberation of the Ukraine could not have been accomplished.[63]

Khrushchev's praise of the Great Russian aid as a decisive factor in winning the war and in the wresting of the Ukraine away from the Germans received still further exaltation from Stalin, in his May 24, 1945 speech at a reception given in the Kremlin in honor of the Red Army commanders. On that occasion, Stalin proposed a toast to the well-being of the Soviet peoples, and above all to the well-being of the Russian people—"the most outstanding nation of all the nations forming the Soviet Union." He singled out Great Russians not only as being the "leading force," but also

as having "a clear mind, a staunch character, and patience." He
commended their trust of "the correctness" of the Party's policies
throughout the hour of despair. He likewise applauded their confidence in the government—confidence which, in his opinion, "proved
to be the decisive force which insured the historic victory over the
enemy of humanity—over fascism." [64]

This elevation of Great Russians from among the equals into
a privileged position, in addition to confirming officially long-
existing reality, signalized also the approaching period of intensified regimentation, of increased stress on the superiority of the
Soviet system, of Soviet isolation, of elimination of all the views
acquired by the population during the war, etc.[65] In the Ukraine,
whose entire territory had been under foreign occupation, and
where armed resistance to Bolshevik return was mounting large
proportions, the new period was marked by a wholesale dismissal
of leading Party and government officials, and a purge of everything that was Ukrainian. According to Khrushchev, who revealed
the scope of the purge at the August, 1946 Plenum of the CC of
the CP(b)U, the chief cause of the turnover lay in the improper
recruitment of officials, their poor qualifications, and their political
unreliability. Khrushchev also bitterly assailed bourgeois nationalist ideology in the Ukraine, whose traces, he said, could be
detected not only in speeches and lectures given by Ukrainian
scholars, but also in newspapers, periodicals, and other publications.
Under his particular attack came the section of Linguistics and
History of the Ukrainian Academy of Sciences, for their idealiza-
tion of the Ukrainian past, and for their complete neglect of the
present. Any writer, Khrushchev argued, who idealized the past
was giving indications of his insufficient knowledge of Marxist-
Leninist theory, and was "making in his work an error of nationalistic nature." [66]

Condemnation of the existence of low ideological standards,
and of traces of Ukrainian nationalistic ideology, was likewise the
main topic at a meeting of Kiev's city writers at the end of
August, 1946. Speaking for the CC of the CP(b)U, K. Z. Litvin,

its Secretary, and a member of the Orgburo, charged that since the war's end there had appeared many works in the Ukrainian language which reflected bourgeois nationalist views. This was especially true, he said, of text books on Ukrainian history and literature, which had been published during and since the war. In those books, Litvin charged, Ukrainian authors had departed from the class struggle principle and had taken the position that national moments were more decisive in the development of the literary process than were internal class contradictions. He scorned those authors who either ignored the decisive influences of progressive ideas and of the writers of Russian literature, or tried to conceal the Russo-Ukrainian literary ties by substituting and overemphasizing Western influence on Ukrainian literature. He likewise condemned, in no uncertain words, those persons who either consciously or unconsciously tried to silence the differences between the "reactionary" and the "progressive" writers of Ukrainian literature of the second half of the XIX and the early part of the XX Century. Finally, after Litvin had warned those writers who underestimated Soviet literature and had reprimanded those editors who published alien ideas, the meeting listened to numerous self-criticisms and adopted a resolution in which it assured the CC of the CP(b)U against the repetition of similar errors.[67]

The criticism and self-criticism, as well as the assurances against repetition of errors, were apparently short-lived, for in July, 1947, a favored literary spokesman of the CP(b)U, O. Ye. Korneichuk, in an article published in *Pravda*, condemned the continuance of "anti-national" and "anti-people" symptoms in Ukrainian literature. He bitterly assailed those contemporary writers who sought inspiration either in the Ukrainian past or in the West. Accordingly, he deplored the fact that very few among the Ukrainian *literati* wrote about contemporary Soviet things, and that only very few took notice of the changes that had taken place in the Ukraine under Soviet rule—in the field of industry, agriculture, and territorial unity of Ukrainian lands, as well as in the Russo-Ukrainian unity.[68]

The problem of Russo-Ukrainian unity and friendship became the most widely discussed and publicized issue, alongside of the accelerated economic reconstruction of the country. It was the main theme of the 30th anniversary of the founding of the UkSSR. It was emphatically stressed by Molotov, in his address before the Jubilee Session of the Supreme Soviet of the UkSSR.[69] It was likewise very heavily underlined by Khrushchev in his speech before the Jubilee Session. There cannot exist, Khrushchev declared on that occasion, any contradictions or antagonisms between the Great Russian and the Ukrainian peoples. Those who oppose the Russo-Ukrainian friendship in any form whatsoever, he announced, oppose also the teachings of Lenin and Stalin, and oppose the building up of Communist society. Consequently, he stated, those who oppose these principles must stand for capitalist servitude and for restoration of the capitalist yoke and exploitation. Those opponents, he declared, are cursed enemies of the Ukrainian people and "we must mercilessly uncover and root them out to the very end . . . [because] they try to reach for the foundation of foundations of our life by trying to undermine the friendship of the Soviet peoples, the friendship between the Russian and the Ukrainian peoples." [70]

The problem of unity between the Russian and the Ukrainian peoples and condemnation of all those who, in one way or another, attempted to disrupt that unity, figured quite prominently at the XVI Congress of the CP(b)U in January, 1949. In his report to the Congress, Khrushchev, while giving primary consideration to economic problems of the country and to the problems of the Party's control of the countryside, also devoted considerable time to the cultural question and to the question of unity between the Russian and the Ukrainian peoples. He scolded all those who maintained that Ukrainian literature had been influenced by the West, and criticized those who either neglected Ukrainian literary traditions, or failed to emphasize Ukrainian ties with the Great

Russian people and with Great Russian literature. All these "shortcomings," he labelled as slavery, and called upon all Party members to wage a determined struggle against such alienisms, as well as against all types of foreign ideology, all expressions of Ukrainian bourgeois nationalism, and all forms of political passivity. In their place, he called for accelerating the creation of a Ukrainian Soviet culture, "national in form and socialist in content." [71]

Criticisms of alien influences on Ukrainian life were also voiced by other high Party spokesmen. Litvin, for example, assailed continued errors in Ukrainian history and historiography.[72] The head of the Propaganda and Agitation Department of the CC of the CP(b)U, P. M. Hapochka, expressed similar indignation in the sphere of general education in the Ukraine, where, he declared, there still existed the remnants of "servile bowing before alienism." [73] An attack against Ukrainian nationalism in Ukrainian history was also unleashed by D. Z. Manuilsky, for many years a high official of the Comintern, and, from 1945 to 1950, the chief spokesman of the UkSSR in the United Nations. He condemned very bitterly the activity of Ukrainian political exiles, labelling them traitors, Utopists, enemies of the Ukrainian people, and servants of the West. Though Manuilsky tried to minimize the scope of Ukrainian national sentiment, he acknowledged that this sentiment was wide-spread and was very dangerous, especially in Galicia. Realizing the force of nationalism, Manuilsky condemned those Party spokesmen who, he charged, saw nationalism in everything that was Ukrainian. The denial of specific features of every nation of the USSR, Manuilsky contended, meant to act contrary to Soviet policy. Such a denial, he declared, was the shortest road to cosmopolitanism and away from internationalism.[74]

The increased emphasis of unity of Ukrainian territory, and of Ukrainian and Russian peoples, and condemnations of Ukrainian nationalism, continued after the XVI Congress of the CP(b)U.[75] At the same time, numerous Ukrainian institutions, publications, editors, and writers, were accused of insufficient presentation of

"Soviet patriotism." Others were condemned for their lack of clarity. Under particular attack came the war-time Stalin Prize-winning poem, "Love the Ukraine," by V. Sosiura. "It is true," declared *Pravda,* [that]

> in his poem, the poet calls for love of the Ukraine. The question arises: *Which* Ukraine is in question, of *which* Ukraine is Sosiura singing? Is he singing of that Ukraine which groaned for centuries under the exploiters' yoke . . . ? Or does Sosiura's poem refer to the new prosperous Soviet Ukraine, created by the will of our people, led by the Party of Bolsheviks?[76]

The problem of inadequate showing and superficial treatment of unity and of "Soviet realism" by the Ukrainians received serious consideration at the November, 1951 Plenum of the CC of the CP(b)U. Speaking for the Party, L. G. Melnikov, the First Secretary of the CC of the CP(b)U, assailed bitterly the libretto of the opera, "Bohdan Khmelnytskyj," by Korneichuk. He also pointed out "serious shortcomings and mistakes" in the work of the Union of Soviet Writers, the Ukrainian Academy of Sciences, various composers, many writers, and some newspapers and periodicals, charging them with inadequate presentation of the influence on the Ukraine of the advanced Russian literature and culture. Melnikov demanded from all organizations of the CP(b)U renewed efforts to destroy "alien ideology of bourgeois nationalism and cosmopolitanism—and in their stead to educate all workers in the spirit of Soviet patriotism, in the spirit of internationalism." [77]

To judge, however, by the many attacks against Ukrainian nationalism in the Soviet press throughout 1952,[78] and by Melnikov's own charges levelled in that direction at the XVII Congress of the CP(b)U in September, 1952, there was very little inclination on the part of the Ukrainians to fall into line and accept Russian culture as the international culture. Though, in his report to the XVII Congress of the CP(b)U, Melnikov pointed out numerous accomplishments in the economic and the cultural fields in the Ukraine (cf. expanded school network, and increased school attendance), he complained that there were many inadequacies.

Among these, he listed: 1) Insufficient ideological training of teaching personnel in higher institutions of learning; 2) Absence of works that would "unmask manifestations of bourgeois ideology, principally Ukrainian bourgeois nationalism, and homeless cosmopolitanism"; 3) Serious shortcomings and absence of works that would disclose "the profoundly beneficial and decisive influence of advanced Russian culture on the development of Ukrainian culture"; 4) Presence of serious "ideological distortions and mistakes in works of various writers and workers in the arts"; and 5) Presence of works that distort the image of Soviet reality and which, thereby, play into the hands of Ukrainian bourgeois nationalism. Accordingly, Melnikov levelled a bitter attack against Ukrainian nationalism for its opposition to the "Leninist-Stalinist friendship and brotherhood of Soviet peoples"; for its attack against "Russian culture and its highest attainment, Leninism"; for its opposition to the policy of the VKP(b); for its attempts to separate the Ukrainian people from the Russian people by "delivering them to colonial bondage of foreign imperialists"; and for its "betrayal of the Ukrainian people." He branded the adherents of Ukrainian nationalism as "spies, saboteurs, and agents of imperialist espionage." Finally, he called upon all members of the CP(b)U to "unmask any manifestation of bourgeois nationalism wherever it may be expressed." Melnikov repeated all of these allegations at the XIX Congress of the VKP(b) in October, 1952.[79]

These condemnations of Ukrainian nationalism, at the XVII Congress of the CP(b)U in September, 1952, and at the XIX Congress of the VKP(b) in October, 1952, marked the peak of the active anti-Ukrainian drive in the post-war years. Thanks to the period of fear, uncertainty, and confusion, which followed Stalin's death in March, 1953, the new leadership of the USSR relaxed its anti-Ukrainian pressure. One of the conciliatory gestures was the removal of Melnikov from his post of Secretary of the CC of the CP(b)U, in June, 1953. Another was the transfer of the Crimea into the UkSSR—a timely move executed on the eve of the preparations for commemoration of the 300th anniversary of the Pereyaslav Act. Being motivated by opportunism and expediency, rather than sincerity or basic change of policy, these "appeasing" acts brought no important innovations. Their immediate effect and significance lies in the fact that, coming as an aftermath of Stalin's death, they mark the passing of an era in the Russian Bolshevik nationality policy in the Ukraine—an era that witnessed on the one hand the unification of all territories inhabited by the Ukrainians, and on the other ruthless extermination of everything Ukrainian.

CHAPTER VII

Economic Relations

In the whole complex of factors that has determined Russian Bolshevik policy in and toward the Ukraine, two fundamental considerations seem to rise above all other motives, and by their force they attract all other elements toward their respective, separate, yet at the same time mutually complementing and dependent, poles. One of these factors is strategic; the other economic. Before World War II, through possession of the Ukraine, the Russian Bolsheviks obtained their only territorial link with the Balkan and Danubian states. Following World War II, that direct link helped considerably in transforming these states (cf. Czechoslovakia, Hungary, Rumania) into Moscow's satellites. By virtue of control of the Ukraine, the Russian Bolsheviks likewise entrenched themselves more firmly on the Black Sea. The Ukraine, thus, served as a vital factor in expanding the revolutionary base; in advancing the world revolution.

However vital these strategic considerations may be, they did not, nor do they now, determine the potential value of the Ukraine. The fame and importance of the Ukraine has been and continues to be in the sphere of economics. Though small in size when compared with the rest of the USSR, comprising only about 2% of the latter's territory, but with about 1/5 of the population, the Ukraine represents a very vital economic region of the USSR. Its black fertile soil ranks among the richest in the world. Under it are located very rich deposits of coal and iron which, though not the largest ones quantitatively, from the quality standpoint and comparative ease of utilization represent a major asset in the economy of the USSR. In addition to coal and iron deposits, the

Ukraine possesses considerable deposits of manganese ore, salt, mercury, potash, natural gas, peat, polymetallic ores, phosphorites, limestone, marl, gypsum, etc. Thus, in the Ukraine are located vital industries of the USSR. There likewise is centered a large portion of the railroad network of the USSR which, running along the meridial lines, connects the North with the South. In view of these factors it would be no exaggeration to state that the Ukraine plays a similarly vital role in the economy of the USSR, though to a lesser degree, than it did in the economy of Imperial Russia.

To evaluate justly the Russian Bolshevik objectives in, and the policy toward, the Ukraine, it is necessary to outline briefly the role and the place Ukrainian economy (*i.e.*, agriculture, resources, industry, etc.) played in the economy of pre-revolutionary Russia.[1] Interchangeably called "the granary of the Empire" and "the bread basket of Europe," the Ukraine, before World War I, was one of the main food-producing centers of the Russian Empire, not only for domestic consumption but also for export. It has been estimated that in the production of wheat between 1909 and 1913, the share of the Ukraine in the Russian Empire was 48%; that of rye 30%; barley 72%; and oats 17%.[2] The role of the Ukraine in Russian grain production can be seen from the fact that 36.1% of all Russian flour mills, wherein 28.9% of all the grain was processed, were located in the Ukraine.[3] A large portion of Ukrainian grain went for export, which according to some estimates was, during the years 1909-1913, on the average as high as 79% of all Russian exports;[4] as low as 15% by other calculations,[5] and less than 50% by still other estimates.[6]

However, the economic importance of the Ukraine was not confined to grain production alone. In the pre-revolutionary economy of Imperial Russia, the Ukraine represented the most important fuel base of the Empire (bituminous coal, anthracite, brown coal, peat, etc.).[7] Though the coal deposits of the Ukraine—of the Donbass—were not the richest in Russia, in actual production for a period of fifty years their share was the largest.[8] In 1860, for example, the share of the Donbass coal output comprised only 6,000,000 puds; by 1890 it had increased to 183,000,000 puds; by

1900 to 672,000,000 puds; and by 1910 to 1,020,000,000 puds.[9] In 1913, the share of the Donbass in Russia's coal output equalled 1,561,000,000 puds out of a total of 2,223,700,000 puds, or 70.2%; the remainder being divided among the Dombrova Basin of Poland (19.2%); Siberia (6.2%); the Urals (3.1%); the Sub-Moscow Region (0.8%); Turkestan (0.3%); and the Caucasus (0.2%). When, in the course of World War I, Germany occupied the Dombrova Basin, the share of the Donbass rose to an all time high, a total of 1,752,200,000 puds, or 87.2% of Russia's total coal production.[10] The main consumer of Donbass coal was industry, which used 56.7%, then railroads with 33.7%, and the remainder of 9.6% went for water transport, utilities, and for export.[11] It would, therefore, be no overstatement to contend that, before the Revolution of 1917, Russian industry and transport relied heavily on Ukrainian coal whose proximity, low cost of transportation, and above all high quality, made a great difference between Russia's technical progress and backwardness.

In addition to its being a vital fuel base for the economy of the Russian Empire, the Ukraine was also one of the major sources of iron ore, especially the deposits of the Krivoy Rog.[12] In many respects the output of iron ore in the Ukraine was similar to that of coal. In 1885, for example, the Ukraine contributed only 12.7% to the total output of iron ore in the Russian Empire. By 1913 this share had risen to 72%.[13] In comparison with other sources of Russian iron ore production, the role of the Ukrainian contribution can be seen from the following table (in millions of puds):[14]

Years	Ukraine	Urals	Others	Total
1891-1900	95	76	16	187
1901-1903	150	85	10	245
1904-1906	209	74	10	293
1907-1909	238	67	8	313
1910-1912	306	93	12	411
1913	420	132	35	587

This rapid growth of the Ukrainian contribution to the total iron output of Russia was due to the high quality of the ore itself (containing from 50% to 70% of iron),[15] as well as to the proximity of the fuel energy source—the Donbass—the prerequisite of a successful development of an industrial base that was either partially or totally absent in all other potential industrial centers of the Russian Empire.

Aside from its rich coal and iron deposits, the Ukraine, before the Revolution, contributed ¼ of Russia's output of manganese ore, most of which went for export.[16] It was the only supplier of mercury for industrial use.[17] It had a considerable share in Russia's salt production, contributing on the average 35,700,000,000 puds per year, or 30.6%, between 1900 and 1914.[18] There were, finally, other minerals whose existence was known but whose full utilization was as yet unrealized.

This exceptionally favorable distribution of fuel and mineral resources (coal and iron)—a distribution which is very rare—contributed greatly to the development of the metallurgical industry in the Ukraine. An important stimulus in this development was agriculture, whose surplus produce in the second half of the XIX Century demanded export; hence the construction of railroads which would connect agricultural centers with the warm sea harbors. This mineral-agricultural-transport complex thus laid the foundation for heavy industry in the Ukraine, whose growth resembled greatly that of other branches of the economy. In 1880, for example, the Ukraine's share in the smelting of pig iron was only 5% of Russia's total. By 1900 that share had risen to 51%, and by 1910 it had climbed to 68%.[19] During the same period the smelting of iron in the Urals, the main competitor of the Ukraine, declined from 71% in 1880, to 28% in 1900, and to 21% in 1910.[20] The chief cause of the growth of Ukrainian iron smelting was the presence of well-balanced supplies of mineral and energy sources.

With the growth of coal and iron industries and with the rapid expansion of the railroad network, there were created in the Ukraine favorable conditions for the development of heavy machine building industry. Before the war, the Ukraine produced 35% of all locomotives in Russia, with Kharkov and Lugansk as chief centers.

Alongside this development there began to take root chemical industries which were able to utilize chiefly local resources. Finally, the Ukraine possessed a well-developed food processing industry—36.1% of all Russian flour mills and about 80% of all sugar refineries.[21] In a word, thanks to its exceptionally well-balanced resources, favorable climatic conditions, and the interest of foreign capital (Belgian, French, English) which helped to develop these resources, the Ukraine represented a very valuable industrial and agricultural economic region of the Russian Empire, which the Russian state could not lose in any form without bringing upon itself almost total economic paralysis.

The demands of World War I only increased the potential value of the Ukraine, in view of the occupation of some industrial areas (the Dombrova Region) by the Germans. Military needs, relatively inexpensive cost of production, proximity to the war theater from the logistical standpoint—all these and many other factors increased the number of industrial enterprises in the Ukraine, some of which were brought in from the war zone (cf. from the Baltic Region). It was during this period that the Ukrainian share in the production of vital materials reached an all time high. Thus, for example, the output of coal climbed to 1,752,200,000 puds in 1916, or 87.2% of Russia's total output.[22] The production of locomotives climbed from 35% before the war to 60% in 1916.[23] Increases were also registered in the output of iron ore and other minerals. It was the absence of well-developed machine and tool building industries and munitions plants that prevented the Imperial Government from fuller utilization of Ukrainian resources in its war efforts[24]—a lesson which the Bolsheviks later took well into consideration. In view of these facts it would be no overestimation to state that, on the eve of the Revolution of 1917, the dependence of Russian economy on Ukrainian resources was so great that without them Russian economy would have experienced almost total paralysis. It was mainly for this reason that the Imperial government and educated Russian public opinion became very agitated whenever Russia's enemies, for the purpose of creating internal dissension within the Empire, expressed their plans about the Ukraine.

With the outbreak of the revolution and the subsequent period of chaos, the paralysis began to set in. Under the stress and strain of war the transportation system yielded, while the output of coal and iron took a downward trend. The absence of fuel energy also affected industry and public utilities. The food situation, the spark that initially ignited the revolution, went from bad to worse as time progressed. Political turmoil and administrative incapacity on the part of the Provisional Government added more fuel to the economic conflagration. To worsen the dilemma, the Bolsheviks helped, through their policies and tactics, to bring about complete territorial dismemberment of the Empire, out of whose ruins new independent states began to rise (Finland, the Baltic States, Poland, the Ukraine, the Caucasus, etc.).

However, no sooner did Russia's territorial dismemberment become a *fait accompli,* than the Russian Bolsheviks who, for propaganda reasons and advantages had promised *Land* to the poor, *Peace* to the idealists, and *Bread* to the hungry, began under the cover of socio-economic unity and liberation to reach for the lost territories, and above all for the lost resources. This they did by force of arms, thrusting aside promises of national self-determination to various nationalities of the Russian State. Thus the burning problem of the stomach, the acute need of Ukrainian grain, sugar, coal, iron and other resources, the utilization of the Black Sea harbors, etc., forced the planners and strategists of the World Revolution to choose first of all the route to Kiev and other Ukrainian cities as a means of self-preservation. Since, upon the successful possession and utilization of these needed resources the outcome of the revolution depended greatly, the Ukraine, whose role in the economy of pre-revolutionary Russia as has been pointed out was very important, became one of the prime objects of the Russian Bolshevik strategy.

To gain the possession of Ukrainian food and mineral resources, the Russian Bolsheviks tried several means. Though numerically insignificant, and disunited, they tried at first to seize power in the Ukraine in the Petrograd fashion. When that attempt failed they tried to force their way into a domineering position by seizing control of one of the then fashionable Congresses of Soviets which they called into being for that purpose. When at the Congress they found themselves outnumbered (2000 to 80) and outvoted, they left the Congress, assembled in Kharkov, proclaimed themselves the sole authority in the country and appealed for help from Petrograd. On December 27, 1917, two days after the new authority was organized, it was officially recognized by the Bolshevik Government in Petrograd, was promised unconditional support, and, in the name of international solidarity and revolutionary obligation, the first invasion of the Ukraine by Bolshevik forces took place.

With the advancing armies the Bolsheviks dispatched into the Ukraine requisitioning brigades. The food procurement brigades were headed by G. K. Ordzhonikidze, who arrived in the Ukraine at the end of December, 1917. Early in January, 1918, he received orders from Lenin to take very energetic and *"revolutionary* measures for the delivery of *bread, bread, bread!!!"* [25] At about the same time Karl Radek, on the pages of *Pravda,* was declaring that if the Russian proletariat wanted to have bread it had to "cry death to the Rada." [26] Another brigade which followed in the footsteps of the advancing Red armies in the Ukraine was charged with the procurement of fuel to aid the situation in Petrograd and Moscow. A special delegation was dispatched to the Donbass at the end of December, 1917, to study means of improving coal delivery to the North, which dropped from 66,000,000 puds in November, 1917 to 30,000,000 puds in January, 1918. [27]

Faced with the first Bolshevik invasion of the Ukraine, the Ukrainian Rada and its government, in search of self-preservation, fell into the waiting arms of the Central Powers. The latter were able to utilize it in negotiations with the Bolsheviks which finally culminated in the Treaty of Brest-Litovsk, on March 3, 1918. By virtue of this treaty signed under German military pressure, the Bolsheviks, in return for their retention of the revolutionary base in Central Russia from which to operate and direct the world revolutionary movement, were forced to recognize a complete separation of the Ukraine, and of the Baltic regions. In this, Russian economy suffered one of its most damaging blows. According to a

Russian estimate, made immediately following the signing of the treaty, Russian losses territorially amounted to 930,000 square kilometers, and population-wise, 56,000,000 or 32% of her total population. In addition, Russia lost ⅛ of her entire railroad network; 28,000,000 desiatins of wheat land of 97,000,000 desiatins; and 100,000 desiatins of 700,000 desiatins of rye land. Her iron mining area decreased by 78.8%, and her coal output by 89%. Russia lost about ½ of all her factory and industrial plants (1,073 or 46.5% of metal-working and machine plants; 615 or 42.8% of paper mills; 233 or 44.4% of chemical plants; 43 or 53.1% of corn brandy distilleries; 1,642 or 56.2% of alcohol distilleries; 113 or 57% of tobacco factories; 574 or 57% of breweries; 918 or 86% of weaving and spinning mills; and 286 or 86% of raw sugar factories). Finally, Russia lost 1,800 savings banks which were said to have provided the government with about 40% of its income [sic].[28]

The loss of the Ukraine, wherein many of the lost enterprises were located, was therefore a shattering blow to the success of world revolution. Though temporary control of the Ukraine by the Bolsheviks had relieved somewhat the economic dilemma—food and fuel—and for a time partially satisfied the needs of the cities in the North, this satisfaction was far from complete. German occupation of the Ukraine, which followed from the provisions of the treaty, relegated Bolshevik hopes for the possession of Ukrainian resources into the unknown future. It forced them on the one hand to follow in other regions the tactics applied in the Ukraine, and on the other hand to rely on their own resources of Central Russia. The evacuated personnel from the Donbass was moved into the Urals and the Sub-Moscow Region in an effort to develop coal resources to meet the emergency.[29] The absence of Ukrainian bread to feed the hungry millions, and the acute shortage of fuel resources for industrial needs were felt very heavily. On May 22, 1918, speaking at the Congress of Commissars of Labor, Lenin frankly acknowledged that the "lack of fuel, after the separation from us of a country rich in fuel [Ukraine], the catastrophe of railroads which are threatened by a standstill—these are the factors which create difficulties for the revolution" and hope for its enemies.[30]

German defeat by the Allies in the West, and the Allied lack of a common policy toward the Bolsheviks saved the latter. No sooner had the victory become known than the Bolsheviks repudiated the Treaty of Brest-Litovsk, withdrew their recognition of Ukrainian independence, and, in search for food and fuel for the approaching winter, undertook the second invasion of the Ukraine. "By conquering the Ukraine and three-fourths of the Donets Basin," wrote *Pravda* on February 6, 1919, "the Red Army, in its bloody struggle, obtained food and coal; it shattered the wall which prevented us from obtaining cotton and it cleared the road to Turkestan." "You all remember," declared a Ukrainian Bolshevik at the session of the Moscow Soviet on March 22, 1919, "that, when, with the advance of Red Armies, the Ukraine became Soviet, for you and for us came a great relief: wealthy, bread-Ukraine became ours! . . . We [in the Ukraine] remember that the entire attention of the proletariat of Russia is directed toward the Ukraine." [31]

Writing on the successes and difficulties of Soviet power in 1919, Lenin expressed great satisfaction that a Ukrainian Soviet Socialist Republic had been created to enable the Russian Bolsheviks to obtain bread in a comradely manner, since the puppet Ukrainian government had taken the position that its "first task was to aid the hungry North. The Ukraine cannot survive if, tired by hunger, the North should not survive. The Ukraine will survive and be victorious if it helps the hungry North." [32] To aid in utilizing the "gigantic" bread reserves in the Ukraine, the Bolsheviks sent, according to Lenin, "the best Soviet forces." Immediately after their arrival they dispatched a communique to the CC of the RCP(b), asking for help in view of the absence of an apparatus, of people capable of forming Soviet rule, and of a proletarian center. The CC of the RCP(b), after considering this "request," arrived at the conclusion that everything possible should be done to organize "an apparatus in the Ukraine, and in return for the work, . . . to demand 50 million puds of bread." [33]

Russian Bolshevik overzealousness in requisitioning and in shipping everything from the Ukraine to the North without compensation, while helping in many ways to improve the almost helpless conditions in Moscow and Petrograd, thereby saving the revolution, created in the Ukraine a wave of peasant uprisings, paved the way for rapid success of General Denikin's forces, and ended as a total fiasco for the Bolsheviks. It was political and administrative blunders of Denikin's administration on the one hand; and on the other, peasant disunity, lack of a far-sighted policy, purpose, and relatively weak national consciousness, that repaired the Bolshevik's hopeless situation and made possible their return to the Ukraine at the end of 1919, placing them again in possession of food, fuel, iron, and other resources.

However, by the end of 1919 and early 1920, Ukrainian economy was in almost complete chaos and destruction. Constant changes of governments, normal war operations, and intentional destruction of supplies and equipment to prevent the opponents' making any use of them, had brought Ukrainian industry and agriculture to a practical standstill. The degree of destruction can be seen from the fact that the output of coal, for example, decreased from 1,752,000,000 puds in 1916 to 1,499,000,000 puds in 1917, to 534,000,000 puds in 1918, and to 200,000,000 puds in 1919.[34] The output of iron ore underwent an even sharper decline, falling from 2,225,000 puds in 1917 to 1,650,000 puds in 1918, to zero from 1919 to 1921.[35] The production of manganese ore fell from 1,380,000 puds in 1916 to 1,070,000 puds in 1917, to 230,000 puds in 1918, to no production at all in 1919 and 1920.[36] The production of pig iron declined from 2,900,000 tons out of Russia's total of 3,700,000 tons in 1916 to 10,000 tons out of Russia's total of 100,000 tons in 1920.[37] Industrial production as a whole dropped to 10% of pre-war level,[38] while in agriculture the sowing area diminished by as much as 70%, and its grain production in 1920 equalled 30% of the pre-war output.[39] In a word, the economy of the Ukraine, as a result of war, revolution, civil war, and intervention, lay in almost complete ruin.

Economic destruction was not an exclusive attribute of the Ukraine. The chaos which war and revolution had brought upon the country affected also other regions of Russia, though perhaps not as totally in fury and duration. If the value, the role, and the contribution of the Ukrainian economy in the economy of the Russian Republic declined as a result of this destruction, the contribution, the value, and the role of various other regions did likewise. It must not be forgotten that the Ukraine, before the revolution, had contributed to Russia's economy far more than all other regions combined. If anything, the value of the Ukraine, destroyed though it may have been, only increased in view of the fact that several regions vital from the industrial and resources standpoint, had succeeded in separating themselves from Russia (Poland, the Baltic States, Finland). As a result the Ukraine, in the eyes of Bolshevik leaders, became their hope for the future, a vital key to post-war reconstruction—the key which was destined to play an important role similarly as it had in the success of the revolution during its early stages.

Speaking at the Fourth Conference of the CP(b)U, on March 17, 1920, Stalin, as the spokesman of the CC of the RCP(b), made it very explicit that without Ukrainian coal the restoration of the national economy of the RSFSR was impossible. He stated that without Ukrainian iron, which "to all intents and purposes" formed "our only source of ore, pig iron and finished products," the work of the revolution was lost; and that without Ukrainian grain to feed the workers, industrial recovery could not be accomplished. "Lack of grain," Stalin declared, "is our chief handicap and the chief cause of our industrial paralysis." [40] On another occasion, Stalin stated that the possession of Ukrainian natural resources (cf. coal) was "as important to Russia as the victory over Denikin." [41]

Speaking at the First All-Russian Mining Congress in Moscow early in April, 1920, Lenin warned the delegates that without coal, which was to be obtained primarily in the Ukraine, neither the post-war economic recovery nor industrial progress was possi-

ble. "Coal: that is bread for the industry. Without that bread
no industry can exist; without that bread the railroad transport
is placed in a very precarious position and cannot recover; without that bread heavy industry of every country collapses, deterio-
rates, turns backwards toward a primitive barbarism." [42] When,
during the second half of 1920, normal conditions began to return
to some parts of the Donbass Region and the monthly coal output rose from 25,000,000 puds to 50,000,000 puds, Lenin, speaking at the VIII All-Russian Congress of Soviets in December,
1920, hailed this increase as one of the great achievements of the
Soviet rule.[43]

At the XI Congress of the RCP(b) in March, 1921, which
inaugurated the period of the New Economic Policy (NEP),
Lenin bitterly criticized the mistakes of the CC of the CP(b)U
in its work in the Donbass and warned that the Donbass was too
vital a thing to allow blunders. The Donbass, he said, was "the
center, the real foundation of our entire economy. There cannot
be any talk about any reconstruction of heavy industry of Russia,
nor [any talk] about the construction of socialism—for it cannot
be built otherwise than through heavy industry—if we do not reconstruct, if we do not elevate the Donbass to its proper heights." [44]
The Donbass, stated a directive of the CC of the RCP(b) to the
CC of the CP(b)U, "is not an ordinary *rayon*—but it is a *rayon*
without which socialist construction will simply remain a wishful
thing." [45] The Donbass in particular, and the Ukraine in general,
became thus vital keys to post-war reconstruction of Russian
economy, of its industries, of its transport and of its food supplies.

The result of this respect for the Donbass was the adoption
of a slogan, "Everything for the Donbass!," which in reality became the official policy of the RCP(b) and of the Soviet government. A special commission was organized by the Council of the
Labor Army to study conditions in the Donbass. In its recom-
mendation the commission advised the Council to increase the
"qualified personnel," which, as a result of revolutionary chaos,
had declined from 250,000 in 1917 to 80,000 in 1920; to increase
the "technical personnel" which had declined by about 50%; to

improve living conditions, food and clothing supplies; to increase pay; to replace technical equipment which had been destroyed; to improve railroad transportation, etc.[46] In the Ukraine itself, for the purpose of the Donbass' quick recovery, a special Labor Army was organized.[47] In view of this emphasis on the recovery of the Donbass as the key to all other recoveries and reconstruction, it would seem reasonable to suggest that the recovery of the Donbass signalized the recovery of the Ukraine, which in turn meant the recovery of the entire economy of post-war revolutionary Russia. Consequently, throughout the entire period of the NEP (1921 through 1928), the Ukraine served as a very valuable barometer of the entire Soviet economy.

The almost unbelievable economic recovery of the Ukraine, under the NEP, from practically total destruction to unprecedented economic health, fully justified Bolshevik expectations and their hopes for the Ukraine. Part of this recovery was due to the incentives the NEP carried within itself. Most, however, was due to the already mentioned mineral-agricultural-transport complex of the Ukraine which, similarly as it had contributed to the rapid industrial growth of the Ukraine in the beginning of the XX Century, was also responsible for this rapid economic recovery.

Since the policy of the ruling party centered on fuel—coal— as the foundation of all the reconstruction, it was only natural that the coal industry of the Ukraine was the first to move ahead. The progress of its recovery can be seen from the following table.[48]

Year	Millions of Puds
1916	1,752
1919	200
1920	272
1921	356
1921-22	387
1922-23	495
1923-24	542
1924-25	761
1925-26	1,182
1926-27	1,507

Thus, as can be seen, by the end of 1927, coal output of the Donbass reached almost the pre-war level, contributing in actual production 80% of the entire coal output of the USSR, although its resources in 1927 were estimated to be only 14% of the total coal deposits of the USSR.[49]

Alongside the recovery of the Ukrainian coal industry went the recovery of the iron industry. Its progress was somewhat slower than that of coal due to its complete breakdown in 1919-1921. Compared with its share in the pre-war output, the Ukrainian iron industry during the NEP period shows the following picture of progress:[50]

Years	Output in Thousands of Tons				Share in Percentage		
	Krivoy Rog	Urals	Other Regions	Total	Krivoy Rog	Urals	Other Regions
1913	6,351	1,764	1,056	9,171	69.3	19.2	11.5
1924-5	1,291	872	61	2,224	58.1	39.3	2.6
1925-6	2,422	944	64	3,430	70.6	27.5	1.9
1926-7	3,538	1,089	—	ca. 4,700	75.3	23.2	1.5

The recovery of the Ukrainian iron industry paralleled quite vividly, as did that of coal, its pre-revolutionary development. The fuller it began to operate, the more it contributed, and accordingly, the lower it placed the share of other regions. This can be seen not only in the coal and iron industry, but also in the output of manganese ore, which, when compared with the pre-war production, presented the following picture (in thousands of tons):[51]

Years	Nikopol	Chiatury	Urals
1913	275.9	(965.8)	3.6
1924-5	175.6	(497.9)	3.0
1925-6	478.3 (861.6)	(848.4)	7.3
1926-7	472.1 (944.0)	365.4 (678.8)	—

The phenomenal progress of recovery under the NEP was also registered in Ukrainian agriculture—the foundation of

Ukrainian economy. Agriculture, in spite of war devastation and one of the severest droughts accompanied by a terrible famine (1921-2), attained pre-war production level ahead of all other branches of Ukrainian economy as well as ahead of all other food-producing regions of the USSR. Compared with the year 1916, the Ukrainian agricultural recovery percentage-wise presented the following picture: [52]

Regions	1923	1924	1925
Northern Caucasus	66.8	68.7	77.5
Kazakhstan	47.9	53.6	71.9
Siberia	80.2	87.1	92.2
Ukraine	86.7	92.5	96.1

Thus, among major food-producing centers, the Ukraine was first to regain full pre-war production level and accordingly was first in the contribution for domestic consumption and export.

This most remarkable all-around recovery of the Ukrainian economy during the NEP, with its great potentials and prospects of ever-increasing output and improvement, entered heavily into the calculations of the architects of the First Five Year Plan. Their fundamental aim was to develop, and at the same time to integrate, economies of all regions of the USSR into one economic entity, in order to be capable of carrying out the world revolution at some future date without fear.[53] The role of the Ukraine in this huge centralizing undertaking became two-fold. As the principal center of fuel energy (supplying 87% of coal); as a vital source of iron ore (producing 70%); as a vital supplier of manganese and pig iron (74% of the total output of the USSR); as the most overpopulated region of the country;[54] as one of the main food-producing centers, especially for export; and as the most completely recovered region of the USSR, the Ukraine was assigned by the First Five Year Plan to share its wealth with other regions, thereby contributing heavily toward their economic development.[55] At the same time, in view of its exceptionally well-distributed resources, the Ukraine was assigned a vital task of industrial self-development (cf. machine building, chemical and

light industries) in order to be able, as the foremost western outpost of the USSR, "to withstand at any moment not only blows
of capitalist intervention, but also to become the starting point
of our economic expansion into the countries of Europe and the
Near East." [56]

The importance of the Ukrainian economy in this tremendous undertaking is self-evident. As a result of this importance,
there developed among the Ukrainian Bolsheviks a two-sided
opposition to the scope as well as the speed of the Five Year
Plan. One group of opponents within the CP(b)U produced a
deviation known as Volobuevism.[57] Another group of opponents,
viewing the Ukrainian resources and their actual contributions
to the economy of the USSR from a political standpoint as well
as from the standpoint of personal advantage, considered these
resources a valuable lever to be used in their arguments and
relations with the central authorities in Moscow. They opposed
the development of other industrial regions at the speed foreseen
by the First Five Year Plan. They feared that once these regions
were developed with Ukrainian aid, their own voice would be
unheard in Moscow, their political importance would diminish
and their semi-privileged status with the central authorities would
decline. To the arguments that rapid construction of other industrial centers was motivated by strategic considerations, these
critics replied that such views were defeatist and unworthy of
revolutionary fighters.[58]

Beyond creating a feeling of annoyance among the proponents
of integral economy, and the disappearance of the critics from
public life, these criticisms had no major effect on the Plan itself,
which went on according to schedule. As the main fuel source of
the entire USSR, the Ukraine, in the First Five Year Plan was to
double its coal output in order to meet demands. Compared with
the contributions of other fuel producing centers of the USSR,
the share of the Ukraine in coal output presented the following
picture on the eve and at the end of the First Five Year Plan:[59]

Regions	1927-28		1932-33				
			In Millions of Tons		Percent in the Entire USSR Output		
	In Millions of Tons	Percent in the Entire Output of the USSR	Amount Expected to be Shipped	Maximum Amount to be Mined	Amount Expected to be Shipped	Maximum Amount to be Mined	
Donbass	27.26	77.0	47.8	52.5	70.4	70.1	
Kuzbass	2.46	7.0	5.2	6.0	7.6	8.1	
Urals	2.00	5.6	5.5	6.1	8.1	8.1	
Sub-Moscow	1.18	3.3	4.2	4.2	6.2	5.6	
East Siberia	1.91	5.4	3.6	4.0	5.2	5.3	
Central Asia	0.23	0.7	0.7	1.0	1.0	1.3	
Caucasus	0.11	0.3	0.5	0.6	0.8	0.8	
Other Regions	0.25	0.7	0.5	0.6	0.7	0.8	
TOTALS	35.40	100.0	68.0	75.0	100.0	100.0 [sic]	

Although percentage-wise the share of the Ukraine in coal output at the end of the First Five Year Plan was to decline because of the development of other regions, it is quite obvious that without Ukrainian coal, the First Five Year Plan—with its broad scope—would have had difficulty in succeeding. This was because the Ukrainian "coal basin was the main supplier of hard mineral fuel for the entire Union and the only source of coke in the entire European part of the USSR." [60] In addition, the Ukraine played a decisive role as a potential source of electric energy, not only for the Ukraine, but for the entire USSR,[61] increasing its output between 1928 and 1931 from 180,000,000 to over 630,000,000 kilowatts.[62]

Aside from its enormous contribution in fuel and energy, the Ukraine played a vital role as the chief supplier of iron ore (over 75% of the All-Union output) in the First Five Year Plan. According to the plan, the output of Ukrainian iron ore was to double between 1928 and 1932—from 5,170,000 tons to 10,190,000 tons.[63] To be sure, the Plan called for the erection of numerous metallurgic centers, but their contribution to the Plan, if any, was not expected until the end of the First Five Year Plan. Therefore, the Ukraine, as a well developed metallurgic base, had to carry the largest burden. The Ukraine likewise contributed heavily in the production of manganese ore, almost doubling its output—from 536,000 tons in 1928-29 to 920,000 tons in 1932-33—half of which went for export.[64] It is only fair to suggest that without these fundamentals, which the Ukraine provided, neither the scope nor the speed of the industrialization of the USSR would have been possible.

Alongside its serving as the main source of fuel, energy, and iron, in the construction and development of other industrial centers of the USSR, the Ukraine, by virtue of its exceptionally well balanced resources—the mineral-agricultural-transportation complex—was assigned by the architects of the First Five Year Plan an important role in self-industrialization. Especially was its role to be important in the expansion of its mining and heavy industries; in expanding its agricultural machinery production; and in expanding its chemical and food processing industries. These expansions were to transfer the Ukraine into a potential base of all kinds of machinery and into a highly industrialized part of the USSR, changing its "agraro-industrial look into industro-agrarian." [65] It is interesting to note in connection with this self-development that the First Five Year Plan placed very little emphasis on the construction of new enterprises in the Ukraine. This factor the Ukrainians tried to exploit in their arguments that the Ukraine was nothing but a colony of the RSFSR.[66]

In this enormous undertaking of building up other industrial regions and carrying on its own industrial self-development, the Plan assigned an important role to Ukrainian agriculture which, in spite of considerable industrial development of the Ukraine, was the foundation of Ukrainian economy. As a region of very fertile soil, with a well-developed railroad network connecting the food-producing centers with warm water harbors on the coast of the Black Sea, Ukrainian agriculture was given the task of producing grain for export rather than for domestic consumption of the USSR, in order to finance a large portion of industrial expenses.[67] In addition, as the most heavily populated rural region, the Ukraine had to provide the main bulk of the labor force for all types of industrial construction.[68] And finally, as one of the largest agricultural regions, it had to serve as "a colossal laboratory of new forms of socio-economic and productive-technical reconstruction of rural economy for the entire Soviet Union." [69]

By virtue of all these factors upon whose smooth functioning depended the success or failure of the First Five Year Plan, the Ukraine, as one of the fundamental keys in the complexity of all these experiments, became the subject of utmost political and administrative attention. Any sign of improper functioning of this elaborate mechanism was immediately interpreted as sabotage, as a sign of counter-revolutionary moves; as a sign of an attempt to separate the Ukraine from the rest of the USSR; and as a sign of foreign conspiracy against the "citadel of the proletariat." The defense of the USSR and of the Ukraine in particular became the everyday slogan, and toward that end the entire apparatus of the Comintern was organized. The Ukraine, in a word, became the region *sine qua non*. When, therefore, in this atmosphere of self-created fear and anxiety, a partial breakdown in agriculture occurred, a considerable number of the Ukrainian peasantry was exterminated, both as a class and as a national enemy. This was done in the most ruthless fashion of recorded history—by an intentionally created famine.

The most heinous feature of the 1932-3 famine in the Ukraine was the fact that it was politically inspired, and that it had the full blessing of the top leadership of the Party and of the Government of the USSR. That this cold-blooded massacre was deliberately engineered can be seen from the fact that every measure taken by the Government of the USSR during this period was intended to increase, rather than to alleviate, the difficulties of the population. Thus, for example, the government, to finance industrialization and to feed the growing city population—though fully aware of the unfavorable climatic conditions in the Ukraine in 1931 and 1932, and though conscious of the decrease of the sowing area—not only forced the peasantry *en masse* into collective farms, but also, without defining what constituted "surplus," arbitrarily intensified the requisitioning of foodstuffs and grain surplus from the peasants. At the same time, it fully enforced the August 7, 1932 decree for the protection of "socialist property." As a result the entire peasantry—in addition to the *kulaks*— was left with no means of support.[70]

Another factor which points vividly to the deliberate administering of the famine was the government's prevention of all attempts and efforts on the part of Ukrainian as well as non-Ukrainian organizations and agencies abroad to aid the famine-stricken population,[71] and its labelling of all references to the famine as "lies circulated by counter-revolutionary organizations abroad." [72] At the same time, however, the Government of the USSR barred all foreign newspaper correspondents stationed in Moscow from entering the famine-stricken Ukraine and Northern Caucasus until the harvest of 1933 was brought in. This was designed to prevent the spread of news to the outside world of this great human tragedy.[73] If the famine were the result of climatic conditions, and not deliberately engineered, there would have been neither need nor cause to hide it from the world— especially since some charitable groups expressed their unconditional willingness and readiness to aid.[74] However, since the famine was a man-made disaster to "teach the peasants a lesson," [75] the Government of the USSR was unwilling to let the truth become known.

The scope of that gigantic tragedy, which today is acknowledged by all observers, except Communists and their sympathizers,[76] is beyond comprehension. One foreign observer, who visited the Ukraine immediately following the lifting of travel restrictions, declared later that

> No one, I am sure, could have made such a trip with an honest desire to learn the truth and escaped the conclusion that the Ukrainian countryside had experienced a gigantic tragedy. What had happened was not hardship, or privation, or distress, or food

shortage, to mention the deceptively euphemistic words that were allowed to pass the Soviet censorship, but stark, outright famine, with its victims counted in millions. No one will probably ever know the exact toll of death, because the Soviet Government preserved the strictest secrecy about the whole question, officially denied that there was any famine, and rebuffed all attempts to organize relief abroad.[77]

Another foreign observer, who spent the winter of 1932-3 in Kharkov, wrote

> I spent the winter of 1932-33 mainly in Kharkov, then capital of the Ukraine. It was the catastrophic winter after the first wave of collectivization of the land; the peasants had killed their cattle, burned or hidden their crops and were dying of starvation and typhoid; the number of deaths in the Ukraine alone is estimated at about two millions. Travelling through the countryside was like running the gauntlet; the stations were lined with begging peasants with swollen hands and feet, the women holding up to the carriage-windows horrible infants with enormous wobbling heads, stick-like limbs, swollen, pointed bellies . . . Under my hotel-room window in Kharkov funeral processions marched past all day.[78]

Because the Soviet government observed the strictest secrecy concerning the entire question, probably no one will ever know the famine's exact toll of lives. According to some Ukrainian observers, who based their findings on the discrepancy between the official census figures of 1926 and of 1939, the decrease in Ukrainian population during that period was approximately 7,500,000.[79] One Western observer, however, interpreted the decrease of Ukrainian population as reflecting, in the main, the change of Ukrainian ethnic affiliation.[80] This theory however gives rise to many questions, particularly that of why there occurred such a sudden desire on the part of the Ukrainian population to be assimilated.

The fear of losing the Ukraine, and the degree or cost this loss would have meant for the planning, can be seen from the actual contribution of Ukrainian production to the production of the USSR. According to the figures computed at the end of the First Five Year Plan in 1932, the share of the Ukrainian economy in production of various commodities and in the supply of raw materials and fuel was: [81]

Product	Quantity		Percent of USSR Total
Coal	44,896,000	tons	69.8
Iron Ore	8,444,000		70.0
Manganese	443,000		75.0
Pig Iron	4,624,000		69.9
Steel	3,546,000		63.3
Finished Steel	2,745,000		64.0
Precious Metals	1,579,600,000	rubles	23.0
Phosphates	63,846	tons	50.0
Cement	1,566,000		45.4
Bricks	1,325,000,000	pieces	28.1
Leather Footwear	17,175,000	pairs	24.3
Meat	120,000	tons	27.7
Fish	207,000		26.4
Sugar	575,000		69.5
Canned Food	197,000,000	cans	60.2
Margarine	140,000	tons	33.3
Sugar Beet Acreage	1,173,800	ha.	76.3
Planted Acreage	33,638,000		25.4

It is self-evident that had the Ukrainian share been eliminated in one form or another, the success of the First Five Year Plan, which was a psychological test of the regime, would have been greatly jeopardized; indeed it might have collapsed. This was frankly admitted by Stalin himself, in his report to the XVI Congress of the VKP(b) in 1930, when he stated that the entire Soviet industry and Soviet economy was dependent exclusively on the coal and iron of the Ukraine. "It is self-evident," he went on, "that without such a base, industrialization of the country is unthinkable. And such a base is our Ukrainian fuel-metallurgic base." [82]

The great psychological victory which the regime had achieved by carrying through the First Five Year Plan in four years did not decrease the value of the Ukraine even though, following the conclusion of the Plan, the Ukrainian share, percentage-wise, began to decline because of the increased contribution of other regions. Official expectations for the end of the First Five Year Plan were for an increased significance of the Ukraine "as one of the industrial centers producing the means of production for the entire Soviet Union . . . Similarly will likewise increase its [the Ukraine's] significance as a supplier of rural agricultural production, especially the production of intensified cultures and livestock for internal markets of the Union as well as for foreign markets." [83]

In spite of the forecast of the significance of the Ukraine at the end of the First Five Year Plan when compared with the expectations of the Second Five Year Plan (1932-7), the projected achievements of the latter somewhat reduced the Ukrainian share as can be seen from the following table: [84]

Product	Percent in 1932	Percent in 1937	Percent of Decrease
Coal	69.8	54.3	− 15.5
Iron Ore	70.0	56.9	− 13.1
Pig Iron	69.9	58.1	− 11.8
Steel	63.3	55.8	− 7.5
Precious Metals	23.0	21.3	− 1.7
Cement	45.4	35.4	− 10.0
Bricks	28.1	22.8	− 5.3
Footwear	24.3	20.0	− 4.3
Fish	26.4	20.7	− 5.7
Canned Food	60.2	59.9	− 0.3

It would be a great mistake to assume that, as a result of the percentage decrease of the Ukrainian share in the total production of the USSR, the importance of the Ukraine in the Bolshevik industrial strategy and planning followed a similar decline. The Ukraine in the Second Five Year Plan was to remain, in the words of V. V. Kuibyshev, "one of the decisive districts of the Union in coal, metallurgical, machine building and chemical production, in electrical construction—the largest in the Union—and in large scale socialist agriculture." [85] By the end of the Second Five Year Plan (1937), the Ukraine was to contribute to the total production of the USSR, 8,900,000 tons of pig iron, or 55.7% of the total; 6,700,000 tons, or 51.6% of rolled metal; 72,000,000 tons of coal, or 48%; 16,000,000 tons, or 47% of iron ore; 50% of aluminum; 36% of tractors; 61.5% of locomotives; 48% of calcinated soda; 44.4% of manganese ore; 9,700,000,000 kilowatts, or 25.8% of electric power; and 27,000,000 ha. of sowing area. In addition, in the sphere of self-development, the Ukraine was to construct three giant pig iron mills with an annual production capacity of over 1,000,000 tons (Zaporozhstal, Azovstal and Krivoyrogstal); a Nikopol pipe rolling mill; complete the Dzerzhynski and Makeyevka iron mill plants with a capacity of over 1,100,-000 tons of pig iron; build 68 new coal pits; complete the Kramatorsk plant; the Kharkov turbine plant; the Lugansk locomotive construction plant; and various other machine building, tool, car, and food producing plants.[86]

As can be seen from this official pronouncement, the role of the Ukraine in the Second Five Year Plan was far from declining. In view of the fact that the First Five Year Plan only laid the incomplete foundation for the industrialization of the USSR, now more than ever the need for possessing the Ukraine, its resources, its well-balanced industry and its know-how became of great importance. Without them the execution of the tasks set forth by the Second Five Year Plan would have been hardly possible. This can be concluded from the fact that while percentage-wise the share of the Ukraine was on a downward trend, in actual contribution the Ukrainian production quota had in many instances more than doubled. Compared with the year 1932, the production of certain commodities in 1937 was to represent the following ratio: [87]

Product	1932	1937	% of 1937 to 1932
Elec. Energy	3,158,300,000 kw. hrs	9,343,400,000 kw. hrs.	295.8
Coal	39,200,000 tons	69,072,000 tons	176.2
Iron Ore	7,925,500	16,414,100	207.1
Manganese	443,300	956,900	215.9
Pig Iron	3,910,800	8,800,300	225.0
Steel	3,127,700	8,466,700	270.7
Metal Indus.	1,788,000,000 rubles	4,721,000,000 rubles	264.0
Locomotives	431 pieces	880 pieces	204.2
Chem. Indus.	209,000,000 rubles	709,000,000 rubles	3.4 times
Sugar	720,000 tons	1,789,800 tons	248.3
Shoes	14,160,000 pairs	31,230,000 pairs	220.6
Sown Area	26,438,400 ha.	25,194,900 ha.	95.0

The increase of Ukrainian production in the Second Five Year Plan was not an accident. Although new centers of raw materials and fuel were being established in various parts of the USSR (Kuzbass, Urals, Karaganda, Sub-Moscow Basin, the Far East, Central Asia in coal), the Ukraine remained the chief supplier of coal for the European part of the USSR, satisfying in addition the needs of export.[88]

In addition to serving as the main fuel and raw material base for other industrial regions, the Ukraine underwent a far reaching self-development and modernization of its own industries during the Second Five Year Plan. As a result of this modernization and thanks to the exceptionally well balanced location of resources, the Ukraine became a highly industrialized region wherein four major industrial areas were to be noticed. The first area was centered around Kharkov which produced transportation, agricultural and electrical machinery and machine tools (a tractor plant; a turbine plant with a capacity of 1,500,000 kilowatts; a railroad car plant with a capacity of 4,000 cars per year; etc.). The second industrial area, containing black metallurgy, heavy transport and agricultural machinery, chemical and electrical plants, centered around Dniepropetrovsk (Dnieprostal: productive capacity 1,230,000 tons of iron, 1,600,000 tons of steel, and

1,000,000 tons of finished steel; Azovstal: productive capacity
1,300,000 tons of iron, 1,140,000 tons of steel and 1,225,000 tons
of finished steel; Nikopol: tubular plant; Novamoskva: tin
plant; and Dnieprostroy: one of the major electricity producing
centers of the USSR with a capacity of 4,000,000,000 kilowatts
in 1938). The third major industrial center was the Donbass,
which, in addition to being the main energy source, became an
important center of heavy industry, agricultural and transport
machinery, and chemical industry (Horlivka chemical and coke
plants; Makeyevka metallurgical, tubular, and coke plants;
Slaviansk machine and chemical plants; Kramatorsk machine
building plant; Lugansk locomotive, tubular and tool plants;
Konstantinovka glass and chemical plants; Mariupol metallurgical
and coke plants). Finally, the Kiev and Odessa areas together
represented the fourth industrial area, wherein mainly food and
food processing industries were located.[89] Thanks to these developments, the Ukraine became a highly industrialized country.

The industrialization of the Ukraine, during the Second Five
Year Plan, *i.e.,* its change from an agricultural and raw material
base into a highly industrialized, raw material and agricultural
base, greatly changed its role in the economy of the USSR. By
virtue of its aid in the development of other regions, and owing
to its industrial self-development, the Ukraine began to change
slowly from a region *sine qua non* into a region of *primus inter
pares.* From then on, without the Ukraine, the economy of the
Soviet Union, given some outside stimulus or incentive, was
capable of taking over many of the responsibilities, while with the
Ukraine the outlook was bright. The loss of the Ukraine at any
time from then on would have been a heavy blow to the economy
of the USSR, but it would not have brought about economic
paralysis. The effect of this fundamental change of the potential
economic value of the Ukraine in the economy of the USSR can
be seen in the assignment of the Ukraine in the Third Five Year
Plan (1937-42).[90]

Product	1937	1942
Electric Energy	28.01%	25.29%
Coal	53.97%	46.22%
Peat	6.33%	7.15%
Pig Iron	60.75%	55.68%
Steel	47.99%	49.64%
Cement	22.37%	13.65%
Meat	17.60%	17.19%
Fats	14.26%	14.14%
Flour Products	22.25%	22.63%
Sewing Articles	16.40%	15.56%
Cotton Cloth	0.21%	1.08%

As the above table indicates, the percentage-wise contribution of the Ukraine to the total production of the USSR during the Third Five Year Plan was slightly reduced. However, the projected reduction of the Ukrainian share did not proportionately decrease its value. The Ukraine, declared the Third Five Year Plan, remained the fundamental coal-metallurgic base of the USSR, and one of the main regions of chemical, machine building, food and light industry, grain and technical cultures and livestock.[91] As an economic region, the Ukraine was surpassed only by the almost limitless RSFSR. However, from the point of view of resources distribution and their utilization, the Ukraine remained one of the most important economic areas of the USSR—"a republic of coal, iron, and many other precious minerals; a republic of widely developed metallurgy and machine building." [92]

In 1940, the Ukraine was supplying into the total productive scheme of the USSR, 24.9% of electric energy; 50.5%, or 83,728,-000 tons of coal; 63%, or 18,900,000 tons of iron ore; 61.2%, or 9,183,100 tons of pig iron; 47.1%, or 8,621,700 tons of steel; 47.7% of rolling iron; 19.6% of metallurgy; 46.8% of agricultural machinery; 30% of glass; 20% of alabaster; 15% to 17% of bricks; 35% of manganese ore, etc.[93] Ukrainian industry "manufactured railway engines and cars, tractors, turbines, harvester combines and mining and agricultural machinery for all parts of the Soviet Union . . . produced mineral fertilizers, soda, glass and cement," and had "attained great dimensions in the output of sugar, meat packing, flour milling, distilling, oil crushing and dairy industries." [94] On the eve of World War II, the Ukraine still formed "one of the largest granaries of the USSR and produced about 50 percent of the winter wheat and 74 percent of the sugar beet crop of the Union." [95] According to the revised Plan of 1941, the Ukraine was to contribute in actual production, the following: [96]

Product	Ukrainian Share	USSR's Total
Coal	83,573,000 tons	171,160,000 tons
Gasoline	353,000	34,300,000
Peat	3,844,000	39,615,000
Iron	21,000,000	34,030,000
Coke	17,106,000	23,800,000
Pig Iron	11,107,000	18,000,000
Steel	10,650,500	22,400,000
Rolling Iron	7,657,500	15,800,000
Cement	1,616,000	7,998,000
Shoes	29,125,000 pairs	167,308,000 pairs
Alcohol	26,725,000 dkl.	101,200,000 dkl.
Salt	1,964,400 tons	4,600,000 tons
Spring Crop	11,485,100 ha.	77,856,899 ha.
Winter Crop	8,124,000	35,355,800
Technical Cultures	2,263,300	10,742,000
Cotton	230,000	2,020,600
Flax	98,000	1,788,000
Hemp for cloth	96,700	482,300
Sugar Beets	770,000	1,136,900
Sun Flowers	594,600	3,099,300
Hemp for seed	39,000	93,200
Soya	51,100	172,800
Tobacco	9,100	94,000
Makhorka	36,900	110,700
Herbs	21,000	41,600
Potatoes & vegetables	949,000	5,028,080

In view of this share of the Ukraine in the economy of the USSR, although reduced in percentage, as well as owing to its strategic value, it is little wonder that with the outbreak of Nazi-Soviet hostilities in June of 1941, German military strategy aimed at a *blitz* occupation of the Ukraine in order to weaken the Soviet Union. It is likewise little wonder that Bolshevik military strategy, following the outbreak of hostilities, aimed at salvaging as much movable wealth as possible in order to utilize it in its war efforts. The result of Bolshevik strategy was the mass Eastward exodus of Ukrainian industry, people and livestock.[97]

It has been reported that between September and December, 1941, more than 1,000 war and machine production enterprises were transferred Eastward from the Ukraine, to the Urals and beyond.[98] This strengthened greatly the newly established industrial centers and, in the final analysis, made it possible for the Soviet Union, with Allied help, to out-produce the German military machine. In view of the displacement of manpower and machinery (tractors, automobiles, horses, etc.), and because of war operations, air attacks, and finally German occupation of the Ukraine, the actual contribution of the Ukraine to the war economy of the USSR, aside from the vital exodus, was insignificant. Comparing the previous food delivery to the state, the Ukrainian share in 1941 was relatively small; while Ukrainian iron and coal, by December, 1941, had completely stopped flowing into the industry of the Soviet Union.[99]

The loss of the Ukraine to Germany from 1941 to 1943 forced the Russian Bolsheviks to accelerate the building up of their more remote industrial centers, factories, mines, electric stations, etc. The Urals, the Chelabinsk *oblast'*, the Kuznetsk, the Altai, and the Uzbek Regions became mass production centers, taking the place of the Ukraine. By the end of 1942, and in the early part of 1943, these areas doubled their pre-war output; while between 1941 and 1945, production of the Urals increased 3.6 times; that of Siberia 2.8 times; and that of the Volga Region 3.4 times.[100] German Eastward penetration of the USSR, in addition to creating heavy losses in industry, incapacitated almost half the total sowing area of the Soviet Union, most of which was located in the Ukraine, thereby forcing the Bolsheviks to develop extensive new sowing areas in the

East.[101] In other words, these losses to Germany forced the Soviet Union to become, with Allied help and maximum effort and self-sacrifice, economically independent of the Ukraine. At the same time the war demonstrated that the loss of the Ukraine, while capable of inflicting a heavy blow to the economy of the USSR, was no longer capable of completely paralyzing it, as had been the case earlier, in 1918-1920.

Evacuation, war operations, and intentional destruction by the Bolsheviks as well as by the Nazis, reduced the Ukrainian economy to ruins. It has been officially reported that, in addition to untold deaths, the fury of the war period damaged 714 cities, and 28,000 villages. More than 2,000,000 dwellings were destroyed leaving over 10,000,000 people homeless. The war disrupted 10,150 industrial establishments, which before the war had employed more than 2,300,000 people. The Donbass coal basin—once the pride and the heart of industrial UkSSR—with its mines flooded, lay in ruins. In total or partial ruins was the machine industry, electric power, chemical, and food industries. War had disrupted 47%, or 9,203 kilometers of railways. Great damage and extensive losses were suffered by Ukrainian agriculture; particularly in equipment and in the decline of the number of livestock. Compared with pre-war conditions, the number of cattle surviving in 1944 was 42%; that of pigs 10%; sheep and goats 18%; and horses 22%. Total losses of the Ukraine were officially set at 285 billion rubles.[102]

However damaged the Ukraine may have found itself at the end of the Second World War, its potential value in post-war reconstruction of the USSR did not appear to have declined. No sooner had the fighting front receded from the Ukraine than a slogan, which in fact became an official policy—"Recovery of the Donbass is a nation-wide task"—was adopted. Men and materiel were sent from Eastern districts of the USSR to begin the reconstruction of the Donbass in order to bolster final Soviet war efforts.[103] Another factor which, if not increasing, at least maintained intact the economic value of the Ukraine, was the considerable expansion of Ukrainian territory following the war; namely the acquisition of Galicia and Volyn from Poland, Trans-Carpathian

Ukraine from Czechoslovakia, Bukovina and Izmail from Rumania, and the more recent transfer of Crimea from the RSFSR to the Ukraine. These additions of territory added considerable resources to the Ukraine's over-all capacity (oil in Boryslav and Drohobych, natural gas in Dashava, salt, and many other industrial enterprises). The final factor which points out that the economic value of the Ukraine remained intact, in spite of its tremendous losses during the war and the development of new industrial and agricultural centers in Asia, was the assignment the Ukraine received in the Fourth Five Year Plan (1946-50), both in the industrial and agricultural fields.

In addition to its economic recovery and complete reconstruction, Ukrainian industry by 1950 was to give in relation to the total production of the USSR: 9,700,000 tons, or 49.7% of pig iron; 8,800,000 tons, or 34.6% of steel; 86,100,000 tons, or 34.4% of coal; 1,637,000 tons, or 68.2% of sugar; 1,000, or 40% of locomotives; 55,500, or 40% of railroad cars; 25,500, or 22.3% of tractors; 5,950, or 33.9% of metallurgic instruments; 325,000 tons of gasoline; 13,690 million kilowatts of electric energy; 15,500,000 tons of coke; 2,065,000 tons of cement; 25,000 automobiles; 860,000 tons of super phosphate; 448,000 tons of calcium soda; 1,930,000 tons of salt; 245,000 tons of meat; 40,000 tons of butter; 80,000 tons of fish; etc.[104] "It is evident from these numbers," stated Khrushchev in his report on the Fourth Five Year Plan, at the Eighth Session of the Supreme Soviet of the UkSSR, "what an important part the industry of the UkSSR plays in the All-Union industry, and this places upon us even greater responsibility for a timely and complete fulfillment of the Five Year Plan in the Union and the Union Republican production." [105] Although it has been reported that privately Khrushchev had doubts as to the success of Ukrainian full recovery, and accordingly its assigned contribution to the post-war Five Year Plan,[106] the official announcement of April 16, 1951, on the fulfillment of the Plan declared, without giving specific data to substantiate the declaration, that the metallurgic industry of the Ukraine had been fully restored by 1950, and that it was producing more than before the war. It went on to say that coal shafts of the Donbass were yielding "more coal than before the war and even more than had been foreseen by the Five Year Plan"; and that "the Donbass is again the greatest and the most mechanized coal basin of the country"; that oil industry, electricity, and other branches of industry were fully recovered and exceeding their pre-war output.[107] Although one must view these statements with skepticism, it would be dangerous, considering past recoveries and performances of Ukrainian economy, to underestimate its capabilities.

The most important factors in all of these performances have been the quality, the distribution and the ease of utilization of Ukrainian natural resources. It was mainly because of this combination that the Ukraine became one of the most vital economic regions of the Russian Empire at the turn of the XX Century, a place which it held until the outbreak of the Second World War. It was likewise due to this favorable combination that the Ukraine became one of the main objects of Bolshevik strategy. Finally, it was likewise because of this favorable combination that the Ukraine was assigned to serve as a major base in the industrialization of the USSR. Although, since the end of the Second Five Year Plan the role of the Ukraine in the economy of the USSR has declined considerably, the favorable combination of Ukrainian natural resources nevertheless makes the Ukraine still one of the most important economic regions of the USSR.

CHAPTER VIII

Federal Ties

From the time of the Bolshevik seizure of power, the main characteristic of constitutional development of the USSR has been a tendency toward centralism. This tendency, often hidden behind a cloak of vagueness and generalities, has been one of the fundamental factors in determining not only the relationship between the center and the border regions—between the centripetal and the centrifugal forces—but also has been the guiding force behind all major constitutional changes. Because of its numerical strength, economic potentials, strategic location, and tradition of independent, though short-lived, existence, the Ukraine, in principle as well as in fact, through its spokesmen, has acted as a deterrent in this centralizing process. For all practical purposes the centralizing process of the USSR was completed by 1936, when a new constitution—Stalin's constitution—went into effect. Subsequent changes, especially the so-called "Constitutional Reform of February 1, 1944," while at first glance seeming to tend in the opposite direction, in reality neither changed the monolithic process nor weakened the authority of the center over the periphery.

Constitutional relations between the RSFSR and the UkSSR began during the second Russian Bolshevik invasion and occupation of the Ukraine in 1918-19. On March 10, 1919, in Kiev, the Third All-Ukrainian Congress of Soviets approved the Ukrainian government, which had been organized in the RSFSR under Stalin's supervision,[1] and ratified a constitution for the UkSSR. Like its creators, who were brought into the Ukraine by the westward advancing Red Army, the Ukrainian constitution was an import from the

215

RSFSR. In many respects it was nothing but a small replica of the RSFSR's constitution. Ten of its thirty-three articles (Articles 24-33) dealt with rights and duties of the laboring and exploited people of the Ukraine, and were verbatim translations of the same declarations made in Articles 14-23 of the RSFSR constitution. There were also other provisions in the Ukrainian constitution which reflected fundamental ideas of the Russian constitution. Like its source and inspiration—the constitution of the RSFSR—the Ukrainian constitution declared the Ukraine "an organization of the dictatorship of the toiling and exploited masses of the proletariat and of the poorer peasantry over their congenital oppressors and exploiters, the capitalists and landowners." The task of the dictatorship, the constitution further proceeded, was to "effect the transition from the bourgeois regime to socialism by carrying out socialist reorganization and systematic oppression of all counter-revolutionary attempts on the part of the possessing classes." Accordingly, and similarly as the constitution of the RSFSR, the Ukrainian constitution called for the destruction of the "existing economic order by eliminating private ownership of land and of all other means of production" (Chapter I, Article 3, a). Like its source, the constitution of the RSFSR, the Ukrainian constitution assured the power to the working class, and only for the laboring masses did it create an exclusive possibility to make use of their political rights, especially freedom of speech, of the press, and of the assembly. (Chapter I, Article 3, b, c.).[2]

Theoretically the Ukrainian constitution retained many vestiges of Ukrainian independence. Within the competence of the central organs of the UkSSR, which were very vaguely formulated, came all questions of national significance. In particular, within its jurisdiction belonged: 1) The ratification, amendment, and supplementing of the constitution; 2) The determination and alteration of the frontiers of the republic; 3) Relations with foreign powers, in particular the declaration of war and conclusion of peace; 4) The establishment of the basis of the organization of the armed forces; 5) General direction of domestic policy; 6) Civil, criminal and lawsuit legislation; 7) The establishment of principles of socialist construction in economy; 8) The management of the monetary system and the organization of the financial economy of the republic; and 9) The control over activities of Soviet authority, in particular over the correctness, legality, and reasonableness of expenses. (Article 6, Sections *a* through *i*).

Like its source, the RSFSR constitution, the Ukrainian constitution placed the supreme authority of the UkSSR into the Congress of Soviets under whose exclusive jurisdiction belonged the ratification, amending and supplementing of the constitution. (Article 10). In the interim between the congresses, which were to meet twice a year, the constitution placed the supreme authority into the hands of the All-Ukrainian Central Executive Committee. Under the exclusive jurisdiction of the latter came the appointment and recall of the People's Commissars and the Chairman of the Sovnarkom; the distribution of state income and revenue between the central and local organs; the determination of time and order of the election of the local Soviet organs, norms of their representation, problems of their internal organization as well as the establishment of the scope of their jurisdiction. (Article 11). In addition, under its exclusive jurisdiction fell "other questions concerning legislation and the general administration of the country," with the exception of those matters which fell under the competence of the Sovnarkom. (Article 13).

Like its source, the constitution of the RSFSR, the Ukrainian constitution provided for a joint jurisdiction exercised equally by the Congress of Soviets and by the Central Executive Committee. Both organs were empowered with "the general direction of the activity . . . of all government organs throughout the country." Both exercised joint jurisdiction over the determination and alteration of frontiers; relations with foreign powers; organization of the armed forces; general direction of domestic policy; and the approval of the annual budget. (Article 11). Both bodies likewise exercised joint jurisdiction in deciding "questions of declaration of war and conclusion of peace,"—a provision valid only in case of urgency if the Congress of Soviets could not be convened in proper time. (Article 13, Note).

Theoretically and constitutionally the Ukraine was an independent state. It had its own territory; it had its own fundamental law; and it had its own government. At the same time, however, by virtue of its declaration of "complete solidarity with the existing Soviet republics," and of readiness to enter with these republics "into the closest political union for the common fight, for the triumph of the world communist revolution," the constitution of the UkSSR had predetermined the transformation of the Ukraine into an integral part of the rising Soviet Empire.[3] For all practical purposes, these declarations, plus the fact that the Ukrainian government itself was imported from the RSFSR, annulled all provisions which to a greater or lesser degree granted to the UkSSR the right and possibility of independent action.

It was on the basis and in pursuance of these declarations—declarations which called for unity of action and purpose—that the central government gradually eliminated all the rights of the so-called independent republics, including the UkSSR. Officially the liquidation of sovereign rights of these republics began on June 1, 1919, with the creation of a commission to formulate a treaty of alliance between the RSFSR on the one hand, and the Ukrainian, Latvian, Lithuanian, and Belorussian republics on the other. The resolution of the All-Russian Central Executive Committee which announced the creation of this commission, after denouncing the outside world for its unwillingness to submit to the dictates of the Communists, called for the creation of a military union, "a close union of the: 1) Military organization and military command; 2) Council of People's Economy; 3) Railway administration and economic structure; 4) Finances; and 5) Commissariats for Labor." [4]

As far as the Ukraine was concerned, formal expressions of these intentions were put into force by a treaty concluded between the RSFSR and the UkSSR on December 28, 1920.[5] By virtue of this act, the RSFSR and the UkSSR entered into a military and an economic union (Article 1). Article 3 of the treaty provided that "both governments declare the following commissariats as being henceforth unified: 1) War and Navy; 2) Supreme Council of People's Economy; 3) Foreign trade; 4) Finance; 5) Labor; 6)

Ways of Communication; and 7) Post and Telegraphs." Both parties agreed that unified commissariats were to be included in the Sovnarkom of the RSFSR (Article 4). They agreed that the unified commissariats be placed under the supervision and control of the All-Russian Congress of Soviets and the All-Russian Central Executive Committee, wherein the UkSSR was allowed to send "its representatives in conformity with the statute of the All-Russian Congress of Soviets." (Article 6). The Ukrainian Congress of Soviets and its Central Executive Committee retained only the right of control over the plenipotentiary representatives of the unified commissariats who became regular members of the Ukrainian Sovnarkom. (Article 4).[6]

In addition to this first major centralization, which for all practical purposes ended the actual independence of the UkSSR as a state, both governments agreed that at a future meeting of "the Congress of Soviets each of the signatory parties has the right to demand that, in regard to the non-unified commissariats, the other party shall have only advisory power." (Article 6). Both governments likewise declared that all of their future actions "in regard to other states can be prefaced only upon the community of interests of the workers and peasants."

Basically, this centralizing process was the logical outcome of many of the provisions of the constitution of the UkSSR. Other provisions of the December, 1920 treaty were nothing but confirmations of the centralizing actions which both governments had agreed upon on previous occasions. Among these actions belonged Order No. 1020 of June 19, 1919, issued by the Revolutionary War Council. It stated that " . . . all decrees, legislative statutes, ordinances, and orders concerning the Red Army and matters within the competence of the people's commissariat for military affairs, such as have already been published, and such as may be published in the future by the corresponding organs of the Russian Soviet Republic, shall be effective throughout the territory of the UkSSR, in so far as they do not contradict existing or future agreements between the All-Russian Central Executive Committee and the Ukrainian Central Excecutive Committee concerning army units, administration, instructions, and officials of the two soviet republics." [7]

Provisions of the December, 1920 treaty, however, served as a foundation for the future rather than as a confirmation of the past centralization. On the basis and in pursuance of the principles established by the December, 1920 treaty, as well as on the basis of the declarations made in the constitution of 1919, the UkSSR, together with other so-called independent republics, on February 22, 1922, delegated its rights in the sphere of foreign relations to the RSFSR. The protocol, by virtue of which this transformation of rights was effected, stated that these republics, in order to guarantee more efficiently their interests "have decided to entrust the R.S.F.S.R., with the representation and protection of the interests of the said eight republics at the conference and with the conclusion of the signature in the names of the Republics; as well as drafting of acts at this conference, the conclusion of all kinds of separate international treaties and agreements, directly or indirectly connected with the said conference, with states represented at said conference as well as any other and the taking of necessary measures therefor." [8] This protocol thus ended the virtual, if not the theoretical, independence of the UkSSR in the sphere of foreign relations. [9]

Since the principle of unity of action and purpose demanded unquestionable obedience to the center, there was very little opposition on the part of Ukrainian spokesmen to this centralizing move. The attempt of the central government to bring foreign trade under its supervision, however, found resentment in the Ukraine. Apparently because the resentment was so great, on June 22, 1923, the Council of Labor and Defense was forced to issue a decree which annulled the original decree issued by the same organ whereby all transactions of foreign trade were to be carried out exclusively through the Commissariat for Foreign Trade of the RSFSR. This repeal affected only the UkSSR. All other republics and territories which were mentioned in the original decree of May 9, 1923, were deprived of their right of foreign trade. [10]

The aim of all these and many other centralizing moves and actions on the part of the central government was to prepare the ground for unification of all former Russian territories. This unification found its first formal expression in a new treaty entered into by the RSFSR, the UkSSR, the Belorussian SSR, and the Trans-Caucasian Federation, on December 30, 1922. On the basis of that treaty the first constitution of the USSR was adopted in 1924. In a very broad and general wording, it placed within the competence of the USSR the following matters: 1) Representation of the Union in international relations; 2) Conduct of diplomatic relations; 3) Conclusion of political and other treaties with foreign states; 4) Alteration of frontiers of the Union and of the Republics; 5) Acceptance of new republics into the Union; 6) Declaration of war and conclusion of peace; 7) Conclusion of foreign loans and control over similar loans in the union republics; 8) Ratification of international agreements; 9) Direction of foreign and internal trade; 10) Control over the national economy; 11) Direction of transport, posts and telegraphs; 12) Organization and direction of the armed forces of the USSR; 13) Approval of a single state budget and determination of taxes and revenues; 14) Establishment of uniform money and credit systems; 15) Establishment of general principle for the development of, and use of, land, mineral deposits, forests and water; 16) Legislation on migration; 17) Establishment of the bases of the courts of justice and legal procedure, and also the civil and criminal legislation; 18) The establishment of the fundamental labor laws; 19) General control over public education and public health; 20) The establishment of a standard system of weights and measures; 21) Organization of general statistics of the Union; 22) Legislation in the matter of citizenship; 23) The right of general amnesty; 24) The repeal of decrees infringing upon the fundamental law of the Union; 25) Settlement of disagreements between union republics; and 26) The exclusive right to alter the fundamental law as well as the competence of the organs of the USSR. (Article I, Sections *a* through *x* of the USSR constitution).[11]

In spite of all these limitations, which in their scope covered the entire field of activity of any government, the constitution of the USSR (Article 3) declared, and the constitution of the UkSSR confirmed (Article 6), that the latter's sovereignty was limited only within the limits indicated. Outside of these limitations, the UkSSR retained the right to exercise its political rights and administrative matters independently—but in conformity with the constitution of the USSR. (Article 6 of the UkSSR constitution). The UkSSR retained the right to ratify and to amend its own constitution which, henceforth, by virtue of Article 5 of the USSR constitution, made the latter a small replica of the former. The UkSSR retained the right of general direction of domestic policy; of control over the administrative-territorial division of the republic; over the organization and general direction of the central and local organs of authority of the UkSSR; and over civil, criminal, material, and lawsuit legislation on the basis determined by the USSR. The UkSSR likewise retained the right of legislation relating to land problems, the use of land, subsoil, forests, waterways, etc., within the territory of the UkSSR in accordance with general provisions determined by the USSR. Similar conditional right of legislation was retained by the UkSSR in the sphere of public education, and also in matters of citizenship, which, by virtue of Article 7 of the USSR constitution, was based on the dual principle. The highest organs of power in the UkSSR likewise retained the right to issue an amnesty effective throughout the territory of the UkSSR and also to elect their delegates to the highest organs of power of the USSR. (Article 6, Part I A, Sections *a* through *n* of the UkSSR constitution).

In addition to these rights which the UkSSR retained for itself and some of which, as has been shown, were made conditional, *i.e.*, were operative only within the framework established by laws of the USSR, the UkSSR preserved for itself at least constitutionally an advisory function pertaining to certain legislative matters of the USSR. Thus, for example, by virtue of Article 6, Part II B, Sections *a* through *k* of the UkSSR constitution, the UkSSR reserved for itself the right to voice its opinion on "all questions falling within the scope of the administration centered in the USSR, in conformity with the legislation of the same and instructions and ordinances of the respective central organs of the USSR." In particular the UkSSR could voice its opinion on: 1) The establishment of the general plan of the whole national economy and individual branches of the same throughout the territory of the UkSSR in conformity with the provisions of the USSR constitution; 2) The approval of the budget of the UkSSR, included in a common state budget of the USSR; 3) The determination of national and local taxes, and other revenues in conformity with the USSR constitution and legislation; 4) The conclusion of foreign and domestic loans of the UkSSR, likewise in conformity with the USSR constitution; 5) The examination and participation in the conclusion of concessionary agreements provided for and in conformity with the USSR constitution and legislation; 6) The supervision of the monetary system, and organization and direction of economy and finances of the UkSSR; 7) The organization and supervision of manufacturing in the UkSSR; 8) The organization and regulation of domestic commerce; 9) The regulation of labor; 10) The supreme control over the state income and expenditure of the UkSSR; and 11) The organization and supervision of the workmen's and peasants' inspection as well as control over the activities of all other organs of the soviet administration throughout the UkSSR.

Finally, the UkSSR retained the right to examine and participate "in settling questions in conformity with the constitution and legislation of the USSR," if those questions fell within the scope of immediate supervision of the USSR. Among those were: 1) Questions relating to participation of the UkSSR in representation of the USSR in foreign relations; 2) The participation in the examination of questions relating to the conclusion of political and other treaties with foreign states, their ratification, and other questions of diplomatic nature; 3) The examination of questions of foreign trade of the USSR and also of participation in such trade of the USSR within the limits determined by the USSR legislation; 4) Participation in discussions of questions relating to conclusion of agreements concerning the admission of new Soviet republics into the USSR; and 5) Participation, within the limits determined by the law of the USSR, in the organization of the armed forces and also in supervision of transport and communication. (Article 6, Part II C, Sections *a* through *e* of the UkSSR constitution).

Compared with the provisions of the Ukrainian constitution of 1919, these rights which the UkSSR retained for itself following the formation of the USSR were considerably reduced. The reduction included such fundamental questions of national significance as the determination and alteration of the frontiers of the UkSSR; relations with foreign powers; declaration of war and conclusion of peace; establishment of the basis of the organization of the armed forces; establishment of principles of socialist construction in the sphere of national economy; and state control over the activity of Soviet authority, the correctness and legality of its actions and reasonableness of its expenses. All of these matters, which had been in the UkSSR constitution of 1919 (Articles *b, c, d, g, h,* and *i*), became the exclusive prerogatives of the central government in Moscow. Compared, however, with the rights and privileges of other union republics entering the USSR, the provisions of the UkSSR constitution included various rights that were conspicuously absent from the constitutions of other union republics, thus making the latter more dependent on the central government.

This privileged constitutional status of the UkSSR did not last long. Between 1924 and 1936 there were numerous changes of and amendments to the constitution of the USSR, which, by virtue of Article 5, made the corresponding changes in the union republican constitutions mandatory.[12] Thus, for example, the Third Congress of Soviets of the USSR in May, 1925, brought changes to the preamble and six articles of the constitution.[13] The Fourth Congress of Soviets of the USSR in April, 1927, made nine changes in the constitution;[14] while the Sixth Congress of Soviets in March, 1931, effected changes in the preamble and fourteen articles of the constitution.[15] The reflection of these changes was fully incorporated into every union republican constitution, including the Ukrainian. The Twelfth All-Ukrainian Congress of Soviets alone effected sixteen changes in March, 1931.[16]

None of these changes of or amendments to the constitution, however, affected either the fundamentals of the constitution or the principles of the dictatorship of the proletariat. These remained unaltered. The changes that were brought about affected primarily the competence of the central organs and their organization, by expanding the jurisdiction of the federal organs at the expense of the union republics. Thus, for example, following the changes of 1931, the Ukrainian Congress of Soviets (which up to that time had exercised jurisdiction over the ratification, amendment and supplementing of the constitution of the UkSSR and the constitution of the Autonomous Moldavian SSR; confirmation and alteration of the boundaries of the UkSSR in conformity with paragraph *b*, article 1 and article 6 of the constitution of the USSR; final decision in questions relating to withdrawal of the UkSSR from the USSR; election of deputies to the All-Ukrainian Central Executive Committee and elections of the members of the Soviet of Nationalities in the Central Executive Committee of the USSR (Article 7 of the UkSSR constitution)) retained only the right to listen and approve the actions of the government; give to the government general direction of activity; change or amend the constitution and also borders, and elect delegates to the Union Congress of Soviets and that of Nationalities. (Article 22 of the amended Ukrainian constitution).

Changes introduced into the Ukrainian constitution between 1925 and 1931 affected likewise the competence of the All-Ukrainian Central Executive Committee of the UkSSR, its jurisdiction being more defined. Accountable to the Congress of Soviets of the UkSSR, the All-Ukrainian Central Executive Committee became the supreme legislative, administrative and executive organ of power in the UkSSR between the sessions of the Congress. (Article 26). By virtue of Article 30 of the amended constitution of the UkSSR, the All-Ukrainian Central Executive Committee was charged with: 1) The guidance of economic, state, and cultural activity; 2) The approval of the budget; 3) The establishment of the state economic plan in accordance and in compliance with the All-Union plan; 4) The problems of foreign trade, a privilege not granted to any

Central Executive Committee of the other union republics; 5) The approval of legislative acts of the Presidium of the All-Ukrainian Central Executive Committee undertaken in the period of recess of the latter; 6) The approval of codes, legislation dealing with general norms of political, economic and cultural life, or those acts which tended to bring changes to the existing government practice; 7) The consideration of problems connected with changes to the constitution of the UkSSR to be brought before the Congress of Soviets; 8) The initiative to consider changes to the constitution of the USSR; 9) A voice in the organization of military affairs, transport, communication; and 10) A check on the activity of the lower organs of authority as well as on those of the Presidium.

Compared with the UkSSR constitution of 1919, or even with that of 1925, the competence of the All-Ukrainian Central Executive Committee as originally presented in the Ukrainian constitution was narrowed by the amendments. Compared, however, with the competence of the Central Executive Committees of other union republics, the competence of the All-Ukrainian Central Executive Committee differed greatly. For example, Article 32 of the Belorussian constitution did not emphasize the particulars and defined the competence of its Central Executive Committee as extending over "the issuing of codes, decrees and decisions on its own initiative," and also confirming legislative acts presented to it by the government.

The constitutional changes brought about between 1925 and 1931 affected also the competence of the Presidium of the All-Ukrainian Central Executive Committee. Named by Article 32 of the UkSSR constitution as a higher legislative, executive and administrative organ of power, the Presidium had the right to issue decrees, decisions, and orders, and to consider and approve (Article 34) or to suspend or reject orders or decrees of the Ukrainian Sovnarkom or individual commissariats. (Article 33). The Presidium could not bring fundamental changes affecting political, economic, and cultural life of the country (Article 35)—an exclusive prerogative of the All-Ukrainian Central Executive Committee. In this respect the Presidium of the Belorussian Central Executive

Committee had no such limitations; its competence, by virtue of Article 34 of the Belorussian constitution, being defined as that of a legislative, administrative and controlling organ of power on the territory of the Belorussian SSR. As a higher organ of power, the Presidium of the All-Ukrainian Central Executive Committee retained important rights not exercised by any other Presidium of union republics. It had the right of legislative initiative in the higher organs of the USSR. It could protest against orders of the All-Union Commissariats, whose plenipotentiaries were in the Ukraine. It could likewise protest against decrees and orders of the Sovnarkom of the USSR. However, it had no power to suspend the execution of these orders unless they definitely violated laws of either the USSR or the UkSSR. (Article 36 of the UkSSR constitution; also implied in Articles 20, 42, 53, and 59 of the USSR constitution). This principle was generally acknowledged, but not mentioned in any other constitution except the UkSSR.

Though reduced by amendments, the privileged status of Ukrainian central organs extended likewise to the Sovnarkom of the UkSSR, which, as an executive and administrative organ of the All-Ukrainian Central Executive Committee and responsible before it, had the right to issue legislative acts and decisions with force throughout the UkSSR. (Articles 38 and 39). And, finally, the privileged status of the UkSSR found its reflection in individual commissariats of the UkSSR. Their orders were binding throughout the territory of the UkSSR, and could be revoked or suspended only by the All-Ukrainian Central Executive Committee or the Sovnarkom of the UkSSR (Articles 47 and 48) but not by the Commissariats of the USSR. Orders of the commissariats of the Belorussian SSR, for example, could have been suspended by the Belorussian Sovnarkom, Central Executive Committee, or its Presidium, as well as by the Sovnarkom and by the Commissariats of the USSR, if the orders of the Belorussian commissariats were not based on exact directives. (Article 52 of the Belorussian constitution). The same was true in the case of the RSFSR. (Article 43 of the RSFSR constitution).

All of these special privileges and rights which the UkSSR enjoyed were brought to an end by Stalin's constitution of 1936. It declared that every union republican constitution, aside from taking into account specific features of the given republic, must be "drawn up in full conformity with the Constitution of the USSR." (Article 16). The end to special treatment came likewise by virtue of Article 14 of the new constitution, which enumerated "the rights" which every union republic had equally delegated to the USSR. According to Soviet jurists, these delegated rights, which placed within the competence of the highest organs of the USSR such unlimited jurisdiction in the field of foreign and domestic policies that all traces of federal principles disappeared, leaving one extremely centralized entity, may be classified into five groups.[17] The *first* group over which the USSR exercises exclusive jurisdiction, embraces matters of foreign relations and defense, or more specifically: 1) Representation of the USSR in international relations; 2) Conclusion, ratification, and denunciation of treaties with other states; 3) Organization of the defense of the USSR and direction of all its armed forces; 4) Questions of war and peace; 5) Foreign trade—on the basis of state monopoly; and 6) Preservation of the security of the state. (Article 14, Sections *a, b, g, h, i*).

The *second* group—the broadest one—covers economic problems over which the exclusive jurisdiction rests within the competence of the USSR organs. In some instances the administration of these problems can be shared by the competent union republican organs if and when these should be called upon to carry out directives of the USSR. This group covers the following problems: 1) Determination of the national economic plans of the USSR; 2) Approval of the single state budget of the USSR and determination of the taxes and revenues going into the USSR, the Union Republican, and local budgets; 3) Administration of banks, industrial, agricultural and trading establishments or enterprises of All-Union importance; 4) Administration of transport and communications; 5) Direction of the monetary and credit systems; 6) Organization of state insurance; 7) Contracting and granting of loans; 8) Establishment of the basic principles for the use of land, natural resources, forests, and water; and 9) Organization of a uniform system of national economic statistics. (Article 14, Sections *j, k, l, m, n, o, p, q, s*).

The *third* group embraces the socio-cultural field (education, public health, labor, marriage and family) in which the central government alone has the right to establish "basic principles" in these spheres as well as "basic principles of legislation." In this group, too, in some instances, the administration or execution of some directives may be shared by the corresponding union republican organs, but only if and when they should be called upon by their corresponding organs of the USSR. (Article 14, Sections *r, t, w*).

The *fourth* group of "delegated rights" deals with problems of inter-relationships between the USSR and the Union Republics and covers the following fields: 1) Admission of new republics into the USSR; 2) Control over the observance and ensuring conformity of the constitutions of the union republics with the constitution of the USSR; 3) Confirmation of boundary changes between union republics; 4) Confirmation of the formation of new territories, regions, or new autonomous republics within the territory of union republics; 5) Establishment of general procedure governing the relations of union republics with foreign states; and 6) Determination of directing principles governing the organization of military formations of the union republics (Articles 14, sections *c, d, e, f, a, g*).

The *fifth* and final group of the "delegated" powers of the USSR places within the jurisdiction of the central organs: 1) Legislation concerning the structure of courts and legal procedure; criminal and civil codes; 2) Legislation concerning union citizenship and the rights of foreigners; and 3) Issuing of All-Union acts of amnesty. (Article 14, Sections *u, v, x*).

In spite of this unlimited jurisdiction of the central organs of the USSR (jurisdiction which can be enlarged by changing the fundamental law (Article 146), and which embraces the entire field of foreign and domestic policy of a state), whose orders are not only equally binding throughout the territory of the USSR (Article

19) but also prevail in case of divergence between the law of the
union and that of a union republic (Article 20), all union republican constitutions, nevertheless, jokingly state that outside of these
provisions every union republic "exercises state authority independently, preserving fully its sovereign rights." (Article 13 of the
UkSSR constitution).[18] An analysis of Article 19 of the Ukrainian
constitution, which enumerates the competence of the higher organs
of state power and organs of state administration, reveals that this
competence is limited to either the approval or the execution of
orders or policies of the agencies of the central government. Thus,
the jurisdiction of the UkSSR embraces: 1) The adoption of the
constitution of the UkSSR and control over its observance; 2) The
submission of new administrative units of the UkSSR to the Supreme
Soviet of the USSR for confirmation; 3) The legislation of the
UkSSR; 4) The maintenance of public order and safeguarding
the rights of citizens; 5) The approval of the national economic
plan of the UkSSR and also of the state budget; 6) The determination of state and local taxes as well as revenues of the UkSSR
in conformity with the laws of the USSR; 7) The direction of the
fulfillment of the local budgets; 8) The direction of insurance and
savings; 9) The administration of the banks, industrial, agricultural,
and trading enterprises and organizations of the UkSSR; 10) The
direction of local industry; 11) Control and supervision of the
condition and administration of enterprises of the USSR; 12) The
establishment of the procedure governing the use of land, mineral
wealth, forests and water; 13) The direction of housing facilities
and municipal services, dwelling houses construction and modernization of cities; 14) Road building; 15) The direction of local
transport and communication; 16) The direction of social welfare;
17) Labor legislation; 18) The direction of elementary, secondary
and higher education; 19) The direction and administration of
cultural, educational, and scientific organizations and institutions
of the UkSSR; 20) The direction of public health and administration of institutions of public health of the UkSSR; 21) The direction and organization of sport; 22) The organization of the juridical organs of the UkSSR; 23) The granting of the rights of citizen-

ship of the UkSSR; 24) The legislation concerning marriage and family; 25) The granting of amnesty to persons convicted by the juridical organs of the UkSSR; 26) The determination of the manner of organization of the military forces of the UkSSR; and 27) The determination of the representation of the UkSSR in international relations. (Article 19, Sections *a* through *zz* of the Ukrainian constitution).

To exercise these supervisory and directive functions, the constitution of the UkSSR designated the Supreme Soviet of the UkSSR as the sole legislative body and authority, insofar as these functions did not come within the jurisdiction of other organs of the UkSSR that were accountable to the Supreme Soviet of the UkSSR. (Articles 22 and 23). Between the sessions of the Supreme Soviet of the UkSSR the constitution of the UkSSR charged the Presidium of the Supreme Soviet with the responsibility over these supervisory and directive functions. (Articles 29 and 30).[19]

The administration of these directive and supervisory functions, the constitution entrusted to the Council of Ministers. Their competence extends over the issuing of "decisions and orders on the basis and in pursuance of the laws of the USSR and the UkSSR, and of decisions and orders of the Council of Ministers of the USSR and verifies their execution." (Article 41). These decisions and orders are binding throughout the territory of the UkSSR (Article 42), and may have the force of suspension and annulment of orders and decisions of lower organs of authority. (Article 44). These decisions, however, if they do not conform to the law, may be annulled by either the Presidium of the Supreme Soviet of the UkSSR (Article 30, Section *e*), or the Council of Ministers of the USSR (Article 69 of the USSR constitution), or by the Presidium of the Supreme Soviet of the USSR. (Article 49, Section *f* of the USSR constitution).

The direction of these supervisory functions, which Article 19 of the UkSSR constitution enumerated, were placed under the jurisdiction of individual ministries (Article 46 of the UkSSR constitution),—union republican and republican (Article 47). Within the limits of their respective jurisdiction they "issue orders and instructions on the basis and in pursuance of the laws of the USSR and the UkSSR, of the decisions and orders of the Council of Ministers of the USSR and the Council of Ministers of the UkSSR and of the orders and instructions of the union republican ministries of the USSR, and verify their execution." (Article 50). Being directly subordinate to the Council of Ministers of the UkSSR and the corresponding union republican ministry of the USSR, each union republican ministry of the UkSSR is allowed to direct its branch of state administration (Article 76 of the USSR constitution and Article 51 of the UkSSR constitution). In other words, each union republican ministry of the UkSSR is nothing more than an extension of the corresponding ministry of the USSR.

In view of this utmost centralization of the governing apparatus of the USSR, it is difficult to agree with the contentions of Soviet legal writers that each union republic preserves fully its sovereign rights in spite of the fact that, by virtue of Article 15 of the USSR constitution, these rights are placed under the protection of the USSR.[20] The number of the protected rights is very flexible and depends upon the particular need or emphasis at a given moment. The most strongly emphasized sovereign right of every union republic is the right to have its own constitution, which, it is claimed, takes into consideration and reflects historical development, peculiarities and specific interests of every union republic.[21] Since, however, Article 16 of the USSR constitution for all practical purposes cancels with the right hand what it extends with the left, undoubtedly the most outstanding peculiarity of this highly appraised right is the language of the given republic in which the constitution is written.

Another protected right which is being heavily underscored by Soviet writers is the "right to free withdrawal" of every union republic from the USSR. (Article 17.)[22] As yet no union republic has attempted to apply that right. There is little doubt that they will not try to do so as long as the central power is strong. Any such attempt, or even thought of it, would violate various articles of the USSR constitution, and above all Article 133, which proclaims that the defense and not the weakening of the country is the sacred duty of every citizen of the USSR. Any act contrary to this sacred duty could be, and on many occasions has been, considered as treason to the state. The same article defines treason, in any form whatsoever, as "the most heinous of crimes." The problem of the right of "free withdrawal" is further complicated by the fact that every citizen of a union republic is at the same time a citizen of the USSR. (Article 21). Since the laws of the USSR have the same force throughout and within the territory of every union republic (Article 19), and in view of the fact that in the event of a divergence between a law of the union republic and the law of the union, the latter prevails (Article 20), it would be a violation of the constitution of the USSR to try to withdraw from the union without co-ordination of this act with the USSR. Furthermore, Article 49, Section *c*, authorizes the Presidium of the Supreme Soviet of the USSR to interpret the constitution; hence the competence to decide when or in what manner a union republic could secede. In view of these factors the right of secession is valueless.

The third protected right of the Union Republics, that is pointed out by Soviet legal writers, is the inviolability of their territories. (Article 18).[23] To be sure, while there cannot be a state without a territory, according to the wording of Article 14, Sections *e* and *q* of the USSR constitution, the sole owner and manager of the territory of the union republics is the central government, which likewise has the final jurisdiction over all territorial changes. Since it, and it alone, can establish fundamental principles for the use of land, natural resources, forests and water, as well as confirm changes of boundaries between, or territorial rearrangements within the union republics, Article 18 of the USSR constitution, as well as similar provisions of all republican constitutions, to the effect that union republican territories cannot be altered without their consent, is superfluous. Thus, the third protected right, sound from a theoretical and propaganda point of view, is useless in practical application.

The fourth guarded right, which every union republic was granted as a result of the "Constitutional Reform of February 1, 1944," is the right and privilege to have its own military forces. (Article 18 B).[24] The wording of this article without making any changes in other provisions of the USSR constitution regarding military forces, makes this privilege inoperative. This is because the USSR retained for itself the exclusive jurisdiction over the establishment of the leading basis of the organization of military formations throughout the country; hence uniform regulations, mobilization plans, and command as well as questions of war and peace. (Article 14, Sections b and g). Moreover, the constitution retained unchanged the power of the Presidium of the Supreme Soviet of the USSR as regards: 1) The institution of military titles; 2) The appointment and removal of the high command of the armed forces of the USSR; 3) The ordering of general or partial mobilization; 4) The proclamation of martial law in separate localities or throughout the territory of the USSR in the interest of the defense of the USSR. (Article 49, Sections k, l, u, r). Neither did the February, 1944 change affect the constitutional jurisdiction of the Council of Ministers of the USSR, which retained: 1) Fixing of the annual contingent of citizens to be called up for military service; 2) Direction of general organization of the armed forces; and 3) Establishment of various committees or central administrations, including that of defense. (Article 68, Sections e and f). Finally, in the present atomic age, it is inconceivable to grant a state the possibility of having a ministry of armed forces while at the same time denying it all means of logistical support, a factor so vividly expressed in Article 77 of the USSR constitution.

The fifth, and final, protected right of every union republic which is being strongly emphasized by Soviet legal writers,[25] is the right "to enter into direct relations with foreign states, to conclude agreements with them and to exchange with them both diplomatic and consular representations." (Article 18 A). It is interesting to note at this point that in Soviet terminology an agreement is defined as a treaty on problems of lesser significance and only of temporary nature, such as agreements on fisheries, use of coastal waters, etc. A treaty is defined as "a more important international legal act, which establishes rights and obligations for the contracting parties in the field of political and economic relations," such as peace treaties, treaties of alliance, friendship, guaranties, mutual aid, neutrality, non-aggression, trade, etc.[26] However, aside from this interpretative curtailment of the rights of union republics in the field of foreign relations, the wording of Article 18 A of the USSR constitution, without making any changes in other provisions of the constitution regarding foreign relations, makes this right inoperative. By virtue of Article 14, Sections *a*, *b*, and *h* of the USSR constitution, the USSR retained for itself exclusive jurisdiction over such vital questions of foreign relations of any sovereign state as that of war and peace; foreign trade; representation of the USSR in international relations; conclusion, ratification and denunciation of treaties as well as "establishment of general procedure governing the relations of Union Republics with foreign states." The Council of Ministers of the USSR retained its co-ordinative and directive functions over the work of all the ministries of the USSR as well as over "the general guidance in the sphere of relations with foreign states." (Article 68, Sections *a* and *d*).

Article 13 of the constitution of the USSR calls this extremely centralized entity a federal state. If, however, federalism means the broadest possible autonomy of the component parts, harmonious with their center only with regard to foreign relations, and if in addition, it presupposes some shades of sovereignty, especially as concerns the right of self-organization, own final jurisdiction and a well-defined share in the formation of at least some of the agencies of federal power, then the claim made by Soviet "federalism" fails to meet these qualifications. In fact it is the antithesis of federalism.

The attainment of this extremely centralized entity, which operates on the principle of upward delegation of power and downward delegation of orders, was gradual. At first, immediately following the revolution, the constitutional order of the RSFSR and that of the UkSSR had in common only broad principles.

Later, this commonness extended over vital economic and military affairs, leaving, however, to the Ukraine certain minor "rights" and "privileges," because of the Ukraine's economic potential, its numerical strength, and its independent, though short-lived existence. With the entrenchment of the power of the central government came the end to all previous concessions and considerations, and the Ukraine was totally engulfed by the forces of centralism.

CHAPTER IX

Composition of the CPU

As the nucleus of the world revolutionary movement, the Communist Party of the Soviet Union (CPSU) completely overshadows all other communist parties throughout the world. Because of this domination, observers of contemporary world affairs have centered their attention on the study of the objectives, the structure and the functioning of the CPSU. While their research has produced many outstanding monographs, too numerous to mention here, they have tended to neglect the CPSU's vital branches—the Communist Parties of the Union Republics. The importance of these parties, however, can neither be overlooked nor underestimated. Being intimate parts of the CPSU, they have acted as instruments of the Kremlin's policies, carrying out its directives and controlling life in the union republics. From insignificant minorities they have grown into large forces. Their membership has alternately received praise and undergone purges. The Union Republican Communist Parties, therefore, are important reflectors of policy changes within the Soviet Union. In addition, they serve as barometers of the successes or failures of the Kremlin's policies in the union republics. An excellent case in point is the Communist Party of the Ukraine (CPU).

In its origins, the CPU was a continuation of various small, un-coordinated regional groups of the RSDRP(b), which had secretly operated in the larger industrial cities of the Ukraine (Kiev, Kharkov, Ekaterinoslav, Odessa, Krivoy Rog, etc.) before the revolution. In strength, unity, force or influence, these organizations were never outstanding.[1] One estimation is that on the eve of the revolution Bolshevik strength in the Ukraine was 1,060 active members.[2] Only a very small percentage was of Ukrainian origin; the overwhelming majority consisted of Russian and Jewish city intelligentsia.

Following the Bolshevik seizure of power in Petrograd, the numerical strength of the CP(b)U began to increase. It has been officially reported that by March, 1918, the membership was 4,364. By October, 1918, it had mounted to 5,014. By March, 1919, it had increased to 16,363. By March, 1920, it had climbed to 25,247, and by October, 1920, it had reached a high of 31,065 members.[3] The most important factor responsible for the increase of the membership of the CP(b)U was the assignment of RCP(b) members to the Ukraine. Unfortunately, war operations, frequent changes of authority, and extreme fluidity of the CP(b)U membership make it impossible to establish with any degree of certainty the actual numerical contribution of the transfer policy. Only vague references are to be found on this problem. Writing in 1919 on the successes and difficulties of Soviet power, Lenin stated, for example, that the Central Committee of the RCP(b) had dispatched "the best Soviet forces" to organize "an apparatus in the Ukraine" in return for "50,000,000 puds of bread." [4] One observer noted that early in 1920, following Denikin's fiasco in the Ukraine, many new Party members came from Central Russia, while a number of Ukrainian Bolsheviks was sent to Central Russia and Asia.[5]

In addition to the transfer policy, the growth and composition of the membership of the CP(b)U was, in part, influenced by the Russian Bolshevik policy of joining and absorbing some Ukrainian political groups of the extreme left. An outstanding example was the absorption of the *Borot'bisty* in 1920,[6] which netted the CP(b)U approximately 4,000 members according to one estimation,[7] and about 20,000 members according to another.[8] From 1918 to 1920, the policy of transferring RCP(b) members from Central Russia into the Ukraine and the practice of absorbing leftist groups were the two main channels of growth of the CP(b)U membership. Thanks to these two tactics, by

1921 the membership of the CP(b)U was said to have risen to 97,321 persons.[9]

In 1921 the growth of the membership of the CP(b)U received its first major setback. This resulted from the purge that followed the Kronstadt rebellion. There is no agreement among Bolshevik spokesmen on the scope of the 1921 purge. According to one, it eradicated half the membership of the CP(b)U.[10] An official estimate asserted that the purge took a toll of 21,430 members, or 22.5% of the total membership, lowering the numerical strength of the CP(b)U from 97,321 to 75,891.[11] Another official source placed the remaining number at 68,092.[12] The *Borot'bisty,* whom the Party leaders in Moscow held indirectly responsible for peasant unrest in the Ukraine and for the Kronstadt rebellion,[13] suffered the most. Many of them were expelled from the Party. Some were sent to Central Russia to replace Russian Party members who had been sent to the Ukraine. Still others were sent to Central Asia. By 1923, according to Skrypnyk, only 119 of the *Borot'bisty* were still in the Ukraine.[14]

Irrespective of the disagreement among official spokesmen on the exact numbers involved, it is clear that as a result of the 1921 purge, the numerical strength of the CP(b)U declined considerably. The official Party census of 1922 shows only 54,818 members in the Ukraine as of April 1, 1922.[15] Territorially they were distributed as follows: the Donets Region, 10,577; Kharkov, 8,641; Kiev, 7,016; Odessa, 4,011; Ekaterinoslav, 3,700; Nikolaev, 3,600; Poltava, 3,399; Kremenchug, 2,859; Zaporozhie, 2,566; Volyn, 2,304; Chernigov, 1,900, etc.[16] Socially, the composition of the CP(b)U was favorably inclined toward workers who were said to comprise 27,437, or 51.3% of the total membership. The remainder was distributed among service people (*sluzhashchie*), 15,404, or 28.9%; peasants, 9,307, or 17.5%; and others, 1,204, or 2.3%. This favorable presentation of the workers' strength in the CP(b)U was more illusion than reality, for only a small percentage of those classified as workers did manual work. An overwhelming majority occupied executive posts in Party, Soviet, and Trade Union organizations.[17]

The national composition of the CP(b)U, according to official census, presented the following picture as of April 1, 1922. Of 54,818 Party members, the Russians comprised 27,490, or 53.6%; the Ukrainians 11,920, or 23.3%; the Jews 6,981, or 13.6%; the Poles 1,241, or 2.6%; and other nationalities 3,604, or 7.1% [sic]. Of the total membership, however, 42,471, or about 79% acknowledged Russian as their native tongue. 6,054, or about 11% chose Ukrainian; 1,887, Jewish, and 514, Polish.[18] The actual percentage of Ukrainians in the CP(b)U was further clarified by Rakovsky. At the VII Conference of the CP(b)U held in Kharkov in April, 1923, he declared that "when we take our Party statistics and examine the relationship of national elements among the members of our Party, then you will see that the Ukrainians—by this word I mean those comrades who have preserved connections with Ukrainian culture and those who are Ukrainians by origin but perhaps do not know the Ukrainian language—comprise 2.37% in our Party." [19]

The absence of Ukrainian membership in the CP(b)U was one of the main factors which brought about the period of so-called "Ukrainization" of the Party and state apparatus. During the Ukrainization period a drive for native members was undertaken. By virtue of this drive, and more so thanks to mass recruitment following Lenin's death in January, 1924, the total membership of the CP(b)U rose from 54,818 in April, 1922 to 98,639 members (49,610 members and 49,029 candidates) in December, 1924.[20] Lenin's death memorial drive alone brought into the CP(b)U about 32,000 members, or approximately 15% of the total of the drive of the entire USSR, which netted about 220,000 new Party members.[21] Over 50% of the new membership were said to be miners and metal workers. In preponderant majority they came from industrial areas where Ukrainians were in a minority. The Donbass, for example, supplied 16,500 of the new members. Kharkov and Ekaterinoslav supplied 6,500.[22] The recruitment of peasants, who were overwhelmingly Ukrainian, into the Party was very low even at the peak of mass recruitment. According to official Party data, 6,861 peasants were accepted into the Party during the second half of 1924. Of these, only 641 were in the Ukraine.[23]

The numerical growth brought some, but not proportionate, changes in the social and national composition of the CP(b)U. Between January 1, and May 1, 1924, the workers' membership in the CP(b)U rose from 52.3% to 62%. This increase was said to have been made at the expense of peasants and service people.[24] The national composition of the CP(b)U likewise reflected some changes. According to the official Party press, the national composition of the CP(b)U on January 1, 1924, was the following: Russians, 48%; Ukrainians, 33.4%; Jews, 14%; and others, 4.6%. By January 1, 1925, the following changes had been registered: Russians, 43%; Ukrainians, 37%; Jews, 11.9%; and others, 8.1%.[25] The slight increase of Ukrainians in the membership of the CP(b)U, in the period under consideration, may be attributed chiefly to the merger of the Ukrainian Communist Party with the CP(b)U on orders from the Comintern.[26] The official press reported, likewise, the presence of Ukrainians all along the Party's organizational pyramid—except for the top positions in the Party. Thus, for example, during 1925 the number of Ukrainians in the Central Committee of the CP(b)U rose from 4 to 22 members. In the *okrug* Party organization, Ukrainian membership climbed from 38.8% to 42.4%. In the instructor apparatus of the Party Committees, the number of Ukrainians rose from 51 to 137 members; while village and *rayon* Party secretaries were "Ukrainized" by 50.1%[27] At the same time, however, the Party press reported that within the Party "the percentage of those able to speak Ukrainian is, on the average, lower than the percentage of Ukrainians by origin. Meetings are still being conducted in many places not in the Ukrainian language." [28]

These contradicting statements of favorable and unfavorable achievements continued to come. However, they had little effect on the numerical growth of the CP(b)U itself. Between January 1, 1925 and January 1, 1927, the number of Party cells in the Ukraine rose from 3,391 to 4,428. Party membership during the same period climbed from 101,852 (53,325 members and

48,527 candidates) to 180,937 (114,160 members and 66,777 candidates).[29] One official Party publication placed the number of Party cells in the UkSSR, as of January 10, 1927, at 4,995, with 168,087 members and candidates. On the basis of this estimate it was reported that Ukrainians formed 87,185 members or 52%; Russians 46,156, or 27.5%; and other nationalities 34,746, or 20.5%.[30] According to the latter set of figures, which are based on the January, 1927 Party census, the social composition of the Party's membership had undergone great changes since 1922 and even since 1924. In 1927, factory workers comprised 55,726, or 33.1% of the membership. Laborers comprised 1,826, or 1.1%; peasants 14,971, or 8.9%; and others 95,564, or 56.9%.[31]

Industrialization, the adoption of integral planning, and above all the collectivization of the countryside, greatly affected the membership of the CP(b)U. Fundamentally, before this, membership had been predominantly confined to the industrial regions of the Ukraine. On the eve of the First Five Year Plan, January 1, 1928 for example, seven industrial centers of the Ukraine (Artemovsk, Dniepropetrovsk, Kiev, Lugansk, Odessa, Stalino and Kharkov) had among them 112,269 Party members,[32] at a time when total membership of the CP(b)U was over 180,000.[33] The difference was spread among other cities of the Ukraine and the rural areas. With minor variations this ratio existed throughout the 1920's.

For all practical purposes, the strength of the CP(b)U was insignificant in Ukrainian villages. On the one hand, the peasantry was not overly anxious to join the CP(b)U; on the other hand the CP(b)U, while not taking an open and official stand against peasant participation, never welcomed or openly encouraged their membership in the Party. This can be seen in data supplied by the official Party census. In 1922, for example, peasant membership in the CP(b)U was 9,307, or 17.5% of the total membership.[34] Peasant membership in 1927, according to one official Party publication, was 33,375, or 18.5% of the total membership of the CP(b)U.[35] According to another official Party report, it comprised only 14,971, or 8.9%.[36] Still another official statement placed the strength of the CP(b)U in Ukrainian villages in January, 1928 at 37,400 members.[37] A resolution of the November, 1929 Plenum of the CC of the VKP(b) placed the number of Communists in Ukrainian villages at 25,000 plus an additional force of 4,434 members in the *sovkhozy* of the UkSSR.[38]

The absence of an agreement on the strength of the CP(b)U in the countryside is not very surprising. Consider the fact that there are great discrepancies regarding its strength in industrial areas which, from the standpoint of the Party's effectiveness, were far easier to supervise. One of the reasons for this lack of uniformity is the fluidity, *i.e.*, considerable turnover, of Party membership. During the first two Five Year Plans (1928-1938), the turnover of membership reached great proportions and affected quite strongly the numerical, social, and national composition of the CP(b)U. Throughout this period official Party records show constant increases in the membership. These same records point as consistently to mass purges and liquidation of Party membership.

It has been officially reported that the membership of the CP(b)U on January 1, 1929, was 231,360 strong. Of that number, 69.5% were reported as workers. 17.3% were peasants; 12.3% were service people; and 0.9% were others.[39] A year later, on January 1, 1930, the membership of the CP(b)U had risen to 250,681 members, or an increase of 19,321.[40] Socialwise, workers are reported to have comprised 122,210, or 48.8% of the total membership; laborers 4,769, or 1.9%; peasants 20,904, or 8.3%; and others 102,799, or 41%.[41] As regards the national composition of the CP(b)U in 1930, the Ukrainians are reported to have formed 131,029, or 52.3% of the total. The Russians had 71,176, or 28.4%, and other nationalities had 48,476, or 19.3%.[42]

These increases in Party membership between 1928 and 1930 were offset by the second major purge of the ranks of the CP(b)U. This fact may, in part, explain the absence of agreement on the Party's strength. During 1929, for example, in the industrial centers of the Ukraine 128,179 members and candidates of the CP(b)U were checked. Of these, 8.9% were expelled from the Party and 13.3% were fined.[43] Percentage-wise, both the expulsion and the fining differed from district to district. However, those members who had entered the CP(b)U since the revolution seem to have been affected most. In Nikolaev, for example, the expulsion embraced 6.2% of the Party's membership; in Kharkov 6.9%; in Odessa 7.2%; in Dniepropetrovsk 8.5%; and in Artemovsk 8.6%. In Stalino it affected 9.7%; in Kiev 10.3%; in Krivoy Rog 10.7%; in Mariupol 11.2%; and in Zaporozhie 12.7%.[44]

Quite interesting also are some of the causes which led to the expulsion of these members. Among the expelled in the industrial areas, 21.6% were charged with passive membership in the Party; 14.8% were declared class and alien elements; and 13.9% were charged with violation of Party discipline. 13.2% were accused of drunkenness; 9.3% of holding non-Communist views; 9.1% of vagrancy; 7.7% of distortion of the Party line; 4.7% of the violation of labor discipline. 3.8% were expelled on religious grounds, and 1.9% for nationalism, chauvinism, and anti-semitism.[45] As could be expected, checking of the rural Party organizations took a heavier toll. Of the 35,841 members checked, 5,831, or 16.3% were expelled from the Party and 5,725 were fined.[46] Again the expulsion differed from district to district. In the Summy district it embraced 10% of the Party's membership; in Lugansk 16.5%; in Kupiansk 18.2%; in Artemovsk 19%; and in Mariupol 20%. In several smaller districts the percentage of expulsion was as high as 76%.[47] Of those expelled from rural party organizations, 27.9% were labelled as ideologically alien elements; 33.5% as decadents; 12.4% as distorters of the Party line and opponents of collectivization; and 16.4% as violators of Party discipline. 5.3% were expelled for religious beliefs; and 4.5% for various other causes.[48]

No sooner had the results of the second major purge been announced, when the third purge of the membership of the CP(b)U was in the making under the personal supervision of Postyshev. According to his own testimony before the November, 1933 Plenum of the CC of the CP(b)U, between January 1, 1933 and October 15, 1933, out of 125,000 members and candidates of the CP(b)U, 27,000, or about 21.6% were expelled as "class enemies and unstable and demoralized elements." [49] In addition to this mass expulsion of rank and file members, the 1933 purge took a heavy toll of the leadership of the Party. During the period under consideration, 237 Secretaries of District Party Committees, and 249 Chairmen of District Control Commissions were relieved of their duties.[50] It has been officially reported that, all in all, the purge of 1933 took a toll of 14% of Party members and 23% of Party candidates.[51] Most of these were of Ukrainian origin; hence a great reduction of Ukrainian membership in the CP(b)U.

A main characteristic of the 1933 purge of the CP(b)U was the fact that practically all the vacancies created were filled not by members of Ukrainian origin or from the Ukraine, but by non-Ukrainian personnel, chiefly from Central Russia. Thus, for example, the purged chairmen of District Party organizations were replaced by 1,340 selected Party members from the VKP(b). An additional 3,000 hand-picked Party members of the VKP(b) were sent into the 643 newly-created Political Departments at the MTS's and 203 at the *sovkhozy*. These were later joined by 17,000 Party men to staff an additional 3,860 Political Departments, whose 4,000 supervisors were very carefully chosen from about 25,000 of the most trusted members. Collective farms were assigned 10,000 Party-trusted men. Of these, 3,000 went for permanent assignment to work as chairmen of collective farms, secretaries, and Party nuclei organizers. Finally, "a huge detachment of strong tried Bolsheviks was sent into the rural districts to act as organizers of collective farm construction." [52]

The influx of VKP(b) members into the Ukraine from other areas was indeed so great that, in spite of the great drop in the CP(b)U membership due to the purge, the Party membership showed a considerable increase. It rose from 291,950 members and candidates as of July 1, 1930 to 468,793 members and candidates as of October 1, 1933.[53] Social-wise, this membership is reported to have possessed the following composition: workers, 70.4%; peasants, 23.3%; and service people, 6.3%.[54] As for the national composition, the percentage of Ukrainians is reported to have increased from 54% in 1930 to 60% in 1933, while Russian membership declined from 26.9% to 22.9%.[55] However, in view of considerable evidence to the contrary, this claim of Ukrainian increase is very doubtful. It would perhaps be proper to interpret this claim as an attempt on the part of the VKP(b) spokesmen to cover up the reality of the purge.

No sooner could the results of the third purge of the CP(b)U be evaluated than a fourth major purge was in the making. Still hidden in a cloud of mystery, the fourth purge of the CP(b)U, unlike its predecessor of 1933, was part of a general purge of the entire apparatus of the VKP(b). The scope of the fourth purge of 1937-8, or the toll it took, is still unknown. However, there are some indications, aside from various accounts that have come to light since the war, which paint a relatively clear picture. For example, between October 1, 1933 and May 1, 1938, according to official reports of the Party, membership of the CP(b)U declined from 468,793 to 285,818 members and candidates. This was a drop of 182,975 members.[56] Social-wise, it is reported, the purge changed the Party's composition very little, while the national composition was not revealed. One of the major innovations of the purge was the introduction into the Party apparatus of a considerable force of newcomers. For example, of the 15,861 Party secretaries in 1938, only 7,376 had previously held that post, while 8,485 were new.[57] A similar ratio existed in the membership of Party Committees of the Party's primary organizations, where new members comprised 55.8%.[58]

The period following the purge of 1937-8 witnessed considerable growth in the membership of the CP(b)U. In fact, one would not be far from the truth to name this the period of mass recruitment into the Party. It surpassed by far the recruitment following Lenin's death in 1924. Between May 1, 1938 and April 1, 1940, membership of the CP(b)U had risen from 285,818 to 521,078 members (319,523 members and 201,555 candidates), or an increase of 235,260 members—roughly 82.3%.[59] These were distributed among 26,502 primary Party organizations. National-wise the new membership of the CP(b)U is reported to have presented the following picture: Ukrainians, 63.1%; Russians, 19.1%; Jews, 13.4%; and others 4.4%.[60] However, it is interesting to note that of the 712 delegates to the XV Congress of the CP(b)U in May, 1940, the Ukrainians formed only 56%; the Jews 4%; and other nationalities 2.8%; while the Russians had 37.2%.[61]

World War II had an important effect on the membership of the CP(b)U. Many of its members perished in the war. Their places were temporarily filled by new recruits, many of whom became subjects of the fifth major purge in the history of the CP(b)U immediately following the war. According to Khrushchev, more than half of "the leading workers" were dismissed from their positions between May, 1945 and August, 1946.[62] The post-World War II purge embraced about 38% of Party secretaries; about 64% of the chairmen of regional executive committees, and about two-thirds of the MTS directors.[63] In some districts the purge of Party organizations ran as high as 83% (in Nikolaev), 88% (in Rovno), and 91% (in Summy).[64]

Simultaneously with the post-war purge, in accordance with established tradition and practice, considerable effort was exerted by the CP(b)U leadership to increase the Party membership and to expand greatly its network in the Ukraine, especially in the countryside. The scope of this effort can be seen from a statement of Kharkov District Party Secretary V. Churaev. Comparing the years 1941 and 1947, he reported that whereas in 1941 there were only 498 primary Party organizations in his district, in 1947 that number had risen to 1,117. As a result, practically every collective farm had either a Party or a Comsomol organization.[65] The increase in the Kiev District Party organization showed even greater efforts. On July 1, 1945, the rural areas of the Kiev District had only 497 Communists in the 47 collective farms. By July 1, 1946, the Kiev District reported 500 primary Party organizations in rural areas, with 4,600 Communists—not including those who were connected with the MTS's.[66] Similar increases were reported in other districts. The result of this drive for expansion of the CP(b)U network was that by 1949 there were in the Ukraine 47,765 primary Party organizations, of which 13,280 were in the countryside.[67]

In spite of the victim-heavy post-war purge, this tremendous expansion of the Party network made possible a sizeable numerical increase in the membership of the CP(b)U. It has been reported that between 1945 and 1949 there were 178,332 new members (94,898 members and 83,434 candidates) accepted into the CP(b) U. This addition brought the total membership of the CP(b)U to 684,275 members (572,950 members and 111,325 candidates) in January, 1949.[68] Social-wise, the new membership was a stern departure from earlier periods, for now the intelligentsia and bureaucracy, rather than the workers, were reported to be the main core. In the Dniepropetrovsk District, for example, students and service people formed 73.2% of the new membership of the CP(b)U, while workers were represented by 17.2% and peasants by 9.6%.[69] This ratio was not universal, for there were some regions in the Stalino district where the percentage of workers among the new members was as high as 31.2%.[70] However, the new trend of social composition found some reflection among the delegates to the XVI Congress of the CP(b)U in January, 1949. Of the 657 delegates, 311, or 47.4%, had higher education. 244, or 37%, had intermediate education. 102, or 15.5%, had lower education only.[71] National composition, so persistently stressed in the official press before World War II, has not, for unexplained reasons, been revealed in the post-war growth of the CP(b)U. The only indication is a statement that among the 657 delegates to the XVI Congress of the CP(b)U in 1949, the Ukrainians had 400, or 60.9%; the Russians 234, or 35.6%; and other nationalities 23, or 3.5%.[72] However, it would be a mistake to assume that this ratio reflects the national composition of the entire membership of the CP(b)U. At no time did the delegates to the Party Congresses ever represent proportionately the national composition of the Party.

Before the XVII Congress of the CP(b)U in September, 1952, the membership of the CP(b)U was 777,832 (676,190 members and 101,642 candidates). This represented an increase of 93,557 since January, 1949.[73] It was dispersed throughout the country in 48,352 primary Party organizations. 36.3% of the membership was reported to be located in the national economy—36.9% in industry, transport, and construction; 17.7% in agriculture; and 9.1% in science, education, and cultural work.[74] The national composition of the entire membership of the CP(b)U was again withheld and only that of its Central Committee was reported. The latter consisted of 61.7% of Ukrainians and 38.3% of Russians and others.[75] Since Stalin's death the membership of the CPU is reported to have grown quite rapidly. It seems not unreasonable to suggest that Khrushchev, to strengthen his recent rise, has been largely responsible for this increase.

Examination of the membership of the CPU throughout the period under review reveals several important characteristics. Although it has posed as a representative of the Ukrainian people, the CPU, from its very origin, has been not only a minority party but also an alien one transplanted and imposed upon the Ukraine. Ukrainian participation both in leadership and in the rank-and-file has grown very slowly and reached larger proportions only after the second World War. This conclusion is noteworthy in view of the persistent assertion by the Communists that neither their ideology nor their membership is exportable.

Another significant characteristic is the size of the CPU. Since its founding, it has had one of the largest party memberships of the USSR. Its influence has been quite weighty, and on occasion it has even been praised and respected by the CPSU leadership in Moscow. This seems to have been true in particular during the latter half of the 1920's when Stalin was rising to power, and it appears to be the case at the present time.

The size and importance of the membership of the CPU has been primarily due to Moscow's respect of Ukrainian economic and strategic potentials. It has also come about because of the policy of using the Ukraine as a testing ground for various national, economic, and social experiments. Since that policy has always been predetermined in Moscow, the task of the CPU has been to supervise the execution of the directives. "Proper" execution has brought praise; "faulty" execution on the other hand has resulted in massive and ruthless purges. Because of this, the evolution of the membership of the CPU serves as a reliable barometer of the successes and failures of many policies of the CPSU in the Soviet Union in general, and in the Ukraine in particular.

CHAPTER X

Conclusion

When Stalin died on March 5, 1953, observers of international affairs agreed that his passing marked the end of one, and signalized the beginning of another, era in the history of the Soviet Union. Since then, this assertion has received repeated confirmation. Rigid, iron-rule, one-man dictatorship has been replaced by the flexible actions and policies of a globe-trotting, "smiling," yet just as dangerous, leadership. In the sphere of international affairs, this change has been responsible for a number of significant developments (the Austrian Peace Treaty; the re-establishment of Soviet-Yugoslav friendship; the meeting of the "summit" at Geneva; the Soviet leaders' tour of Southeast Asia and the United Kingdom; the intensified Soviet interest in Africa, Latin America, and other parts of the world; etc.). No less important changes have taken place inside the Soviet Union (the execution of L. P. Beria; the public admission of weakness in agriculture; the demotion of G. M. Malenkov; the rise of N. S. Khrushchev; the de-Stalinization process; etc.). While some of these developments came as a surprise to observers of Soviet affairs, many were, and still others are, expected to emerge sooner or later, inasmuch as they were rooted in the bankrupt policies of the Stalin era.

There is little doubt that one of the most empty of those policies has been the complex nationality policy. As depicted in the preceding pages, the Russian Bolshevik nationality policy in the Ukraine has a distinguished record of almost total failure. One of the fundamental causes for that failure has been on the one hand the Bolshevik inability to comprehend the inner nature of Ukrainian nationalism (as evidenced by their failure to fulfill promises or satisfy the legitimate needs of the Ukrainian people); and, on the other hand, Bolshevik recognition of the potential force of Ukrainian nationalism and their readiness to utilize that force, first in the disintegration of Russia, and then in the expansion of the territorial base of the revolution.

This paradox, a product of Marxism and of Russian extremism, forms the basic core of the impracticability of the Russian Bolshevik nationality policy. Though present before the revolution, this incompatibility was not fully revealed until the Bolshevik seizure of power. It was greatly strengthened by Russian national forces which had witnessed the inglorious ending of the war and the territorial disintegration of Imperial Russia. It was likewise stimulated by Ukrainian and other non-Russian forces which, capitalizing on Great Russian failures, raised their hopes and increased their national feelings.

The Party, however, being centralist in its objectives, preponderantly Russian in composition and violently anti-Ukrainian in sentiment, after the seizure of power, minimized the national problem. In addition, it entrusted the execution of its nationality policy to persons hostile to the Ukrainian idea. As a result there followed the period of an intensified anti-Ukrainian drive conducted in the name of centralism. However, thanks to the Ukrainian silent, but firm, determination, this policy ended as a total fiasco, and forced the Party on several occasions to admit its errors. The impatient centralization, the anti-Ukrainian drive, and the ruthless economic exploitation of Ukrainian resources, contributed heavily to forcing the adoption of the Ukrainization policy. These factors were also responsible for the appearance of national deviations (Khvylovism, Shumskyism, Volobuevism, etc.) which, because of their exposure of the bankruptcy of the Russian Bolshevik nationality policy, were denounced as being foreign inspired and were ruthlessly exterminated.

The utter inability of the Russian Bolsheviks to reconcile Ukrainian national forces with those of centralism—one of the main characteristics of the Russian Bolshevik nationality policy in the Ukraine

—has been greatly aggravated thanks to the adoption of the erroneous belief that satisfaction of national needs and the solution of the national problem could be realized through ruthless imposition of an artificial formula—"national in form and socialist in content." In practice, this formula has resulted in the forceful imposition, in the name of "progress," of a carefully selected Russian cultural heritage, and accordingly in the purge of everything Ukrainian that even in the slightest way might resemble disharmony in Russo-Ukrainian relations.

The incompatability between Russian Bolshevik nationality theory and practice in the Ukraine has also been strongly influenced by economic factors. The natural resources of the Ukraine—so important to the success of the Revolution, then to the reconstruction period, later to the industrialization and collectivization of the USSR, and finally to the post-World War II reconstruction—have been a strong lever for the Ukrainians against Moscow, but at the same time they have been the cause of ruthless political and administrative strangulation by Moscow of the Ukrainian population.

The Ukraine, in the period under consideration, has undergone great changes in all phases of life. However, in spite of the many public assurances by high Party spokesmen of monolithic unity within the USSR, and of their asserted solution of the national problem, that problem still remains, and is one of the weakest pillars upon which the entire Soviet structure rests. In the present total ideological struggle between the Communist and the non-Communist worlds, the failure to win over the Ukrainians should not only be understood, but also fully exploited.

If national freedom is good for Indonesia, India, Egypt, Sudan, Morocco, and other former Western colonies—Soviet spokesmen have been quite vociferous on that issue—why is it not also good for Kazakhstan, Uzbekistan, Armenia, the Ukraine, Latvia, and for all the peoples within the Communist orbit? Western cognizance or willingness to take careful note of the real national movements within the Communist orbit, which are constantly being denounced for their Western orientation, may yet prove to be a decisive factor in the Cold War.

Abbreviations

CC	Central Committee
CEC	Central Executive Committee
CP(b)U	Communist Party (bolshevik) of the Ukraine
CPSU	Communist Party of the Soviet Union
EC	Executive Committee
KPZU	Communist Party of Western Ukraine
LKSMU	Comsomol Organization of the Ukraine
Obkom	Area Committee
PCP	Polish Communist Party
Rayispolkom	District Executive Committee
RCP(b)	Russian Communist Party (bolshevik)
RSDRP(b)	Russian Social Democratic Workers' Party (bolshevik)
RSFSR	Russian Soviet Federated Socialist Republic
SVU	Union for the Liberation of the Ukraine
TsIK	Central Executive Committee
UkSSR	Ukrainian Soviet Socialist Republic
UNDO	Ukrainian National Democratic Union
VKP(b)	All-Union Communist Party (bolshevik)
VTsIK	All-Union Central Executive Committee
VUTsVK (or VUTsIK or UkTsIK)	All-Ukrainian Central Executive Committee

Notes

Chapter 1: THE EVOLUTION OF THEORY

1 "The Leninist Party had its own clear and concise program on the national question, a program which was closely linked up with the main task of over-throwing the power of the landlords and the bourgeoisie." From a speech of S. V. Kosior, the First Secretary of the Communist Party (bolshevik) of the Ukraine, at the November, 1933 Plenum of the Central Committee of that Party. P. P. Postyshev and S. V. Kosior, *Soviet Ukraine Today* (New York: International Publishers, 1934), p. 61.

2 For a classic treatment of the ideas of Russian intellectuals of the XIX century, see Thomas G. Masaryk, *The Spirit of Russia. Studies in History, Litera-ture and Philosophy*. Translated from the German by Eden and Cedar Paul (London: George Allen & Unwin, Ltd., 1919), 2 vols. Pan-Slavism is treated by Hans Kohn, *Pan-Slavism. Its History and Ideology* (Notre Dame: University Press, 1953), 356 pp.

2a For a valuable interpretation of the Marxist view of the national problem, see Thomas G. Masaryk, *Die philosophischen und sociologischen Grundlagen des Marxismus* (Vienna: C. Konegen, 1899), pp. 426-54.

3 V. I. Lenin, *Sochineniia*. 4th ed. (Moscow: Gosudarstvennoe Izdatelstvo Politicheskoi Literatury, 1946), VI, 294-5. Italics Lenin's.

4 *CPSU. Kommunisticheskaia partiia sovetskogo soiuza v rezolutsiiakh i resheniiakh s'ezdov, konferentsii i plenumov TsK, 1898-1953*. 7th ed. (Moscow: Gosudarstvennoe Izdatelstvo Politicheskoi Literatury, 1953), I, 40. Hereinafter cited as *KPSS v rezolutsiiakh*.

5 As quoted by V. Sadovskyj, *Natsionalna Polityka Sovitiv na Ukraini* (War-saw: Pratsi Ukrainskoho Naukovoho Instytutu, 1937), p. 16.

6 Lenin, *Sochineniia*, VI, 412. Italics Lenin's.

7 *Ibid.*, XIX, 384.

8 *Ibid.*, XIX, 384-5.

9 *Ibid.*, XIX, 386. Compare the entire resolution with the pre-conference thesis worked out by Lenin in *ibid.*, XIX, 213-21.

10 *Leninskii Sbornik*. Edited by L. B. Kamenev (Leningrad: Gosudarstvennoe Izdatelstvo, 1925), III, 472-3.

11 Lenin, *Sochineniia*, XXII, 342. Italics Lenin's.

12 Among the most important treatments of the national problem during this period belong: *Kriticheskie zametki po natsionalnom voprosu* (1913); *O natsionalnoi gordosti velikorossov* (1914); *O prave natsii na samoopredelenie* (1914); *O*

natsionalnoi programe RSDRP (1915); *Sotsialisticheskaia revolutsiia i pravo natsii na samoopredelenie* (1916).

13 Lenin, *Sochineniia*, XXII, 142.
14 *Ibid.*, XXII, 331. Italics Lenin's.
15 *Ibid.*, XXIII, 56. Italics Lenin's.
16 *Ibid.*, XXII, 135.
17 *Ibid.*, XXII, 331-2. On April 29, 1917, Lenin outlined the tactics to be pursued in the Russo-Polish plan in these words: "In Russia we must stress the freedom of separation of the oppressed nations and in Poland we must underline the freedom of unity. The freedom of unity presupposes the freedom of separation. We, the Russians, must underline the freedom of separation, and in Poland [the Poles must underline] the freedom of unity." *Ibid.*, XXIV, 265.

18 The principle "through destruction to unity" became one of the main parts of Communist tactics throughout the world. It became the foundation upon, and around which, Lenin built his *State and Revolution*. It also became an important factor in bringing about the decomposition of the Imperial Army. "In place of severe imperial subordination," wrote N. Bukharin after the revolution, "there was put forth a principle for wide election; numerous committees were created in all branches of the military apparatus; army matters became subjects of wide discussions and conversations . . . What was the aim of this process? The first and foremost: *the decomposition; destruction of the old imperial army.*" N. Bukharin, *Ekonomika perekhodovogo perioda* (Moscow: 1920), pp. 117-8, as cited by Sadovskyj, *op. cit.*, p. 26.

19 Cf. S. N. Shchegolev, *Ukrainskoe dvizhenie kak sovremennyi etap iuzhno-russkogo separatizma* (Kiev: 1912), 588 pp. and M. Hrushevskyj, *Ukrainstvo v Rossii, ego zaprosy i nuzhdy* (St. Petersburg: 1906), in *Leninskii Sbornik*, XXX, 10-21, 25-6.

20 Cf. "Kadety ob ukrainskom voprose" (1913); "Kak episkop Nikon zashchyshchaet ukraintsev," (1913); Lenin, *Sochineniia*, XIX, 236-7, 341-2.

21 P. Struve expressed the thought of Ukrainian assimilation in these words: "One must not forget that [Russian] language is not only the language of the state but also [it is the language] of the new economic culture. Capitalism speaks and will speak not in Little Russian [Ukranian] but in Russian. In addition, since capitalism brings to the Ukrainian soil 'Great Russian' population, by the very same token it indirectly brings into the ethnic unity of the Ukraine a decomposition and strengthens greatly the Russian element at the expense of the Little Russian [Ukrainian]." P. Struve, "Obshcherusskaia kultura i ukrainskii partikularizm," *Russkaia Mysl'*, XXXIII (1912), p. 72. Lenin expressed the same idea in these words: "For the past decades the process of rapid economic development of the South, *i.e.*, the Ukraine, which attracts from Great Russia hundreds and thousands of peasants and workers into capitalist economies, mines and cities has increased. In these conditions the factor of assimilation of the great Russian and Ukrainian proletariat is unavoidable. *And this* fact is *doubtless* a progressive one. Capitalism puts the proletariat, both Great Russian and Ukrainian, whose conditions of life break down particular national narrowness, in place of a dull, rusty, settled and wild peasant, Russian or Ukrainian." Lenin, *Sochineniia*, XX, 14-5. Italics Lenin's.

22 Lenin, *Sochineniia*, XXIX, 236-7; 341-2; XX, 39-41, 91-2.

23 *Ibid., XX*, 14-15. Italics Lenin's.

24 *Ibid.*, XX, 199.

25 Alexander Lototsky, *Storinki Minuloho* (Warsaw: 1933-34), II, 422f, as quoted by John S. Reshetar, Jr., *The Ukrainian Revolution, 1917-1920. A Study in Nationalism* (Princeton: University Press, 1952), pp. 42-3. See P. N. Miliukov, *Natsionalnyi vopros (Proiskhozhdenie natsionalnosti i natsionalnye voprosy v Rossii)* (Prague: "Svobodna Rossiia," 1925), p. 175.

26 Lenin, *Sochineniia*, XXIV, 269-70; *KPSS v resolutsiiakh*, I, 345-6.

27 Mykola Kovalevskyj, *Ukraina Pid Chervonym Yarmom. Dokumenty i Fakty* (Warsaw-Lvov: "Skhid," 1936), pp. 16-17.

28 For an excellent treatment of the period from February to October, 1917, see Reshetar, *op. cit.*, pp. 47-85.

29 On the June, 1917 crisis, see William Henry Chamberlin, *The Russian Revolution, 1917-1921* (New York: Macmillan, 1935), I, 454-5. Adriana Tyrkova-Williams, *From Liberty to Brest-Litovsk* (London: Macmillan, 1919), pp. 135-41.

30 Lenin, *Sochineniia*, XXV, 73-4.

31 *Ibid.*, XXV, 82.

32 *Ibid.*, XXV, 82-3.

33 *KPSS v resolutsiiakh*, I, 361.

34 Kovalevskyj, *op. cit.*, pp. 171-2. It is interesting to note that the Bolsheviks refused to accept positions in the Russian Provisional Government, although they willingly joined the Government of the Ukrainian Central Rada.

Chapter II: THEORY VERSUS PRACTICE

1 *Izvestiia*, November 16, 1917, as reproduced by James H. Meisel and Edward S. Kozera, *Materials for the Study of the Soviet System*. 2nd ed. (Ann Arbor: The George Wahr Publishing Co., 1953), pp. 25-6.

2 Mykola Skrypnyk, *Stati i Promovy* (Kharkov: Derzhavne Vydavnytstvo Ukrainy, 1930), I, 290-1. Compare these views with those expressed by Struve in his May, 1917 proposal for an Autonomy Statute, as cited *supra*, pp. 21-2.

3 Akademiia Nauk URSR. Instytut Istorii. *Istoriia Ukrainy. Korotkyj Kurs* (Kiev: Akademiia Nauk URSR, 1941), pp. 294-6.

4 Provinces of Kiev, Podolia, Volyn, Chernigov, Poltava, Kharkov, Ekaterinoslav, Kherson, and Tauride, except the Crimea.

5 P. Khrystiuk, *Zamitky i Materialy do Ukrainskoi Revolutsii, 1917-1920* (Vienna: Ukrainskyj Sotsiologichnyj Instytut, 1921), II, 51-3.

6 W. E. D. Allen, *The Ukraine. A History* (Cambridge: The University Press, 1940), p. 282.

7 From Stalin's interview with a Ukrainian representative as reported in *Pravda*, December 7, 1917, p. 3. It is interesting to note that this interview does not appear in Stalin's works.

8 M. Ravich-Cherkasskii, *Istoriia kommunisticheskoi partii (b-ov) Ukrainy* (Kharkov: Gosudarstvennoe Izdatelstvo Ukrainy, 1923), p. 24.

9 M. Shapoval, *Sotsiografiia Ukrainy. Sotsialna Struktura Ukrainy* (Prague: "Vilna Spilka," 1933), I, 77.

10 Mykola Skrypnyk, "Narys Istorii Proletarskoi Revolutsii na Ukraini," *Chervonyj Shliakh*, No. 1 (1923), as quoted by Sadovskyj, *op. cit.*, p. 67.

11 Comintern. *Ezhegodnik kominterna. Spravochnaia kniga po istorii mezhdunarodnogo rabochego politicheskogo i professionalnogo dvizheniia, statistike i ekonomike vsekh stran mira na 1923 god* (Petrograd-Moscow: Kommunisticheskii Internatsional, 1923), p. 476. Hereinafter cited as *Ezhegodnik kominterna.*

12 Lenin never expressed trust in the Ukrainians. In 1922, speaking at the XI Congress of the RCP(b), he characterized the Ukrainian situation in these words: "The Ukraine is an independent republic; that is very fine, but in Party relations it sometimes takes a round-about way and we must somehow get to them because these are very clever people, and I would not say that the CC [of the CP(b)U] tries to cheat us, but it tries to deviate from us." Lenin, *Sochineniia,* XXXIII, 267.

13 For details, see Reshetar, *op. cit.*, pp. 93-7; Chamberlin, *op. cit.*, I, 490.

14 Sadovskyj, *op. cit.*, p. 68.

15 *Leninskii Sbornik,* XXXIV, 102. N. I. Suprunenko, "Obrazovanie ukrainskoi sovetskoi sotsialisticheskoi respubliki," *Voprosy Istorii,* No. 2 (February, 1954), pp. 39-40.

16 *Pravda,* December 18, 1917, p. 1; Lenin, *Sochineniia,* XXVI, 323-5.

17 *Pravda,* December 21, 1917, pp. 1-2.

18 *Ibid.,* December 20, 1917, p. 3.

19 *Loc. cit.*

20 J. V. Stalin, *Works* (Moscow: Foreign Languages Publishing House, 1948), IV, 22. See also *Pravda,* December 22, 1917, p. 3; December 23, 1917, p. 1.

21 *Ibid.,* December 22, 1917, p. 1.

22 *Ibid.,* December 30, 1917, p. 3; Stalin, *Works,* IV, 29-30.

23 Erich von Ludendorff, *Ludendorff's Own Story, August 1914-November 1918* (New York-London: Harper, 1919), II, 128.

24 Dmytro Doroshenko, *Istoriia Ukrainy 1917-1923* (Uzhhorod: 1932), I, 295-6.

25 Major-General Max Hoffmann, *War Diaries and Other Papers.* Translated from the German by Eric Sutton (London: Martin Secker, 1929), II, 214-5.

26 *Graf* Ottokar Czernin, *Im Weltkriege* (Vienna-Berlin: Ullstein & Co., 1919), pp. 316, 322, 325-31.

27 Leon Trotsky, *My Life: An Attempt at an Autobiography* (New York: Charles Scribner's Sons, 1930), pp. 376-8.

28 Hoffmann, *op. cit.*, II, 215.

29 *Loc. cit.*

30 *Ibid.,* II, 209.

31 John W. Wheeler-Bennett, *The Forgotten Peace: Brest-Litovsk March 1918* (New York: William Morrow & Co., 1939), p. 166.

32 Hoffmann, *op. cit.*, II, 213-4.

33 For the complete German text of the treaty, see Adolf Weissler, ed., *Preussisches Archiv; Sammlung der Gesetze und der das Rechtswesen betreffenden Verordnungen und Verfügungen Preussens und des Reichs* (Freiburg/Breisgau: J.

Bielefelds Verlag, 1918), XXV, Pt. I, 959-77. For English text, see Ukraine. Secretariat for Foreign Affairs. *Texts of the Ukraine "Peace." With Maps.* (Washington: Government Printing Office, 1918), 160 pp.

34 For excerpts of the German press reaction to the Treaty and the Reichstag debates, see W. M. Knight-Patterson, *Germany from Defeat to Conquest 1913-1933.* Foreword by Lord Vanisittart (London: George Allen and Unwin Ltd., 1945), pp. 147-52.

35 Germany. Reichstag. *Untersuchungsausschuss über die Weltkriegsverantwortlichkeit. 4. Unterasschuss. Die Ursachen des deutschen Zusammenbruches im Jahre 1918. Erste Abteilung der militärische und aussenpolitische Zusammenbruch. Vierte Reihe im Werk des Untersuchungsausschuss. Unter Mitwirkung von Dr. Eugen Fischer . . . Dr. Walther Bloch . . . im Auftrage des Vierten Unterausschusses hrsg. von Dr. Albrecht Philipp . . .* (Berlin: Deutsche Verlagsgesellschaft für Politik und Geschichte m.b.H., 1925-1929), III, 20-1.

36 Dmytro Solovei, *Holhota Ukrainy* (Winnipeg: "Ukrainskyj Holos," 1953), I, 33.

37 *Ezhegodnik kominterna,* p. 476. See also Iwan Majstrenko, *Borot'bism A Chapter in the History of Ukrainian Communism* (New York: Research Program on the U. S. S. R., 1954), p. 107.

38 Skrypnyk, *Stati i Promovy,* II, 7.

39 N. Popov, "SSSR i natsionalnaia politika sovetskoi vlasti," *Kommunisticheskaia Revolutsiia,* No. 4 (43), February 15, 1923, p. 42.

40 Jurij Lawrynenko, *Ukrainian Communism and Soviet Russian Policy Toward the Ukraine. An Annoted Bibliography 1917-1953* (New York: Research Program on the U.S.S.R., 1953), pp. xvi-xvii.

41 Skrypnyk, *Stati i Promovy,* I, 81-2.

42 *Ibid.,* I, 84-5.

43 *KPSS v rezolutsiiakh,* I, 443.

44 *Ibid.,* I, 416-7. Italics mine.

45 *RCP(b). VIII s'ezd rossiiskoi kommunisticheskoi partii (bolshevikov). Stenograficheskii otchet* (Saratov: Sovgrafiia, 1919), p. 70.

46 *Ibid.,* p. 40.

47 Stalin, *Works,* IV, 385-6.

48 As reproduced in full by E. F. Girchak, *Na dva fronta v borbe s natsionalizmom* (Moscow: Gosizdat, 1930), pp. 199-200.

49 Solovei, basing himself on various statements of Rakovsky, estimated that between April 1, and June 19, 1919, there were 328 peasant uprisings in the Ukraine. Solovei, *op. cit.,* I, 22. See also Chamberlin, *op. cit.,* II, 221-41; Majstrenko, *op. cit.,* pp. 119-23.

50 *Ezhegodnik kominterna,* p. 463.

51 According to a recent biography of Trotsky, following Denikin's victory in the Ukraine many Party members adopted the view that it was not a bad idea for Denikin's forces to occupy the Ukraine for the time being in order to teach the peasants a good lesson, as they held that this occupation would turn them from opponents into supporters of the Bolsheviks, choosing the latter as the lesser of two evils. Isaac Deutscher, *The Prophet Armed. Trotsky 1879-1921* (New York: Oxford University Press, 1954), p. 440. For a similar philosophy,

see also Lenin, *Sochineniia*, XXIX, 172. On Denikin's occupation of the Ukraine, see Majstrenko, *op. cit.*, pp. 147-57.

52 *KPSS v rezolutsiiakh*, I, 458-61; Lenin, *Sochineniia*, XXX, 142-4.

53 It is reported that the Bolshevik agitators who followed in the steps of the retreating forces of Denikin had secret orders from Trotsky not to talk to Ukrainian peasants about communes until the Bolshevik rule gained strength; to introduce communes very carefully under the name of artels and co-operatives; to stress the non-existence of communes in Russia; and to underline that Russia did recognize the independence of the Ukraine, but only under Soviet rule, in contrast to the Ukrainian bourgeois independence of Petliura. See cf. Oleksander Dotsenko, *Zymovyj Pokhid* (Warsaw: Pratsi Ukrainskoho Naukovoho Instytutu, 1932), p. xcv.

54 For full text of Lenin's appeal, see Lenin, *Sochineniia*, XXX, 267-73. For Lenin's caution of Party members at the VIII All-Russian Conference of the RCP(b) regarding dealings with Ukrainians, see *ibid.*, XXX, 156-7.

55 Kovalevskyj, *op. cit.*, pp. 26-7; Majstrenko, *op. cit.*, pp. 171-2.

56 *Sobranie uzakonenii*, (1920), No. 24, Statute 509, as fully reproduced by A. Khvylia, *Natsionalnyi vopros na Ukraine* (Kharkov: Gosudarstvennoe Izdatelstvo Ukrainy, 1926), pp. 121-2.

57 See cf. Majstrenko, *op. cit.*, pp. 212-17.

58 *Soviet Russia*, December 11, 1920, as quoted by Alfred L. P. Dennis, *The Foreign Policies of Soviet Russia* (New York: Dutton & Co., 1924), p. 177.

59 For full text, see *Pravda*, October 10, 1920, as reproduced in Stalin, *Works*, IV, 363-76.

60 Compare these views with Lenin's statement on organizing Soviet rule in the Ukraine in 1919, when he declared that, in return for organizational aid to the Ukraine, the CC of the RCP(b) should demand 50,000,000 puds of grain. Lenin, *Sochineniia*, XXIX, 64-5.

61 At the X Congress, Stalin was accused by the pro-Russian faction of artificially cultivating non-existing nationalities, to which he made the following reply: "I have received a note alleging that we Communists are artificially cultivating a Byelorussian nationality. That is not true, for there exists a Byelorussian nation, which has its own language, different from Russian. Consequently, the culture of the Byelorussian people can be raised only in its native language. We heard similar talk five years ago about the Ukraine, about the Ukrainian nation. And only recently it was said that the Ukrainian Republic and the Ukrainian nation were inventions of the Germans. It is obvious, however, that there is a Ukrainian nation, and it is the duty of the Communists to develop its culture. You cannot go against history. It is obvious that although Russian elements still predominate in the Ukrainian towns, in the course of time these towns will inevitably be Ukrainized." Stalin, *Works*, V, 48-9.

62 At the V Conference of the CP(b)U, in November, 1920, Skrypnyk charged that the resolution of the CC of the RCP(b) of December, 1919, had become a "lost document." He repeated this charge on several other occasions. Skrypnyk, *Stati i Promovy*, II, 7; Lawrynenko, *op. cit.*, p. xviii.

63 For full text, see *KPSS v rezolutsiiakh*, I, 553-63.

64 "Of all the Soviet Republics that have thus far existed, only Soviet Russia has been able victoriously to resist international and internal counter-revolution, and to deal smashing blows to its opponents. Soviet Russia alone holds the geographical conditions, as well as the economic and political resources, which make of it an impregnable fortress against all the attacks of international imperialism, . . . the leader and organizer of the international proletariat in the struggle against international imperialism. Each new Soviet republic, impelled by the instinct of self-preservation, will seek support and aid from Soviet Russia. An effective alliance with Soviet Russia is the revolutionary duty of every new Soviet state." From a thesis of the CC of the CP(b)U defining the relationship between the RSFSR and the UkSSR, November, 1920. *Soviet Russia*, December 11, 1920, p. 572, as quoted by Dennis, *op. cit.*, p. 191.

65 Khristian Rakovsky, "Soviet Russia and Soviet Ukraine," *Soviet Russia*, December 11, 1920, p. 571, as quoted by Dennis, *op. cit.*, p. 187.

66 Solovei, *op. cit.*, I, 31-2; Lawrynenko, *op. cit.*, pp. 102-13. For a well-documented study of the rise and fall of the *Borot'bisty*, including numerous biographical sketches of their leaders, by a former member of the *Borot'bisty* group, see Majstrenko, *op. cit.*, pp. 1-286.

67 At the VIII All-Russian Conference of the RCP(b), in December, 1919, Lenin attacked the *Borot'bisty* in these words: "The Borot'bisty talk a great deal about the national question, but they do not mention *partizanstvo* [partisan warfare]. We should demand that the Borot'bisty dissolve the Union of Teachers—even if it uses the Ukrainian language and the official Ukrainian state seal—in the name of the same principles of proletarian communist policy in the name of which we dissolved our All-Russian Teachers' Union, since it has not applied the principles of proletarian dictatorship, but has defended the interest and applied the policy of the petty bourgeoisie." Lenin, *Sochineniia*, XXX, 171-2.

68 *Ibid.*, XXX, 270. Italics Lenin's.

69 *Ibid.*, XXX, 438-9. Majstrenko makes no reference to this statement.

70 On March 15, 1927, *Dilo* (Lvov), the official newspaper of the Ukrainian National Democratic Union (UNDO), made the following observation on the objectives of the *Borot'bisty* in joining the CP(b)U: "In the period of post-war communism, there entered into the membership of the CP(b)U a numerically small, but qualitatively very selected number of nationally conscious Ukrainians who placed for themselves as a task to protect in the Party not only the interests of Ukrainian national culture, but also to propagate in its midst the idea of Ukrainian statehood, even though of communist nature. In this category of members of the CP(b)U one ought to count also former Independent Ukrainian Socialists, and Socialist Revolutionaries, the Borot'bisty, who entered the Communist Party [(bolshevik) of the Ukraine] already in the period of War Communism." As quoted by Mykola Skrypnyk, *Dzherela ta Prychyny Rozlamu v KPZU* (Kharkov: Derzhavne Vydavnytstvo Ukrainy, 1928), p. 30. On September 8, 1937, the IV Plenum of the Kiev Party *Obkom* gave the following interpretation of the aim of the *Borot'bisty* in entering the CP(b)U: "The Plenum of the *Obkom* considers as established [fact] that a considerable part of the leading core of the former Borot'bisty entered the Bolshevik Party with double purpose: in order to preserve their forces from defeat and to continue counter-revolutionary

nationalist work inside the Party." Lenin and Stalin, *O borbe za ustavlenie sovetskoi vlasti na Ukraine* (Kiev: Partyzdat, 1938), p. 91.

71 Skrypnyk, *Stati i Promovy*, II, 12.

72 N. Bukharin, "The New Economic Policies of Soviet Russia," in *The New Policies of Soviet Russia* (Chicago: Charles H. Kerr & Co., 1921), p. 56. From the speech at the Third Congress of the Communist International on July 8, 1921, which implied the connection of the *Borot'bisty* with the rebellious sailors, "mostly sons of peasants, especially Ukrainian peasants."

73 See cf. Majstrenko, *op. cit.*, pp. 271-6.

74 Solovei, *op. cit.*, I, 36-8. The *Dniprosoiuz* was a consumer cooperative; the *Tsentral*, an agricultural cooperative; the *Ukrainbank*, a credit cooperative; and the *Koopstrakh*, a Ukrainian cooperative publishing center.

75 *Ibid.*, I, 41-2. Lenin, *Sochineniia*, XXX, 171-2.

76 Solovei, *op. cit.*, I, 40; H. Vashchenko, *Ukrainskyj Renesans XX Stolittia* (Toronto: "Na Varti," 1953), pp. 12-6.

77 See cf. *KPSS v rezolutsiiakh*, I, 419.

Chapter III: UKRAINIZATION POLICY

1 For the full text of Trotsky's speech see *Pravda*, April 11, 1923, p. 4, and April 12, 1923, pp. 4-5. For a few excerpts of other speeches see *Nova Ukraina*, No. 7-8 (July-August, 1923), p. 263.

2 *Pravda*, April 12, 1923, p. 4.

3 N. N. Popov, "Natsionalnaia problema na Ukraine," *Kommunist* (Kharkov), No. 969, April 5, 1923, as reproduced fully in *Nova Ukraina*, No. 7-8 (July-August, 1923), p. 314.

4 *Ibid.*, p. 316.

5 Walter Russell Batsell, *Soviet Rule in Russia* (New York: Macmillan, 1929), p. 643.

6 *Ibid.*, p. 645.

7 At the XI Congress of the RCP(b) in 1922, Skrypnyk complained that there was a tendency among Russian members of the Party to liquidate the statehood of the Ukraine. Skrypnyk, *Stati i Promovy*, II, 6-7.

8 For the full text of the resolution see *KPSS v rezolutsiiakh*, I, 709-18.

9 Stalin, *Works*, V, 241-68.

10 Skrypnyk, *Stati i Promovy*, II, 11.

11 *Pravda*, April 25, 1923, p. 3.

12 As reproduced in *Nova Ukraina*, No. 7-8 (July-August, 1923), pp. 288-9.

13 Stalin, *Works*, V, 269-70. For other arguments see *ibid.*, V, 270-85.

14 As cited in the resolution of the June, 1926 Plenum of the CC of the CP(b)U and reproduced by Girchak, *op. cit.*, pp. 179-80.

15 Compare this assertion of Stalin with the statements made by Lenin and Struve in *supra*, p. 256, note 21.

16 Stalin, *Works*, V, 336-7. The attention accorded to, and the rather favorable treatment of, the Ukrainian problem by Stalin was undoubtedly prompted by the

renewal of criticism by the Ukrainian Bolsheviks of Stalin's machinations in the preparation of the constitution of the USSR and by their demands that Union Republics be left wider authority.

17 *Ibid.*, V. 299-300; *KPSS v rezolutsiiakh*, I, 761-6.

18 *Sobranie Uzakonenii USSR* [UkSSR], (1923), No. 29, Statute 435; *Visti VUTsVK*, No. 190, August 28, 1923, as reproduced in full by Khvylia, *op. cit.*, pp. 115-21.

19 William Henry Chamberlin, *Soviet Rule in Russia. A Living Record and a History* (Boston: Little, Brown & Co., 1931), p. 221.

20 As quoted by Mykola Halij and Bohdan Novytskyj, *Het' Maskul Natsionalna Polityka na Radianskij Ukraini v Svitli Dokumentiv* (Prague: "Vsetecky," 1934), p. 16. At the IX All-Ukrainian Congress of Soviets in May, 1925, Kaganovich characterized the need for Ukrainization in these words: "Without culture and without education we shall not move toward socialism. Our task centers not only on the elevation of the economy to its pre-war level, but also on moving forward, toward socialist economy. But without culture we shall not achieve it." UkSSR. [Central Executive Committee.] *IX-j Vseukrainskyj z'izd Rad Robitnychykh, Selianskykh ta Chervonoarmijskykh Deputativ (Stenografichnyj Zvit)* (Kharkov: Orgviddil VUTsVK, 1925), p. 11.

21 Skrypnyk, *Dzherela ta Prychyny Rozlamu v KPZU*, pp. 59-60. Italics Skrypnyk's.

22 Girchak, *op. cit.*, pp. 39-40.

23 S. Kosior, *Itogi noiabr'skogo plenuma TsK VKP(b) i zadachi kulturnogo stroitelstva na Ukraine* (Kharkov: Gosudarstvennoe Izdatelstvo Ukrainy, 1929), pp. 21-3.

24 Vol. P. Zatonskyj, *Natsionalna Problema na Ukraini. Dopovid na Plenumi TsK LKSMU (May, 1926)* (Kharkov: Derzhavne Vydavnytstvo Ukrainy, 1926), pp. 31-2.

25 *Kommunist*, No. 120, (1927), as quoted by Mykola Sciborsky, "The 'Ukrainianization' of Ukraine by Soviet Russia," *The Trident*, III, No. 12 (December, 1939), 32-3. For Popov's treatment of the national problem on the eve of Ukrainization, see N. N. Popov, "Ocherednye zadachi partii v natsionalnom voprose," *Kommunisticheskaia Revolutsiia*, No. 12 (51), July 1, 1923, pp. 65-78.

26 *Visti VUTsVK*, October 26, 1923, as cited in *Nova Ukraina*, No. 12 (December, 1923), p. 184. On January 16, 1923, *Pravda* reported that in the Kharkov Gubernia there were only 1,102 schools.

27 N. N. Popov, "Ocherednye zadachi partii v natsionalnom voprose," *Kommunisticheskaia Revolutsiia*, No. 12 (51), July 1, 1923, p. 72.

28 V. P. Zatonskyj, *Natsionalno-kulturnoe stroitelstvo i borba protiv natsionalizma* (Kharkov: "Ukrainskyj Robitnyk," 1934), p. 11.

29 *Vsesoiuznyj shkilnyj perepis 15, XII, 1927 roku. Shkilni ustanovy sotsialnoho vykhovannia na Ukraini*, p. 196, as cited by S. Siropolko, *Narodnia Osvita na Sovetskij Ukraini* (Warsaw: Pratsi Ukrainskoho Naukovoho Institutu, 1934), p. 25. In some cases the percentages cited by Siropolko are not one hundred per cent accurate. The difference, however, is not enough to alter the overall picture.

30 *Loc. cit.*

31 V. Chubar, *Sovetskaia Ukraina* (Kharkov: "Proletarii," 1925), p. 37.

32 *Ibid.*, p. 38.

33 Adopted from Siropolko, *op. cit.*, p. 92.

34 Adopted from *ibid.*, p. 122. Most of the Ukrainian scholars had left the country and established their institutions abroad (Prague, Vienna, Warsaw, Berlin). One of the tasks of Ukrainization was to silence these institutions abroad by attracting their scholars to return to the Ukraine.

35 Chubar, *op. cit.*, p. 38; *Kommunist* (Kharkov), June 24, 1923, as reproduced in *Nova Ukraina*, No. 9 (September, 1923), pp. 127-8.

36 *Loc. cit.*

37 Adopted from Siropolko, *op. cit.*, p. 98.

38 Adopted from *ibid.*, p. 99.

39 Adopted from *ibid.*, p. 66. This table gives the distribution for the year 1929.

40 *Proletarskaia Pravda*, No. 58, March 9, 1924, as quoted by Ivan Kravchenko, "Fashystski Kontseptsii Hrushevskoho i Joho Shkoly v Ukrainskij Istoriohrafii," *Zapysky Istorychno-Arkheohrafichnoho Instytutu*, No. 1 (Kiev: Akademiia Nauk, 1934), pp. 13-4.

41 N. N. Popov, "Natsionalnaia problema na Ukraine," *Kommunist* (Kharkov), No. 969, April 5, 1923, as reproduced in *Nova Ukraina*, No. 7-8 (July-August, 1923), p. 316.

42 N. N. Popov, "Ocherednye zadachi partii v natsionalnom voprose," *Kommunisticheskaia Revolutsiia*, No. 12 (51), July 1, 1923, p. 71.

43 Adopted from Siropolko, *op. cit.*, p. 184. Much credit for the increase of Ukrainian publications is due the Ukrainian Academy of Sciences, in whose name were issued, between 1918-29, 888 separate works. Solovei, *op. cit.*, I, 51. For a valuable study of the Ukrainian Academy of Sciences, see N. Polonska-Vasilenko, *Ukrainska Akademiia Nauk (Narys Istorii) (1918-1930)*, (Munich: Institute for the Study of the History and Culture of the USSR, 1955), Part I, 148 pp.

44 Chubar, *op. cit.*, p. 38.

45 *Bulletin périodique de la presse russe*, No. 164, April 29-May 25, 1927, as cited by Batsell, *op. cit.*, p. 654.

46 As reproduced by Girchak, *op. cit.*, p. 45.

47 *Ibid.*, p. 46.

48 P. A. Khromov, *Promyslovist' Ukrainy Pered Vitchyznianoiu Vijnoiu* (Kiev: Derzhavne Vydavnytstvo, 1945), p. 26.

49 Kommunisticheskaia Akademiia. [Commission on the Study of the National Problem.] *Natsionalna politika VKP(b) v tsifrakh* (Moscow: Kommunisticheskaia Akademiia, 1930), p. 126.

50 N. N. Popov, "Ocherednye zadachi partii v natsionalnom voprose," *Kommunisticheskaia Revolutsiia*, No. 12 (51) July 1, 1923, p. 68.

51 *Natsionalna politika VKP(b) v tsifrakh*, p. 126.

52 Chubar, *op. cit.*, pp. 36-7.

53 S. Vlasenko, "O X vseukrainskom s'ezde sovetov," *Sovetskoe Stroitelstvo*, No. 5-6 (10-1), (May-June, 1927), p. 104. One *desiatin* equals 2.7 acres.

54 *Izvestiia tsentralnogo komiteta rossiiskoi kommunisticheskoi partii (bolshevikov)*, No. 9 (17), as cited by Ravich-Cherkasskii, *op. cit.*, pp. 241-2. See

also A. Hylynsky, "Sostoianie KP(b)U k piatiletiiu oktiabrskoi revolutsii," *Oktiabrskaia Revolutsiia. Pervoe Piatiletie* (Kharkov: Gosudarstvennoe Izdatelstvo Ukrainy, 1923), pp. 167-83.

55 *Natsionalna politika VKP(b) v tsifrakh*, pp. 137-8.

56 UkSSR. [Statistical Department.] *Ukraina. Statystychnyj Spravochnyk* (Kharkov: Derzhavne Vydavnytstvo Ukrainy, 1925), p. 3.

57 M. Shapoval, "Khto kerue Ukrainoiu?", *Nova Ukraina*, IV, No. 2-3 (June-July, 1925), pp. 2-3.

58 V. Chubar, *Khoziaistvo Ukrainy* (Moscow: 1926), p. 3, as reproduced in *Nova Ukraina*, VI, No. 8-9 (August-September, 1927), p. 72.

59 *IX-j Vseukrainskyj Z'izd Rad*, pp. 389-94.

60 According to one set of Soviet data, in 1924-5, Ukrainians had only 27.6% of the members of the All-Ukrainian Central Executive Committee. In the following year their number rose to 55.5%. Mikh. Katsenelenbogen, "Ob 'uklonakh' v natsionalnoi politike VKP(b)," *Bolshevik*, No. 22 (November 30, 1927), pp. 25-6.

61 Chubar, *Khoziaistvo Ukrainy*, p. 3, as reproduced in *Nova Ukraina*, VI, No. 8-9 (August-September, 1927), p. 72.

62 S. Vlasenko, "Itogi perevyborov v sovety na Ukraine," *Sovetskoe Stroitelstvo*, No. 7 (July, 1927), pp. 75-6.

63 *Ibid.*, p. 80.

64 *Loc. cit.*

65 S. Vlasenko, "O X vseukrainskom s'ezde sovetov," *ibid.*, No. 5-6 (10-1) (May-June, 1927), p. 105.

66 *Kommunist* (Kharkov), No. 73, March 27, 1923, as quoted by Girchak, *op. cit.*, pp. 21 and 92. Italics Lebed's.

67 N. N. Popov, "Natsionalnaia problema na Ukraine," *Kommunist* (Kharkov), No. 69, April 5, 1923, as reproduced in *Nova Ukraina*, No. 7-8 (July-August, 1923), p. 315.

68 Vaganian's book met numerous protests in the Ukraine. For some arguments, see A. Krinitski, "K voprosu a natsionalnoi kulture," *Bolshevik*, No. 9 (May 1, 1927), pp. 51-63; K. Tabolov, "O natsionalnoi kulture, ob ukrainizatsii i o literaturnoi esterike Vaganiana i Larina," *ibid.*, No. 11- 2(June 15, 1927), pp. 69-77.

69 Iu. Larin, "Ob izvrashcheniiakh pri provednii natsionalnoi politiki," *Bolshevik*, No. 23-4 (December 31, 1926), p. 59.

70 *Ibid.*, pp. 64-5.

71 *Ibid.*, pp. 52-3.

72 *Itogi raboty sredi natsmen Ukrainy* . . . (Kharkov. 1927), as cited by A. Arsharuni, "Natsionalnaia kultura za 10 let," *Kommunisticheskaia Revolutsiia*, No. 20 (October, 1927), p. 45.

73 Arsharuni, *op. cit.*, p. 46; Girchak, *op. cit.*, p. 46.

74 *Loc. cit.* See also Ia. Rives, "Rabota sredi natsmen na Ukraine," *Vlast Sovetov*, No. 21 (May 22, 1927), p. 9.

75 A. Butsenko, "Rabota sredi natsmenshinstv na Ukraine," *Sovetskoe Stroitelstvo*, No. 1 (January, 1927), pp. 81-2.

76 Girchak, *op. cit.*, p. 46; Arsharuni, *op. cit.*, pp. 47-8.

266   MOSCOW AND THE UKRAINE

77 Khvylia, *op. cit.*, p. 108. For the full text of the resolution, see *ibid.*, pp. 108-14.

78 *Sobranie Uzakonenii USSR* [UkSSR], (1925), No. 26, Statute 202; *Visti VUTsVK*, No. 112, May 20, 1925, as reproduced in full by Khvylia, *op. cit.*, pp. 123-8.

79 See cf. Larin, *op. cit.*, pp. 64-5. In 1926, at the Second Session of the Central Executive Committee of the USSR, G. Ye. Zinoviev charged that "in the Ukraine such a 'Ukrainization' is being conducted as clearly contradicts our national policy, hurts our line in this problem and aids Petliurism, and there is no remedy for actual chauvinism." As cited by Girchak, *op. cit.*, pp. 31-2.

80 Kovalevskyj, *op. cit.*, p. 44; Mykola Sciborsky, "The 'De-Ukrainianization' of the Ukraine by Soviet Russia," *The Trident*, IV, No. 1 (January-February, 1940), 15.

81 Ukrainization—its tempo, its scope, and its force—made a strong impression on other nationalities, which expressed a desire to initiate a similar program. However, being a centrifugal trend, Ukrainization was incompatible with the Party's centralism. At the Second Session of the Central Executive Committee of the USSR, A. Enukidze warned other nationalities not to seek to imitate either the scope or the tempo of Ukrainization, since their situation differed from the Ukrainian. A. Enukidze, "K voprosu o natsionalnykh iazykakh," *Sovetskoe Stroitelstvo*, No. 1 (August, 1926), p. 43.

Chapter IV: NATIONAL DEVIATIONS

1 These biographical data were taken from Vashchenko, *op. cit.*, pp. 54-5; also Vasyl Pliushch, *Pravda Pro Khvylovyzm* (Munich: Spilka Vyzvolennia Ukrainy, 1954), pp. 5-10.

1a There are some who deny Khvylovyj served with the *CHEKA*. See in particular *Vpered*, No. 12 (61), December, 1955, pp. 7-8.

2 Girchak, *op. cit.*, p. 49.

3 Mykola Khvylovyj, *Ukraina chy Malorosiia?*, as quoted in *ibid.*, p. 55.

4 *Loc. cit.*

5 M. Khvylovyj, "Apologety Pisaryzmu," *Kultura i Pobut*, No. 13 (1926), as cited in *ibid.*, p. 51. Italics Khvylovyj's.

6 M. Khvylovyj, *Kamo Hriadeshy?*, p. 44, as cited by Girchak, *op. cit.*, p. 51. See also S. Nykolyshyn, *Kulturna Polityka Bolshevykiv i Ukrainskyj Kulturnyj Protses* (Na Chuzhyni: n. p., 1947), p. 24; Clarence A. Manning, *Ukraine Under the Soviets* (New York: Bookman Associates, 1953), pp. 80-1.

7 Stalin, *Works*, VIII, 161.

8 As fully reproduced by Girchak, *op. cit.*, p. 204.

9 *Proletarskaia Pravda*, No. 149 (1762), July 5, 1927, as fully reproduced in *Nova Ukraina*, VI, No. 8-9 (August-September, 1927), 83-4.

10 Girchak, *op. cit.*, p. 93.

11 Manning, *op. cit.*, p. 82.

12 *Vaplite*, No. 5 (1927), as cited by Girchak, *op. cit.*, p. 83.

13 *Vaplite*, No. 5 (1927), as cited in *ibid.*, p. 86.

14 Nykolyshyn, *op. cit.*, pp. 37-8; Solovei, *op. cit.*, I, 64-7; P. Harmash, *Politychna Ideia 'Vaplitian' i Ukrainska Politychna Dumka* (n. p.: Krytychna Dumka, n.d.p.), 114 pp.

15 Vashchenko, *op. cit.*, pp. 44-57; Pliushch, *op. cit.*, pp. 11-6.

16 Khvylovyj, *Ukraina chy Malorosiia?*, as quoted by Girchak, *op. cit.*, pp. 58-9.

17 See cf. *ibid.*, p. 59.

18 Pliushch, *op. cit.*, pp. 8-11.

19 *Ibid.*, pp. 11-2.

20 *Kommunist* (Kharkov), February 29, 1928, as fully reproduced in Girchak, *op. cit.*, pp. 213-4. Italics Khvylovyj's.

21 *Loc. cit.*

22 Vashchenko, *op. cit.*, pp. 56-7; Solovei, *op. cit.*, I, 71.

23 See *supra*, pp. 52-5.

24 Khvylia, *op. cit.*, p. 109.

25 I. V. Stalin, *Sochineniia* (Moscow: Gosizdat, 1948), VIII, 149-50.

26 *Ibid.*, VIII, 150-2.

27 *Ibid.*, VIII, 153-4.

28 Skrypnyk, *Dzherela ta Prychyny Rozlamu v KPZU*, p. 22.

29 For full text of the resolution, see Girchak, *op. cit.*, pp. 176-85; also E. F. Hirchak, *Natsionalne Pytannia to Pravyj Ukhyl* (Kharkov: Derzhavne Vydavnytstvo Ukrainy, 1930), pp. 142-5.

30 See cf. Solovei, *op. cit.*, I, 72.

31 As cited by Girchak, *op. cit.*, p. 105.

32 As cited in Point 10 of the resolution of the July, 1927 Plenum of the CC of the CP(b)U. *Proletarskaia Pravda*, No. 149 (1762), July 5, 1927, and fully reproduced in *Nova Ukraina*, No. 8-9 (August-September, 1927), p. 82.

33 Girchak, *op. cit.*, p. 105; M. Shapoval, "Cherez Desiat Rokiv," *Nova Ukraina*, No. 10-1 (October-November, 1927), pp. 32-3.

34 Skrypnyk, *Dzherela ta Prychyny Rozlamu v KPZU*, p. 5.

35 For full text of the resolution, see *Proletarskaia Pravda*, No. 149 (1762), July 5, 1927, as reproduced in *Nova Ukraina*, No. 8-9 (August-September, 1927), pp. 78-84.

36 *Proletarskaia Pravda*, No. 153 (1766), July 9, 1927, as fully reproduced in *Nova Ukraina*, No. 8-9 (August-September, 1927), p. 85.

37 Skrypnyk, *Stati i Promovy*, II, 102.

38 *Proletarskaia Pravda*, No. 153 (1766), July 9, 1927, as fully reproduced in *Nova Ukraina*, No. 8-9 (August-September, 1927), pp. 85-9.

39 See cf. Skrypnyk, *Dzherela ta Prychyny Rozlamu v KPZU*, p. 68.

40 *Dilo* (Lvov), No. 57, March 15, 1927, as cited in Skrypnyk, *Dzherela ta Prychny Rozlamu v KPZU*, p. 30. See *supra*, p. 261, note 70.

41 *Nova Ukraina*, No. 8-9 (August-September, 1927), p. 74. See also Iu. Bratkowski, "Na novom etape borby," *Kommunisticheskii Internatsional*, No. 8 (February 22, 1929), p. 17.

42   A congress of the Second International held in Marseille in 1925, adopted a resolution calling for self-determination of the Ukraine as well as other Union Republics.

43   Emil Strauss, "Die Freiheitskampf der Ukrainer," *Die Gesellschaft*, (1927), p. 273.

44   Skrypnyk, *Dzherela ta Prychyny Rozlamu v KPZU*, p. 88.

45   See cf. Lenin, *Sochineniia*, XXII, 331-2; XXIV, 265.

46   Poland. Ministry for Foreign Affairs. *Official Documents Concerning Polish-German and Polish-Soviet Relations, 1933-1939* (London: 1940), p. 164. Article 3 of the Treaty.

47   Comintern. [Congress.] *Piatyi vsemirnyi kongress kommunisticheskogo internatsional 17 iunia 8 iulia 1924 g. Stenograficheskii otchet* (Moscow: Gosizdat, 1925), I, 595.

48   *Ibid.*, I, 663-4.

49   *International Press Correspondence*, IV, No. 62 (September 5, 1924), 683.

50   *Ibid.*, IV, No. 62 (September 5, 1924), 684. Point 4 of the resolution.

51   Comintern. [Enlarged Executive.] *Erweiterte Exekutive der Kommunistichen Internationale Moskau, 17 Februar bis 15 März, 1926. Protokoll* (Berlin: Carl Hoym Verlag, 1926), pp. 48-50; 267-74; Skrypnyk, *Stati i Promovy*, II, 35-41.

52   K. Danylovych, "III s'ezd KPZU," *Kommunisticheskii Internatsional*, No. 48 (November 30, 1928), p. 21; Ev. Kosmin, "Ukrainskie plany polskogo fashizma," *Bolshevik*, No. 23-4 (December 31, 1928), pp. 112-25; see also Comintern. [Congress.] *VI Kongress kominterna. Mezhdunarodnoe polozhenie i zadachi kominterna. Stenograficheskii otchet* (Moscow: Gosizdat, 1929), pp. 516-7.

53   For complete text, see Girchak, *op. cit.*, pp. 193-202.

54   *Ibid.*, pp. 202-6.

55   *Ibid.*, pp. 206-10.

56   *Ibid.*, pp. 185-92.

57   As fully reproduced in *ibid.*, pp. 216-8.

58   *Pravda*, May 16, 1929, p. 5.

59   Girchak, *op. cit.*, p. 217.

60   *Ibid.*, p. 219.

61   *Loc. cit.*

62   Majstrenko, *op. cit.*, p. 261.

63   For full text of the first article, see Mykhailo Volobuev, "Do Problemy Ukrainskoi Ekonomiky," *Bilshovyk Ukrainy*, No. 2 (January, 1928), pp. 46-72. For other treatments of Volobuev's views, see Girchak, *op. cit.*, pp. 110-22; Solovei, *op. cit.*, I, 74-8.

64   Mykhailo Volobuev, "Do Problemy Ukrainskoi Ekonomiky," *Bilshovyk Ukrainy*, No. 3 (February, 1928), pp. 42-63.

65   "Volobuev studied fundamentally a whole series of published articles and materials and also various plans on the construction of economy in the Ukraine and in the Soviet Union, and on the basis of the examined materials came to the conclusion that the USSR keeps the Ukraine in a colonial dependency, exploits it by every means and provides no possibility for a formal development of economic life of the Ukraine." *Dilo*, February 21, 1928, as cited by Girchak, *op. cit.*, pp. 121-2.

See also E. Vlasenko, "Finansy Ukrainy," *Nova Ukraina*, No. 12 (December, 1927), pp. 1-20.

66 VKP(b). [Congress.] *XVI s'ezd vsesouiznoi kommunisticheskoi partii (bolshevikov)*. *Stenograficheskii otchet* (Moscow: Gosudarstvennoe Izdatelstvo, 1930), pp. 241-2.

67 And. Richytskyj, *Do Problemy Likvidatsii Perezhytkiv Kolonialnosty ta Natsionalizmu* (Kharkov: Derzhavne Vydavnytstvo Ukrainy, 1928), pp. 38-9.

68 *Ibid.*, pp. 12-3.

69 *Ibid.*, p. 13.

70 *Ibid.*, pp. 14-5.

71 The only statement Volobuev made on this matter was the following: "The opposition considers that it is impossible to build socialism in one country. But do we build it in one country?" Volobuev, *op. cit.*, No. 3 (February, 1928), p. 44.

72 Girchak, *op. cit.*, p. 110.

73 *Ibid.*, pp. 117-8.

74 M. Volobuev, "Proty Ekonomichnoi Pliatformy Natsionalizmu," *Bilshovyk Ukrainy*, No. 5-6 (March, 1930), pp. 54-69; No. 7 (April, 1930), pp. 28-40.

75 As reproduced fully by Girchak, *op. cit.*, pp. 215-6.

Chapter V: INTEGRAL STANDARDIZATION

1 N. N. Popov, "Natsionalna politika partii v period sotsialisticheskoi rekonstruktsii," *Pravda*, October 31, 1929, p. 3. Italics Popov's.

2 Skrypnyk, *Stati i Promovy*, II, 351. Italics Skrypnyk's.

3 For full text, see Girchak, *op. cit.*, pp. 223-6.

4 Skrypnyk, *Stati i Promovy*, II, 359.

5 Girchak, *op. cit.*, p. 225.

6 *Ibid.*, pp. 225-6.

7 For full test, see *ibid.*, pp. 220-3.

8 *Istoriia Ukrainy. Korotkyj Kurs*, p. 357.

9 *Loc. cit.*

10 Skrypnyk, *Stati i Promovy*, II, 353.

11 UkSSR. Gosplan. *Puti narodno-khoziaistvennogo razvitiia USSR. Materialy k postroeniiu piatiletnego plana* (Kharkov: Ukrgosplan, 1928), p. 449. Hereinafter cited as *Puti razvitiia*.

12 Skrypnyk, *Stati i Promovy*, II, 356.

13 *Ibid.*, II, 357.

14 See cf. S. M. Dimanshtein, "Problemy natsionalnoi kultury i kulturnogo stroitelstvo v natsionalnykh respublikakh," *Vestnik Kommunisticheskoi Akademii*, No. 31 (1929), p. 122.

15 *Visti*, No. 6, January 8, 1929, as cited by Halij, *op. cit.*, p. 19; see also Girchak, *op. cit.*, p. 14.

16 *Natsionalna politika VKP(b) v tsifrakh*, pp. 230-3.

17 For a very valuable treatment of the trial, see Kovalevskyj, *op. cit.*,

pp. 72-108; Solovei, *op. cit.*, I, 119-124; see also Skrypnyk, *Stati i Promovy*, I, 413-36. For an official Bolshevik appraisal of the trials, see *Spilka Vyzvolennia Ukrainy* (Kharkov: Derzhavne Vydavnytstvo Ukrainy, 1930), 97 pp.

18 I. V. Stalin, *Voprosy Leninizma*, 10th ed. (Moscow: Gosizdat, 1936), pp. 429-33.

19 As cited by Michael Pap, "Soviet Difficulties in the Ukraine," *The Review of Politics*, XIV, No. 2 (April, 1952), 220-1.

20 Stalin, *Voprosy Leninizma*, pp. 432-3. In 1951, commenting on this, one Soviet writer said Stalin's words were a reminder to the West Ukrainians that the USSR remembered them. S. M. Belousov, *Vozz'ednannia Ukrainskoho Narodu v Edynij Ukrainskij Radianskij Derzhavi* (Kiev: Akademiia Nauk, 1951), p. 34.

21 UkSSR. [Administration of Economic Outlook.] *Sotsialistychna Ukraina. Statystychnyj Zbirnyk* (Kiev: Derzhavne Vydavnytstvo Ukrainy, 1937), p. 3.

22 *Izvestiia*, February 12, 1934, p. 1.

23 Kovalevskyj, *op. cit.*, p. 127. One pud equals 36.113 pounds.

24 *Loc. cit.*

25 *Loc. cit.*

26 *Izvestiia*, August 8, 1932, p. 1; see also Nestor Olezhko, *Ahrarna Polityka Bolshevykiv* (Munich: "Nasha Knyhozbirnia," 1947), pp. 59-60.

27 As cited by Kovalevskyj, *op. cit.*, pp. 127-8.

28 As cited in *ibid.*, p. 129.

29 As reproduced in part in the speech of Postyshev, at the November, 1933 Plenum of the CC of the CP(b)U, *Pravda*, December 6, 1933, p. 3.

30 As cited by Kovalevskyj, *op. cit.*, p. 117.

31 S. V. Kosior, *Statti i Promovy, 1933-1936* (Kiev: Partvydav, 1936), p. 30.

32 *Ibid.*, p. 182.

33 P. P. Postyshev, "Mobilizuemo Masy na Svoechasnu Postavku Zerna Derzhavi," *Hospodarstvo Ukrainy*, No. 5-6, (May-June, 1933), p. 11.

34 See *supra*, pp. 201-3.

35 See *supra*, p. 135.

36 *Visti*, No. 164, July 28, 1933, as cited by Sadovskyj, *op. cit.*, p. 65.

37 Postyshev and Kosior, *op. cit.*, p. 10.

38 For complete text of Kosior's speech, see *Pravda*, December 2, 1933, pp. 2-4; also Postyshev and Kosior, *op. cit.*, pp. 34-101.

39 For full text of Postyshev's speech, see *Pravda*, December 6, 1933, p. 3.

40 As cited by Kovalevskyj, *op. cit.*, p. 146.

41 *Ibid.*, p. 147.

42 For full text of the resolution, see *Pravda*, November 27, 1933, p. 2; also Postyshev and Kosior, *op. cit.*, pp. 102-16.

43 For a condensed text of Kosior's speech, see *Izvestiia*, January 22, 1934, pp. 4-5.

44 For a condensed text of Postyshev's speech, see *ibid.*, January 24, 1934, p. 4.

45 *Ibid.*, January 28, 1934, p. 3.

46 *Loc. cit.*

Chapter VI: TOTAL REGIMENTATION

1 P. P. Postyshev, "Podniat rabotu marksistsko-leninskikh nauchnykh institutov Ukrainy na uroven trebovanii nashei velikoi sotsialisticheskoi stroiki," *Bolshevik*, No. 3-4 (February, 1934), pp. 10-8.

2 S. V. Kosior, "Chotyry Roky Borot'by za Sotsializm ta Zavdannia Radianskoi Ukrainy," *Radianska Ukraina*, No. 2 (February, 1935), p. 15.

3 I. Trainin, "Leninskaia partiia v borbe na dva fronta po natsionalnomu voprosu," *Sovetskoe Gosudarstvo*, No. 1 (1934), p. 73.

4 See cf. Solovei, *op. cit.*, I, 222-8; T. Postolovskaia, "Borba za leninskuiu politiku na teoreticheskom fronte sovetskoi Ukrainy," *Vestnik Kommunisticheskoi Akademii*, No. 4 (1934), pp. 53-9; N. Shelkoplias, "K itogam borby na filosofskom fronte Ukrainy," *Pod Znamenem Marksizma*, No. 1 (1936), pp. 66-83; A. Smirnov, "O natsionalisticheskikh izvrashcheniiakh v geograficheskoi nauke na Ukraine," *ibid.*, No. 2 (March-April, 1934), pp. 127-39.

5 I. Levin, "Natsionalnyi vopros v evrope i ugroza voiny," *Sovetskoe Gosudarstvo*, No. 4 (1934), p. 26.

6 Postolovskaia, *op. cit.*, pp. 54-5; S. Bondarchuk, "Ukraina v planakh germanskogo imperializma," *Borba Klassov*, No. 12 (December, 1933), pp. 20-3; Zatonskyj, *Natsionalno-kulturnoe stroitelstvo*, pp. 37-9. See also Alfred Rosenberg, *Der Zukunftsweg einer deutschen Aussenpolitik* (Munich: F. Eher, 1927), pp. 93-7; also Adolf Hitler, *Mein Kampf* (New York: Reynal and Hitchcock, 1939), pp. 889, 950-1, 963-5.

7 Trainin, *op. cit.*, p. 74.

8 *Loc. cit.*; Postolovskaia, *op. cit.*, pp. 55-8.

9 P. P. Postyshev, *Sovetskaia Ukraina na poroge 1936 goda* (Moscow: Partyzdat, 1936), p. 38; Iu. O. Voitsekhivskyj, "Peremohy Leninsko-Stalinskoi Natsionalnoi Polityky Partii," *Radianska Ukraina*, No. 6 (June, 1935), pp. 16-7.

10 Akademiia Nauk UkSSR. Instytut Ekonomiki. *Radianska Ukraina za 20 Rokiv* (Kiev: Partvydav, 1937), p. 98; see also *Sotsialistychna Ukraina*, p. 133.

11 Postyshev, *Sovetskaia Ukraina*, pp. 38-40.

12 *Sotsialistychna Ukraina*, p. 154.

13 *Loc. cit.*

14 *Loc. cit.*

15 *Radianska Ukraina za 20 Rokiv*, p. 103.

16 Adopted from *Sotsialistychna Ukraina*, p. 151.

17 See *supra*, pp. 82-3.

18 P. P. Liubchenko, *Stalinskaia konstitutsiia i sovetskaia Ukraina* (Moscow: Partyzdat, 1936), pp. 1-29; see also his speech at the XVI Extraordinary Session of the All-Ukrainian Congress of Soviets, "O proekte konstitutsii UkSSR," *Revolutsiia i Natsionalnosti*, No. 3 (March, 1937), pp. 30-7.

19 S. V. Kosior, *Konstitutsiia torzhestvuiushchego sotsializma* (Moscow: Partyzdat, 1936), pp. 1-14.

20 For an excellent study of Postyshev's fall, see Hryhory Kostiuk, *The Fall of Postyshev* (New York: Research Program on the U.S.S.R., 1954), pp. 1-25. Mimeographed Series No. 69.

21   For full text of Kosior's speech, see *Pravda,* May 29, 1937, p. 2. For a preview of Kosior's arguments at the XIII Congress of the CP(b)U, see his article in *ibid.,* May 26, 1937, p. 2.

22   For Stalin's criticism of the Kiev Party apparatus, see his speech at the March, 1937 Plenum of the CC of the VKP(b) in *ibid.,* April 1, 1937, p. 2.

23   For full text of the resolution, see *ibid.,* June 6, 1937, p. 2.

24   *Ibid.,* June 9, 1938, p. 2.

25   *Loc. cit.*

26   *Ibid.,* June 13, 1938, p. 1.

27   *Ibid.,* June 16, 1938, p. 3.

28   For full text of the resolution, see *ibid.,* June 21, 1938, p. 3.

29   Munich, and its aftermath, has produced voluminous literature. For an extremely valuable collection of documents on German policy toward the Ukrainian problem during this period, see Germany. Foreign Office. *Documents on German Foreign Policy, 1918-1945. Series D. (1937-1945). The Aftermath of Munich, October, 1938-March, 1939.* (Washington: Government Printing Office, 1949-1951), Vol. IV. These documents refute positively the contention of many observers that the Nazis supported the idea of an independent Ukraine.

30   *Pravda,* March 11, 1939, p. 2.

31   *Ibid.,* March 11, 1939, p. 3.

32   *Ibid.,* March 15, 1939, p. 9.

33   *Ibid.,* March 17, 1939, p. 1.

34   *Ibid.,* March 17, 1939, p. 7.

35   *Ibid.,* March 17, 1939, p. 10.

36   *Ibid.,* March 22, 1939, p. 4.

37   *Ibid.,* March 22, 1939, p. 7.

38   *Izvestiia,* October 26, 1939, p. 1.

39   *Ibid.,* October 28, 1939, p. 1.

40   *Loc. cit.* Italics in the original.

41   *Ibid.,* October 29, 1939, p. 1.

42   *Loc. cit.*

43   *Ibid.,* November 4, 1939, p. 1.

44   *Ibid.,* November 16, 1939, p. 1.

45   *Ibid.,* November 1, 1939, p. 1.

46   See cf. editorial in *ibid.,* November 15, 1939, p. 1.

47   At the XV Congress of the CP(b)U in May, 1940, Khrushchev reported that prior to May, 1940, there were organized in Western Ukraine 155 collective farms, 100 MTS's, and 31 Soviet farms. *Pravda,* May 18, 1940, p. 3.

48   *Ibid.,* May 12, 1940, p. 1.

49   For full text of Khrushchev's speech, see *ibid.,* May 18, 1940, pp. 3-4.

50   See cf. *Izvestiia,* June 29, 1940, p. 1.

51   *Loc. cit.*

52   *Ibid.,* August 2, 1940, p. 1.

52a   For a sound study of the Ukrainian problem during World War II, see John A. Armstrong, *Ukrainian Nationalism, 1939-1945* (New York: Columbia University Press, 1955), 322 pp.

53 For full text, see Akademiia Nauk URSR. Instytut Istorii i Arkheologii. *Naukovi Zapysky* (Ufa: Vydavnytstvo Akademii Nauk URSR, 1943), Bk. 1, pp. 5-7.

54 *Ibid.*, Bk. 1, pp. 10-14.

55 *Ibid.*, Bk. 1, pp. 14-21.

56 *Ibid.*, Bk. 1, pp. 21-6.

57 See *supra*, p. 180.

58 For arguments on the non-practicability of constitutional concessions, see *supra*, pp. 234-5.

59 For a well documented treatment of this story, see Vsevolod Holub, *Ukraina v Ob'ednanykh Natsiiakh* (Munich: "Suchasna Ukraina," 1953), pp. 3-82.

60 For Russo-Polish arguments, see Waclaw Lednicki and N. S. Timasheff, "The Russo-Polish Dispute," *The Review of Politics*, VI, No. 2 (April, 1944), pp. 151-92. The Ukrainian side of the story is well summarized by N. D. Czubatyj, "The Ukrainians and the Polish-Russian Border Dispute," *The Ukrainian Quarterly*, No. 1 (October, 1944), pp. 57-71. For Bolshevik arguments, see N. S. Khrushchev, *Osvobozhdenie ukrainskikh zemel ot nemetskikh zakhvatchikov i ocherednye zadachi vosstanovleniia narodnogo khoziaistva Sovetskoi Ukrainy* (Moscow: Gospolitzdat, 1944), pp. 4-8. For an abridged version see *Bolshevik*, No. 6 (March, 1944), pp. 9-10. See also Nik. Petrovskii, "Vossoedinenie ukrainskogo naroda v edinom ukrainskom gosudarstve," *ibid.*, No. 2 (January, 1944), pp. 42-55.

61 See cf. Edward Toborsky, "Benes and the Soviets," *Foreign Affairs*, XXVII, No. 2 (January, 1949), pp. 302-14. In addition to the wide publicity given the acquisition of the Carpatho-Ukraine, there was called a special Session of the Supreme Soviet of the UkSSR to approve this act. Speaking at this Session, on June 29, 1945, Khrushchev declared that "From today until forever, the Ukrainian people for the first time in their history are united in a single Ukrainian state. Now free Ukrainian Soviet people are masters on all Ukrainian territories. From now on all territories of the Ukraine are united under a Soviet flag, under the flag of the Ukrainian Soviet Socialist Republic. This is a result of a wise Stalinist policy of the Soviet Government and of the Bolshevik Party." UkSSR. [Supreme Soviet.] *Sioma Sesiia Verkhovnoi Rady Ukrainskoi RSR. Stenografichnyi Zvit* (Kiev: 1945), pp. 110-1, as cited by Belousov, *op. cit.*, pp. 124-5.

62 For a detailed Ukrainian account of the activities of the Insurgent Army, see Petro Mirchuk, *Ukrainska Povstanska Armiia, 1942-1952* (Munich: n. p., 1953), 319 pp.

63 For complete text, see Khrushchev, *Osvobozhdenie ukrainskikh zemel*, 40 pp. For an abridged version, see *Bolshevik*, No. 6 (March, 1944), pp. 7-35.

64 For full text, see *ibid.*, No. 10 (May, 1945), pp. 1-2.

65 See cf. the editorial in *ibid.*, No. 17-18 (September, 1945), p. 4.

66 *Pravda*, August 23, 1946, p. 2.

67 See cf. *ibid.*, September 2, 1946, p. 2. For further elaboration of Litvin's views on the history of the Ukrainian people and their relations with the Russians, see K. Litvin, "Ob istorii Ukrainskogo naroda," *Bolshevik*, No. 7 (April, 1947), pp. 41-56.

68 *Pravda,* July 4, 1947, pp. 3-4. See also A. Korneichuk, "Ukrainian Literature Today," *Soviet Literature,* No. 3 (1949), pp. 145-55.

69 *Pravda,* January 25, 1948, p. 1. See also editorial in *ibid.,* January 26, 1948, p. 1.

70 *Ibid.,* January 25, 1948, p. 2.

71 For full text of Khrushchev's speech, see CP(b)U. [Congress.] *XVI Z'izd Komunistychnoi Partii (bilshovykiv) Ukrainy 25-28 Sichnia 1949 r. Materialy Z'izdu* (Kiev: Derzhavne Vydavnytstvo Politychnoi Literatury URSR, 1949), pp. 10 ff. For an abridged version of Khrushchev's speech, see *Bolshevik,* No. 3 (February 15, 1949), pp. 7-38.

72 *XVI Z'izd,* p. 141.

73 *Ibid.,* p. 107.

74 *Ibid.,* pp. 71-4.

75 See cf. F. P. Shevchenko, "Piat' Rokiv Vozz'ednannia Zakarpattia z Ukrainskoiu RSR," *Vistnyk Akademii Nauk* (URSR), XXII, No. 6 (June, 1950), pp. 27-40; also I. I. Kompaniets, "Desiatyrichchia Vozz'ednannia Pivnichnoi Bukovyny z Radianskoiu Ukrainoiu," *ibid.,* XXII, No. 6 (June, 1950), pp. 41-51.

76 *Pravda,* July 2, 1951, p. 2.

77 *Ibid.,* November 26, 1951, p. 2.

78 See cf. *Literaturnaia Gazeta,* November 10, 1951, p. 2, as reproduced in the *Current Digest of the Soviet Press (CDSP),* III, No. 45 (December 22, 1951), pp. 33-4; *Pravda,* June 16, 1952, p. 2, as reproduced in *ibid.,* IV, No. 24 (July 26, 1952), pp. 23-4; *Radianska Ukraina,* June 29, 1952, as reproduced in *ibid.,* IV, No. 26 (August 9, 1952), pp. 5-6; *Sovetskoe Iskusstvo,* September 13, 1952, as reproduced in *ibid.,* IV, No. 43 (December 6, 1952), pp. 26-7.

79 *Pravda Ukrainy,* September 25, 1952, pp. 1-5, as reproduced in *CDSP,* IV, No. 41 (November 22, 1952), pp. 21-6. For a thumbnail sketch of the discussion which followed Melinkov's report, see *ibid.,* IV, No. 41 (November 22, 1952), pp. 22 ff. For Melmikov's speech at the XIX Congress of the VKP(b), see *Pravda,* October 7, 1952, pp. 3-4; for Korneichuk's, *ibid.,* October 11, 1952, p. 2; and for D. S. Korotchenko's, *ibid.,* October 12, 1952, pp. 3-4.

Chapter VII: ECONOMIC RELATIONS

1 To determine the role a part plays in a whole complex is always difficult and often dangerous, as it may involve either underestimation or overemphasis of the contribution of a given part. In this particular case it may involve both, plus a possible objection as to the validity of such a separation, as the Ukraine existed neither legally, nor politically, nor administratively before the Revolution of 1917. This writer is of the opinion that political motives, likes or dislikes, in themselves of temporary character and often products of emotion, cannot be determining factors in the world of reality; for though there was no Ukraine in the political sense, there were Ukrainian people who, on the territory under consideration, formed an overwhelming majority. For a very valuable treatment of Russian

economic policy toward the Ukraine, see E. Glovinskyj, K. Matsievych, V. Sadovskyj, *Suchasni Problemy Ekonomiki Ukrainy* (Warsaw: Pratsi Ukrainskoho Naukovoho Institutu, 1931), pp. 128-41. Hereinafter cited as *Suchasni Problemy*.

2 I. Mirchuk, ed. *Ukraine and Its People. A Handbook with Maps, Statistical Tables and Diagrams* (Munich: Ukrainian Free University Press, 1949), p. 134; see also Pierre Bregy and Prince Serge Obolensky, *The Ukraine—A Russian Land*. Translated by George Knupffer (London: Selwyn & Blount, 1940), p. 150.

3 *Puti razvitiia*, p. 46.

4 Mirchuk, *op. cit.*, p. 135.

5 A. A. Koropskii, "Dovoennyi eksport Ukrainy," *Sbornik statei po voprosam vneshnei torgovli* (Kharkov: Ukrvneshtorg, 1923), pp. 106-27. There is no agreement on the Ukrainian contribution to Russian export of grain. One Soviet observer placed the Ukrainian share for the year 1913 at 61.8% of the Russian total. A. Polianskii, "Itogi vneshnei torgovli Ukrainy," *ibid.*, p. 23. Another Soviet observer, calculating the Ukrainian share for the years 1909-11, in rubles, came to the conclusion that it equalled 3/5 of the total, or 326,757,000 rubles. Khvylia, *op. cit.*, p. 11. One English student of Ukrainian history, treating the Ukrainian economy along administrative lines, arrived at extremely low estimates. Allen, *op. cit.*, pp. 345-56.

6 Voldemar Timoshenko, *Ukraine and Russia. A Survey of Their Economic Relations* (Washington: Friends of Ukraine, 1919), p. 5.

7 The brown coal deposits in the Ukraine are located in the southern part of the Kiev *oblast'*, Cherkassy, Uman, Krivoy Rog and Dniepropetrovsk. The usage of brown coal declined after 1896 due to competition of the Donbass' hard coal. *Puti razvitiia*, pp. 13-4. Peat deposits, located in the Polesie Region, had limited utilization before the revolution. *Ibid.*, pp. 14-5.

8 The estimation of the Donbass coal deposits varied from time to time as can be seen from the following table:

1869	1,765,175,000 tons
1899	3,442,623,000 tons
1912	55,613,000,000 tons
1927	68,167,000,000 tons
1937	88,872,210,000 tons

Adopted from D. F. Virnyk, *Kompleksnoe narodnokhoziaistvennoe ispolzovanie vodnykh resursov Donbassa* (Kiev: Akademiia Nauk URSR, 1940), p. 82.

9 *Puti razvitiia*, p. 12. One pud equals 36.113 pounds.

10 B. L. Lychkov, "Rudnye i nerudnye bogatstva Ukrainy," *Pratsi Pershoho Z'izdu Doslidzhennia Produktsiinykh Syl ta Narodnoho Hospodarstva Ukrainy* (Kiev: Derzhavne Vydavnytstvo Ukrainy, 1926), I, 9. Practically all of Lychkov's data was incorporated into the First Five Year Plan.

11 *Puti razvitiia*, p. 11.

12 Before World War I, Russian geologist A. Faas had estimated that the resources of high quality iron ore of the Krivoy Rog amounted to 86,000,000 tons. A later estimation, by lowering the standard of percentage of iron to 35-40% of Fe, placed the figure at 163,800,000 puds. Lychkov, *op. cit.*, p. 14.

13 *Loc. cit.*

14   Adopted from N. K., "Novoi rynok zheleznoi rudy i vopros ob eksporte krivorozhskoi rudy," *Sbornik statei po voprosam vneshnei torgovli,* p. 147. See also *Puti razvitiia,* p. 15; Lychkov, *op. cit.,* p. 14.

15   *Loc. cit.*

16   *Ibid.,* p. 16. Most of the export went to Germany. In 1913, the Ukrainian production of manganese ore represented 11.9% of the total world production of manganese. *Puti razvitiia,* p. 19.

17   Lychkov, *op. cit.,* pp. 16-7.

18   *Ibid.,* pp. 17-8. In the production of salt, the Ukraine was surpassed only by the United States, Germany, England, France, and the East Indies.

19   *Ibid.,* p. 15.

20   *Loc. cit.*

21   *Puti razvitiia,* p. 46.

22   Lychkov, *op. cit.,* p. 9.

23   *Puti razvitiia,* p. 46.

24   *Ibid.,* p. 49.

25   *Leninskii Sbornik,* XXXIV, 13. Italics Lenin's. Ekaterinoslav, between January 5-11, 1918, dispatched into the RSFSR 200 railroad cars of bread. Suprunenko, *op. cit.,* p. 40.

26   *Pravda,* January 15, 1918, p. 1.

27   Cf. I. A. Gladkov, *Ocherki stroitelstva sovetskogo planovogo khoziaistva v 1917-1918 gg.* (Moscow: Gospolitzdat, 1950), p. 230. One of the findings of the delegation was that General Kaledin's forces received more coal than Petrograd. This may in part explain the charge of the Sovnarkom in its declaration of war against the Ukrainian Rada, that the latter had conspired with Kaledin.

28   *Petrogradskii Golos,* as reproduced in U. S. Department of State. *Papers Relating to the Foreign Relations of the United States, 1918. Russia.* (Washington: Government Printing Office, 1931), I, 476. For a full English text of the treaty, see *ibid.,* I, 442-75.

29   Gladkov, *Ocherki stroitelstva,* p. 233.

30   Lenin, *Sochineniia,* XXVII, 364.

31   From the speech of A. G. Shlikhter, as cited by Solovei, *op. cit.,* I, 21-2.

32   Lenin, *Sochineniia,* XXIX, 64.

33   *Ibid.,* XXIX, 64-5.

34   Lychkov, *op. cit.,* p. 9.

35   *Puti razvitiia,* p. 15.

36   *Ibid.,* p. 18; Lychkov, *op. cit.,* p. 16.

37   *Ibid.,* p. 15.

38   *Puti razvitiia,* p. 51; D. F. Virnyk, *Ekonomichnyi Rozkvit Ukrainskoi RSR —Torzhestvo Leninsko-Stalinskoi Natsionalnoi Polityky* (Kiev: Akademiia Nauk, 1951), p. 22.

39   *Loc. cit.;* Khromov, *op. cit.,* p. 25.

40   Stalin, *Works,* IV, 308-10.

41   *Ibid.,* IV, 305.

42   Lenin, *Sochineniia,* XXX, 461.

43 *Ibid.*, XXXI, 254.

44 *Ibid.*, XXXIII, 267.

45 *Ibid.*, XXXIII, 269.

46 *Ekonomicheskaia Zhizn*, No. 42 (February 25, 1920), as cited by A. Kulikova, "Iz istorii ukrainskoi trudovoi armii," *Proletarskaia Revolutsiia*, No. 3 (1940), p. 162.

47 *Trudova Armiia* (Kharkov) No. 1 (March 5, 1920), as reproduced in *ibid.*, No. 3 (1940), p. 163.. Point 2 of the decree which formed the Ukrainian Labor Army outlined its tasks in these words: "The tasks of the Ukrainian Council of Labor Army are the maximum increase of labor production, fuel, raw materials, the setting up of labor discipline in enterprises, [and] supply of enterprises with labor force."

48 Adopted from *Puti razvitiia*, p. 12.

49 *Ibid.*, p. 96.

50 Adopted from *ibid.*, p. 16.

51 *Ibid.*, p. 18. Numbers in parenthesis indicate the output of raw ore.

52 N. D. Kondratev, ed. *Koniunktura narodnogo khoziaistva SSSR i mirovogo v 1925-26 g.* (Moscow: Izdatelstvo NKF-SSSR, 1927), p. 39.

53 USSR. Gosplan. *Piatiletnyi plan narodno-khoziaistvennogo stroitelstva SSSR.* 3rd ed. (Moscow: "Planovoe Khoziaistvo," 1930), III, 113-64.

54 *Ibid.*, III, 116-7.

55 *Ibid.*, III, 119.

56 *Ibid.*, III, 120. See also H. Hrynko, "Zapadnyi upor SSSR," *Khoziaistvo Ukrainy*, No. 10 (October, 1925), p. 4.

57 See *supra*, pp. 116-21.

58 The Ukrainian opposition toward the Eastward movement of industry was rather loud at the XV Congress of the VKP(b) in 1928. See cf. VKP(b). [Congress.] *XV s'ezd vsesoiuznoi kommunisticheskoi partii (bolshevikov). Stenograficheskii otchet* (Moscow: Gosizdat, 1928), pp. 850, 905, 942, 990. On the discussion of the same problem in Ukrainian Bolshevik circles, see Ia. Tun, "Problemy Narodno-Hospodarskoho Budivnytstva na XI Z'izdi KP(b)U," *Hospodarstvo Ukrainy*, No. 5-6 (May-June, 1930), pp. 5-29. For an excellent appraisal of these arguments see *Suchasni Problemy*, pp. 93-5. At the XVI Congress of the VKP(b), Skrypnyk revealed that following Kuibyshev's publication of his thesis on the industrialization of other regions of the USSR, there developed considerable opposition in the Ukraine which had to be suppressed. VKP(b). [Congress.] *XVI s'ezd vsesoiuznoi kommunisticheskoi partii (bolshevikov). Stenograficheskii otchet* (Moscow: Gosizdat, 1930), pp. 241-2.

59 Adopted from *Piatiletnyi Plan*, I, 34.

60 *Ibid.*, III, 135.

61 Khromov, *Promyslovist' Ukrainy*, p. 45.

62 *Piatiletnyi Plan*, I, 29-30.

63 *Ibid.*, III, 136.

64 *Ibid.*, III, 137.

65 *Ibid.*, III, 164.

MOSCOW AND THE UKRAINE

66 See cf. *Suchasni Problemy,* pp. 98-104.

67 G. T. Grinko, *The Five-Year Plan of the Soviet Union. A Political Interpretation* (New York: International Publishers, 1930), p. 319; *Piatiletnyi Plan,* III, 121.

68 *Ibid.,* III, 116-9.

69 *Ibid.,* III, 127; see also the resolution of the November 16, 1929 Plenum of the CC of the VKP(b) in M. Savelev and A. Poskrebyshev, ed. *Direktivy VKP(b) po khoziaistvennym voprosam* (Moscow-Leningrad: Gosizdat, 1931), p. 629.

70 See *supra,* p. 134. For a well documented account of the famine, see Solovei, *op. cit.,* I, 174-200; see also Manning, *Ukraine Under the Soviets,* pp. 93-102; K. Michael, *Die Agrarpolitik der Sowjet-Union und deren Ergebnisse* (Berlin: Nibelungen Verlag, 1936), pp. 126-167.

71 On July 25, 1933 there was formed in Lvov a Ukrainian Social Committee for Relief of the Suffering Ukraine. The famine likewise received some attention at the Congress of European Minorities held in September, 1933, in Bern, Switzerland. It was also placed, by the Prime Minister of Norway, on the agenda of the September, 1933 meeting of the Council of the League of Nations, which referred the matter to the International Red Cross. None of these efforts, however, produced any positive results; for the Government of the USSR, denying the existence of its own creation, did not allow any aid to be brought to the suffering victims of the famine. See cf. Manning, *Ukraine Under the Soviets,* p. 105; *The Golgotha of Ukraine* (New York: Ukrainian Congress Committee of America, 1953), p. 4; William Henry Chamberlin, *The Ukraine: A Submerged Nation* (New York: Macmillan, 1944), pp. 61-2.

72 From a letter of Soviet Commissar for Foreign Affairs Maxim Litvinov to Herman P. Copleman, U. S. Congressman from Connecticut, dated January 3, 1934, as reproduced in part in *The Golgotha of Ukraine,* p. 5. See also Solovei, *op. cit.,* I, 195.

73 See cf. Chamberlin, *The Ukraine,* p. 60. William Henry Chamberlin, *Russia's Iron Age* (Boston: Little, Brown & Co., 1934), pp. 367-9.

74 Solovei, *op. cit.,* I, 195.

75 Chamberlin, *The Ukraine,* pp. 59-60. See also excerpts from M. I. Kalinin's speech at the All-Union Soviet Executive Committee in December, 1933, as cited in Chamberlin, *Russia's Iron Age,* p. 369.

76 Among those denying the occurrence of the famine is Professor F. L. Schuman, who argues that the stories of human sufferings in the Ukraine were nothing but "lurid accounts, mostly fictional" fabricated by the Nazi and the Hearst Press. Though Schuman acknowledges that the Ukraine was "off limits" for foreign correspondents in the USSR, he stresses strongly the fact that "tourists," of which he was one, were allowed to enter the Ukraine. Frederick L. Schuman, *Soviet Politics at Home and Abroad* (New York: Alfred A. Knopf, 1946), pp. 218-9.

77 Chamberlin, *The Ukraine,* p. 60; Chamberlin, *Russia's Iron Age,* pp. 367-8. In the latter work, Chamberlin gives an excerpt from his diary, wherein he wrote under the date of October, 1933: "What we found was little short of the worst

we had heard, and certainly explains the extraordinary action of the Soviet authorities in forbidding, over a period of several months, all travel in the famine regions by foreign correspondents. Everywhere a death rate that ranged remarkably close around the average figure of 10 per cent, according to the testimony of responsible local officials."

78 Arthur Koestler, *The Yogi and the Commissar and Other Essays* (London: Jonathan Cape, 1945), p. 142; see also Alexander Weissberg, *The Accused*. Translated by Edward Fitzgerald (New York: Simon and Schuster, 1951), pp. 145-8; 188-93.

79 For an extensive and well documented treatment of the losses of Ukrainian population, see Solovei, *op. cit.*, I, 201-16.

80 See cf. Frank Lorimer, *The Population of the Soviet Union: History and Prospects* (Geneva: League of Nations, 1946), pp. 137-9. Lorimer's conclusions were upheld by N. S. Timashev, "Obrechena li Rossia?" *Novyi Zhurnal*, XVII (1947), p. 165.

81 Adopted from Mykola Sciborsky, "Ukraine in Figures," *The Trident*, IV, No. 10 (December, 1940), 31-2. See also Khromov, *Promyslovist' Ukrainy*, p. 36.

82 I. V. Stalin, *Voprosy Leninizma*. 10th ed. (Moscow: Partyzdat, 1936), p. 399.

83 *Piatiletnyi Plan*, III, 163-4.

84 Adopted from Mykola Sciborsky, "Ukraine in Figures," *The Trident*, V, No. 1 (January-February, 1941), 38.

85 V. V. Kuibyshev, *Vtoroi piatiletnyi plan. Doklad na XVII s'ezde VKP(b) 3-4 fevralia 1934* (Moscow: Partyizdat, 1934), p. 57.

86 *Ibid.*, pp. 57-8.

87 USSR. Gosplan. *Itogi vypolneniia vtorogo piatiletnego plana razvitiia narodnogo khoziaistva soiuza SSR* (Moscow: Gosplanizdat, 1939), pp. 141-3. Note the discrepancy between these figures and those adopted from Sciborsky, and cited *supra*, p. 204.

88 The quality of Ukrainian coal as well as the proximity to other industrial centers (Moscow, Leningrad, Stalingrad, Gorky, Kuibyshev, Ufa, Chkalov), made the Donbass a very, very vital base. Although in the Ural industrial centers the coal from the Karaganda region could be utilized due to the latter's proximity, the Karaganda region was as yet undeveloped fully and, in addition, it had "to meet the demands of the rail and the industrial centers of Kazakhstan and Central Asia and the growing metallurgical base of Magnitogorsk, . . . and secondly, as a result of the incorrect building of the rail connections between Karaganda and the industrial regions of the Bashkir Republic (a costly roundabout route through Chelyabinsk), the cost of transporting Karaganda coal was too great to be practical." Stephen Protsiuk, "Ukrainian Donbass at the Close of the Fourth Five Year Plan," *The Ukrainian Quarterly*, VI, No. 3 (Summer, 1950), 222; Khromov, *Promyslovist' Ukrainy*, p. 51.

89 Mykola Sciborsky, "Ukraine in Figures," *The Trident*, IV, No. 10 (December, 1940), 30-1.

90 USSR. Gosplan. *Tretii piatiletnyi plan razvitiia narodnogo khoziaistva soiuza SSR (1938-1942 gg.)* (Moscow: Gosplanizdat, 1939), pp. 211-2.

91 *Ibid.*, pp. 160-1.

92 *Pravda*, May 12, 1940, p. 1. (Editorial.)

93 *Partrobitnyk Ukrainy*, No. 9 (September, 1946), p. 34; S. Chervonenko, *Ukraina do Zhovtnevoi Revolutsii i v Roky Radianskoi Vlady* (Kiev: Derzhavne Vydavnytstvo Ukrainy, 1951), pp. 31-2; Khromov, *Promyslovist' Ukrainy*, pp. 41-4; Virnyk, *Ekonomichnyj Rozkvit*, p. 87; Belousov, *op. cit.*, p. 29.

94 USSR. Embassy (London). *The Sixteen Soviet Republics* (London: Embassy Press, 1945), p. 6.

95 *Loc. cit.;* Chervonenko, *op. cit.*, p. 37; Belousov, *op. cit.*, p. 31; *Partrobitnyk Ukrainy*, No. 9 (September, 1946), p. 34.

96 USSR. Gosplan. *Gosudarstvennyi plan razvitiia narodnogo Khoziaistva SSSR no 1941 god (Prilozheniia k postanovleniiu SNK SSSR i TsK VKP(b) No. 127 ot 17 ianvaria 1941 g)* (Baltimore: University Press for the American Council of Learned Societies, n.d.), pp. 223-33, 251-70.

97 For an interesting account, see Stephen Protsiuk, "The Evacuation of Industry in 1941 and the Postwar Economy of Ukraine," *The Ukrainian Quarterly*, V, No. 3 (Summer, 1949), 210-18.

98 D. F. Virnyk, ed. *Narysy Rozvytku Narodnoho Hospodarstva URSR* (Kiev: Akademiia Nauk, 1949), p. 468; Belousov, *op. cit.*, p. 111.

99 See cf. *Narysy Rozvytku*, pp. 468, 471, and 476.

100 N. Voznesenskii, *Voennaia ekonomika SSSR v period otechestvennoi voiny* (Moscow: Gosizdat, 1948), pp. 33-63; M. Seredenko, *Vidbudova Promyslovosty Ukrainy* (Kiev: Derzhavne Vydavnytstvo Ukrainy, 1945), pp. 20-1; *Narysy Rozvytku*, pp. 492-4.

101 *Ibid.*, p. 471.

102 *Ibid.*, pp. 487-91; Khrushchev, *Osvobozhdenie ukrainskikh zemel*, p. 23; *Bolshaia Sovetskaia Entsiklopedia (1947) (SSSR)*, col. 1811. In his report to the London Conference of Foreign Ministers in 1947, Ukrainian representative I. S. Senin, placed the entire blame for the destruction of the Ukraine on the Germans. While the German share in this operation was great, they received considerable help from the Bolsheviks, who, in their retreat, when unable to evacuate equipment, etc., destroyed it. *Pravda*, February 13, 1947, p. 4.

103 *Narysy Rozvytku*, p. 506.

104 *Pravda*, March 6, 1946, p. 6; *Partrobitnyk Ukrainy*, No. 9 (September, 1946), p. 37; N. S. Khrushchev, *O piatiletnem plane vosstanovleniia i razvitiia narodnogo khoziaistva USSR na 1946-1950 gg. Rech na VIII Sessii verkhovnogo soveta ukrainskoi SSR 28 avgusta 1946 g.* (Kiev: Ukrainskoe Izdatelstvo Politicheskoi Literatury, 1946), p. 6.

105 *Ibid.*, p. 10.

106 John Fisher, *Why They Behave Like Russians* (New York: Harper, 1947), p. 11.

107 "Soobshcheniie gosudarstvennogo planovogo komiteta SSSR i tsentralnogo upravleniia SSSR ob itogakh vypolneniia chetvertogo (pervogo poslevoennogo) piatiletnogo plana SSSR na 1946-1950 gody," *Voprosy Ekonomiki*, No. 5 (May, 1951), pp. 3-4.

Chapter VIII: FEDERAL TIES

1 The government was organized at the end of November, 1918, in Sudja (Kursk). On November 29, 1918, it issued a Manifesto announcing the overthrow of the rule of Hetman Skoropadsky and proclaiming the establishment of Soviet rule in the Ukraine. In December, 1918, it appealed for revolt in the Ukraine. Stalin, *Works*, IV, 177-80, 436.

2 There is unanimous agreement among Soviet legal writers on the influence of the Constitution of the RSFSR on the constitutions of the other Union Republics. "The Constitution of the RSFSR of 1918 was the example for the constitutions of the other soviet socialist republics both within and outside the RSFSR. Its fundamental principles . . . entered into the constitutions of brotherly soviet republics (Ukrainian, Belorussian, Azerbaidzhanian, Armenian, and Georgian) . . ." A. I. Denisov and M.G. Kirichenko, *Osnovy sovetskogo gosudarstva i prava* (Moscow: Gosudarstvennoe Uchebnopedagogicheskoe Izdatelstvo Ministerstva Prosveshcheniia RSFSR, 1950), pp. 46-7; A. I. Denisov, *Sovetskoe gosudarstvennoe pravo* (Moscow: Iuridicheskoe Izdatelstvo Ministerstva Iustitsii SSSR, 1947), p. 147; *Osnovy sovetskogo gosudarstva i prava* (Moscow: Iuridicheskoe Izdatelstvo Ministerstva Iustitsii SSSR, 1947), p. 102; Andrei Y. Vyshinsky, *The Law of the Soviet State*. Translated from the Russian by Hugh W. Babb. Introduction by John N. Hazard (New York: Macmillan, 1948), pp. 99-100; S. I. Iakubovskaia, *Ob'edinitelnoe dvizhenie za obrazovanie SSSR (1917-1922)* (Moscow: Gosudarstvennoe Izdatelstvo Politicheskoi Literatury, 1947), pp. 24-5.

3 For further discussion, see Denisov, *op. cit.*, pp. 209-10.

4 *Sobranie uzakonenii i rasporiazhenii rabochego i krest'ianskogo pravitelstva,* 1919, No. 21, Art. 264, as reproduced by Batsell, *op. cit.*, p. 244. See also Vyshinsky, *op. cit.*, pp. 253-4.

5 RSFSR. [Commissariat for Foreign Affairs.] *Sbornik deistvuiushchikh dogovorov, soglashenii i konventsii R.S.F.S.R. s inostrannymi gosudarstvami* (Peterburg: Gosizdat, 1922), I, No. 8, pp. 15-6. For a concise treatment, see Batsell, *op. cit.*, p. 240.

6 Denisov characterized the Russo-Ukrainian treaty of December 28, 1920 in these words: "It was a treaty on [the problem of] federal union in the form of a military and economic alliance, stressing independence and sovereignty of each contracting party, and establishing the fact that there were no obligations on the part of the UkSSR in view of its having previously belonged to the former Russian Empire." Denisov, *op. cit.*, p. 210. See also Iakubovskaia, *op. cit.*, p. 92.

7 *Sobranie uzakonenii i rasporiazhenii rabochego i krest'ianskogo pravitelstva,* 1919, No. 30, Art. 322, as reproduced by Batsell, *op. cit.*, p. 245; also Denisov, *op. cit.*, p. 208.

8 For the complete text of the protocol, see *Sbornik deistvuiushchikh dogovorov*, III, No. 74, pp. 1-3.

9 For some Soviet comments on the February 22, 1922 agreement, see Vyshinsky, *op. cit.*, pp. 261-2. Iakubovskaia made the following comment on this unifying action: "The delegation [of rights] to the delegation of the Russian Republic to represent and to protect the interests of all Soviet Republics at the Genoa

Conference was fully natural. The Russian Republic . . . had united and strengthened Soviet Republics in the process of unification. In the war years it had led the military union of Soviet Republics. Now it was to head the diplomatic union. The interests of all union republics toward foreign states dictated it." Iakubovskaia, *op. cit.*, pp. 154-5. See also Batsell, *op. cit.*, pp. 241-2.

10 RSFSR. [Commissariat for Justice.] *Sobranie uzakonenii i rasporiazhenii rabochego i krestianskogo pravitelstva*, August 1, 1923, No. 51, Article 508. See also the decree of May 9, 1923, in *ibid.*, No. 17, Article 219.

11 For Soviet treatment of the 1924 Constitution of the USSR, see Vyshinsky, *op. cit.*, pp. 104-12; Denisov, *op. cit.*, p. 154; Denisov and Kirichenko, *op. cit.*, p. 54; *Osnovy sovetskogo gosudarstva i prava*, p. 103. For treatment of the evolution of the federal union, see Batsell, *op. cit.*, pp. 270-99; also Julian Towster, *Political Power in the U.S.S.R., 1917-1947* (New York: Oxford University Press, 1948), pp. 102-6.

12 For an appraisal of constitutional changes in the UkSSR between 1925 and 1929, see Professor Palijenko, "Die neue Staatsverfassung der Räte-Ukraine," *Ost-Europa*, V. No. 11-2 (August-September, 1930), pp. 810-27; also Batsell, *op. cit.*, pp. 343-4.

13 Articles 14, 15, 25, 26, 27, and 45.

14 Articles 9, 10, 11, 37, 44, 51, 52, 67, and 68.

15 Articles 1, 9, 10, 21, 34, 37, 44, 45, 51, 52, 67, 68, and 70.

16 Articles 22, 24, 31, 33, 42, 44, 49, 51, 52, 54, 56, 58, 66, 77, and the annulment of 57 and 65.

17 See cf. N. P. Farberov, *O suverenitete soiuznikh respublik* (Moscow: "Pravda," 1946), pp. 12-3; Denisov and Kirichenko, *op. cit.*, pp. 94-6; Denisov, *op. cit.*, pp. 247-51; Vyshinsky, *op. cit.*, pp. 279-84; *Osnovy sovetskogo gosudarstva i prava*, pp. 136-42; V. Karpinsky, *The Social and State Structure of the U.S.S.R.* (Moscow: Foreign Languages Publishing House, 1952), pp. 70-6. For an authoritative treatment of the nature of Soviet federalism, see Vladimir Gsovski, *Soviet Civil Law* (Ann Arbor: University of Michigan Law School, 1948), I, 81-91; also George C. Guins, *Soviet Law and Soviet Society* (The Hague: Martinus Nijhoff, 1954), pp. 213-25; Towster, *op. cit.*, pp. 83-7.

18 For further elaboration of the problem of the competence of the Union and of the Republics, see Vyshinsky, *op. cit.*, pp. 284-8; I. N. Ananov, *Systema organov gosudarstvennogo upravleniia v sovetskoi sotsialisticheskoi federatsii* (Moscow: Akademiia Nauk SSSR, 1951), pp. 114-21. Ananov argues that it makes no difference whether the competence of the Republics is increased or decreased, for the end result—the strengthening of the USSR—remains the same. See also Denisov, *op. cit.*, pp. 235-7.

19 According to Ananov, the *ukaz* of the Presidium of the Supreme Soviet of a union republic has no legal base for acts of the Council of Ministers of the USSR. Ananov, *op. cit.*, p. 150.

20 See cf. Vyshinsky, *op. cit.*, pp. 288-9; Farberov, *op. cit.*, p. 14; Denisov, *op. cit.*, pp. 234-7; Ananov, *op. cit.*, p. 155.

21 Vyshinsky, *op. cit.*, p. 284; Karpinsky, *op. cit.*, p. 72; *Osnovy sovetskogo gosudarstva i prava*, p. 139.

22 Vyshinsky, *op. cit.*, p. 285; Karpinsky, *op. cit.*, p. 72; *Osnovy sovetskogo gosudarstva i prava*, p. 139; Farberov, *op. cit.*, pp. 15-6. Speaking at the VIII Extraordinary All-Union Congress of Soviets on November 25, 1936, Stalin expressed himself on the problem of "withdrawal" from the Union in these words: "To exclude from the Constitution the article on the right of free withdrawal from the USSR means to violate the free character of that union. Can we take that step? I think that we cannot and should not take such a step. They say that in the USSR there is not one republic which would like to withdraw from the USSR and as a result Article 17 has no practical significance. That we do not have any republic which would like to withdraw from the USSR is, of course, true. But this does not at all mean that we should not include in the Constitution the right of union republics to a free withdrawal from the USSR." I. V. Stalin, "O proekte konstitutsii Soiuza SSR," *Bolshevik*, No. 23 (December 1, 1936), p. 16.

23 Vyshinsky, *op. cit.*, p. 284; Karpinsky, *op. cit.*, p. 73; Farberov, *op. cit.*, pp. 16-7.

24 See cf. Ananov, *op. cit.*, p. 208; Farberov, *op. cit.*, pp. 17-23; Denisov, *op. cit.*, p. 236; Karpinsky, *op. cit.*, pp. 73-4; *Osnovy sovetskogo gosudarstva i prava*, p. 139. For Molotov's report, on February 1, 1944, on constitutional changes, to the X Session of the Supreme Soviet of the USSR, see V. M. Molotov, "O preobrazovanii Narkomata Oborony i Narkomindela iz obshchesoiuznykh v soiuzno-respublikanskie narkomaty," *Bolshevik*, No. 2 (January, 1944), pp. 8-9.

25 Ananov, *op. cit.*, p. 209; Farberov, *op. cit.*, pp. 17-23; Karpinsky, *op. cit.*, p. 74; Molotov, *op. cit.*, pp. 9-11; Denisov, *op. cit.*, p. 236; *Osnovy sovetskogo gosudarstva i prava*, p. 139.

26 V. P. Potemkin, ed. *Istoriia diplomatii* (Moscow: Gosizdat, 1945), III, 803-4.

Chapter IX: COMPOSITION OF THE COMMUNIST PARTY OF THE UKRAINE

1 See *supra*, pp. 28-9.

2 Shapoval, *Sotsiografia Ukrainy*, I, 77.

3 *Ezhegodnik kominterna*, p. 477. The reported figure for the entire Communist Party was 40,000 in April, 1917; 313,766 in March, 1919; and 611,978 in March, 1920. *Ibid.*, p. 414.

4 Lenin, *Sochineniia*, XXIX, 64-5.

5 Sadovskyj, *op. cit.*, p. 71.

6 For a discussion, see *supra*, pp. 52-5.

7 Skrypnyk, *Stati i Promovy*, II, 12.

8 Solovei, *op. cit.*, I, 32.

9 *Ezhegodnik kominterna*, p. 418. For the entire Soviet controlled area, Communist strength in 1921 was reported to be 730,051. *Ibid.*, p. 414.

10 Mykola Skrypnyk, *Neprymyrenym Shliakhom* (Kharkov: Derzhavne Vydavnytstvo Ukrainy, 1929), p. 40.

11 *Ezhegodnik kominterna,* p. 418. This source declared that overall Communist Party membership, as a result of the purge, dropped from 725,077 to 549,511. *Loc. cit.* Another source reported that drop to have been from 658,839 to 499,484. RCP(b). [Central Committee.] *Izvestiia tsentralnogo komiteta rossiiskoi kommunisticheskoi partii (bolshevikov),* No. 4 (40), March, 1922, pp. 20 ff. Hereinafter cited as *Izvestiia CC RCP(b).* Soviet statistics in general, and those pertaining to the Party in particular, leave much to be desired. They are usually incomplete, and the accuracy of some figures, especially in the percentage breakdowns, is questionable. It will be noted that official statistics often contradict each other. The more serious of these defects are pointed out in the text.

12 CP(b)U. [Commission on the Study of the History of the October Revolution.] *Oktiabrskaia revolutsiia. Pervoe piatiletie* (Kharkov: Gosudarstvennoe Izdatelstvo Ukrainy, 1922), p. 129.

13 See especially Bukharin's comments at the Third Congress of the Comintern in 1921. Bukharin, *op. cit.,* p. 56.

14 Skrypnyk, *Stati i Promovy,* II, 12.

15 *Izvestiia CC RCP(b),* January, 1923, p. 44; Ravich-Cherkasskii, *op. cit.,* pp. 239-42; *Nova Ukraina,* No. 7-8 (July-August, 1923), pp. 289-90. In March, 1922, the overall strength of the Communist Party was said to be 485,909. *Ezhegodnik kominterna,* p. 414.

16 For a different set of figures on this distribution, see *loc. cit.*

17 *Izvestiia CC RCP(b),* January, 1923, p. 44.

18 As reported by Ravich-Cherkasskii, *op. cit.,* pp. 241-2; see also *Oktiabrskaia revolutsiia,* pp. 167-83.

19 *Visti,* No. 77 (1923), as quoted in *Nova Ukraina,* No. 7-8 (July-August, 1923), p. 262.

20 VKP(b). [Central Committee.] *Izvestiia tsentralnogo komiteta vsesoiuznoi kommunisticheskoi partii (bolshevikov),* No. 8 (83), February 23, 1925, p. 8. Hereinafter cited as *Izvestiia CC VKP(b).* On the All-Union scale, the increase was from 485,909 in 1922 to 735,881 in 1924.

21 *Izvestiia CC RCP(b),* No. 9 (14), December 1, 1924, p. 5.

22 *Loc. cit.*

23 *Izvestiia CC VKP(b),* No. 9 (84), March 2, 1925, p. 12.

24 *Izvestiia CC RCP(b),* No. 9 (14), December 1, 1924, p. 5.

25 Khvylia, *op. cit.,* p. 54.

26 For a full account of the activities of the Ukrainian Communist Party and its absorption by the CP(b)U, see M. Halahan, "Likvidatsiia U.K.P.," *Nova Ukraina,* IV, No. 1 (May, 1925), 26-38.

27 *Izvestiia CC VKP(b),* No. 9 (180), March 8, 1926, p. 6.

28 *Loc. cit.*

29 *Ibid.,* No. 13-4 (88-9), April 6, 1925, p. 16, and No. 14-5 (187-8), April 21, 1927, p. 12. Total membership for the entire USSR was about 1,130,000.

30 *Natsionalna politika VKP(b) v tsifrakh,* pp. 137-8.

31 *Ibid.,* p. 148.

32 *Izvestiia CC VKP(b),* No. 19 (240), June 20, 1928, p. 28.

33 *Ibid.,* No. 6-7 (227-8), March 5, 1928, p. 16. In 1929 total membership for the USSR was 1,551,238 members, of whom 73.4% had been admitted after 1923. It has been reported that as early as 1917, the industrial areas of the Ukraine accounted for 67% of the total membership of the CP(b)U. See cf. Suprunenko, *op. cit.,* p. 24.

34 *Izvestiia CC RCP(b),* No. 1 (49), January, 1923, p. 44.

35 *Izvestiia CC VKP(b),* No. 6-7 (227-8), March 5, 1928, p. 16.

36 *Natsionalna politika VKP(b) v tsifrakh,* pp. 144-5.

37 V. Chubar, *Do Novykh Peremoh* (Kharkov: "Proletarii," 1930), p. 15.

38 Savelev and Poskrebyshev, *op. cit.,* p. 631.

39 *Izvestiia CC VKP(b),* No. 10 (269), April 12, 1929, p. 28. For the entire USSR, membership was 1,551,238.

40 *Natsionalna politika VKP(b) v tsifrakh,* pp. 144-5.

41 *Loc. cit.*

42 *Loc. cit.*

43 *Pravda,* October 30, 1929, p. 3. See also S. Kats and S. Horskii, "Vyrobni Oseredky KP(b)U v Svitli Chystky," *Bilshovyk Ukrainy,* No. 8 (April, 1930), p. 58.

44 *Loc. cit.*

45 *Ibid.,* p. 59.

46 S. Kats and S. Horskii, "Osnovni Pidsumky Chystky Silpartorganizatsii KP(b)U i Nashi Zavdannia," *Bilshovyk Ukrainy,* No. 5-6 (March, 1930), p. 87.

47 *Loc. cit.*

48 *Ibid.,* p. 88.

49 Postyshev and Kosior, *op. cit.,* p. 10.

50 *Ibid.,* pp. 11-2.

51 Kosior, *Statti i Promovy,* 1933-1936, p. 57.

52 Postyshev and Kosior, *op. cit.,* pp. 10-3.

53 *Pravda,* January 24, 1934, p. 4. Total Party strength in 1934 was 1,874,488.

54 *Loc. cit.*

55 *Loc. cit.*

56 Ibid., June 16, 1938, p. 3. At the XVIII Congress of the VKP(b) in March, 1939, Stalin said that the overall drop in membership between 1934 and 1939 was over 270,000. *Bolshevik,* No. 5-6 (March, 1939), pp. 28-9. The actual drop in membership was from 1,874,488 to 1,588,852.

57 *Pravda,* June 16, 1938, p. 3.

58 *Loc. cit.*

59 *Ibid.,* May 18, 1940, p. 4.

60 *Loc. cit.*

61 *Ibid.,* May 16, 1940, p. 2.

62 *Ibid.,* August 23, 1946, p. 2.

63 *Loc. cit.*

64 *Loc. cit.*

65 *Ibid.,* September 17, 1947, p. 3.

66 Z. Serdiuk, "Bilshovyky Kyivshchyny v Borot'bi za Vidbudovu i Pidnesennia Silskoho Hospodarstva," *Partrobitnyk Ukrainy,* No. 7 (July, 1946), pp. 57-8.

67 *XVI Z'izd Komunistychnoi Partii,* p. 47.

68 *Ibid.,* pp. 46-7.

69 *Loc. cit.*

70 *Loc. cit.*

71 *Ibid.,* pp. 110-1.

72 *Ibid.,* p. 111.

73 The total strength of the CPSU at that time was 6,882,145 (6,013,259 members and 868,886 candidates. *Pravda,* October 6, 1952, p. 7.

74 *Pravda Ukrainy,* September 24, 1952, as reproduced in *CDSP,* IV, No. 41 (November 22, 1952), 24.

75 B. Levitskyj, "Komunistychna partiia Ukrainy—1955 rik," *Ukrainskyj Zbirnyk,* Bk. 3 (1955), p. 111.

Bibliography

The preparation of a bibliography on the problem of the Russian Bolshevik nationality policy and the developments within the Ukraine from 1918 to 1953 is a very complicated task. The difficulty is twofold. On the one hand there is a distinct absence of source material because the archival records have never been published or made accessible to the researcher. The sources which are available have been carefully selected and officially approved. Since 1933 this limited and irregularly issued material has been greatly reduced, in volume as well as in content, and only those items which emphasize monolithism and denounce heterogeneity in the nationality policy have appeared.

The second difficulty in the preparation of such a bibliography is the dispersal of the available material throughout various libraries in this country and abroad, a factor which makes it very difficult for the researcher to investigate thoroughly the content of that material. Until quite recently no attempts had been made to locate or to compile this scattered and half-forgotten evidence. Though it does not include the economic side of the national problem, Lawrynenko's *Ukrainian Communism and Soviet Russian Policy Toward the Ukraine. An Annotated Bibliography, 1917-1953,* represents an outstanding contribution to historiography, and serves as an indispensable tool in investigating the national problem in the Ukraine.

To the extent that it has been possible, this study is based on the available documentary evidence, chiefly on the major resolutions of the Congresses of the CP(b)U, the RCP(b), and the VKP(b); Party Conferences; Plenums of the Central Committees; governments' decrees; and declarations of responsible Party and government spokesmen. Of great value were the stenographic reports of various government and Party proceedings, especially those of the VIII, X, and the XII Congresses of the RCP(b); XV and XVI Congresses of the VKP(b); the I Congress of the CP(b)U; and the V Congress of the Comintern. At all of these sessions, the national problem in gen-

287

eral, and the Ukrainian problem in particular, received considerable attention during the debates and in the resolutions which were adopted. These debates provide a vivid revelation of the struggle between the centripetal and the centrifugal forces inside the USSR.

Because the November, 1933 Plenum of the CC of the CP(b)U inaugurated a new period in the history of the Russian Bolshevik nationality policy in the Ukraine—a period which, with some modification, is still in effect—the speeches and resolutions of that Plenum are very important. They have been reported verbatim in *Pravda*. An English translation of the two key speeches and of a resolution was published in 1934 under the title *Soviet Ukraine Today*, with the names of Postyshev and Kosior appearing as the authors.

In the preparation of this study, extensive use was made of Lenin's *Sochineniia*, 4th edition. However, since there has been a strong tendency to "doctor" Lenin's writings to fit the changing Party line, Lenin's treatment of the national problem, as presented in the latest edition of his works, was checked against earlier editions, and in particular with that recorded in *Leninskii Sbornik*. A similar problem was encountered in the use of Stalin's *Sochineniia*, and *Works*. In cases where conflicts or omissions were found, the original version was cited.

An indispensable source in the preparation of this study was Skrypnyk's *Stati i Promovy*, a compilation of the most important declarations of Skrypnyk, many of which were adopted verbatim as Party resolutions. An important source, though of lesser value because it lacks an inner understanding of the Ukrainian national problem, was Kosior's *Statti i Promovy, 1933-1936*. A like description characterizes the numerous speeches on the Ukrainian problem by Postyshev and Khrushchev. Their significance and value lies only in the fact that, as principal spokesmen of the CP(b)U, these men expressed the then prevailing official policy.

Of immense help in understanding the role of the Ukrainian economy in the post-revolutionary reconstruction and in the projected Five Year Plans was *Puti narodno-khoziaistvennogo razvitiia USSR*. Published by the Ukrainian State Planning Commission in 1928, this survey of Ukrainian economic potentials by outstanding authorities was fully incorporated into *Piatiletnyi plan narodno-khoziaistvennogo stroitelstva SSSR*.

Because of the scarcity, obscurity and inaccessibility of source material, as well as for political and other reasons, the problem of the

Russian Bolshevik nationality policy in the Ukraine has not received adequate attention from students of the Soviet Union. Such treatments as have been written are basically incomplete, inadequately documented and one-sided—either violently anti- or extremely pro-Ukrainian. In English, Manning's *Ukraine Under the Soviets* is perhaps the most up-to-date treatment of the Ukrainian problem in the Soviet Union. However, Manning's work, aside from not being documented, deals primarily with the cultural side of the problem. In the Ukrainian language, and expressing the official post-World War II Bolshevik interpretation of the Ukrainian problem, is Belousov's *Vozz'ednannia Ukrainskoho Narodu v Edynij Ukrainskij Radianskij Derzhavi.* Among other inadequacies, this work stresses only the monolithic aspect of the national problem, and accordingly credits Stalin with all achievements and denounces all persons and forces who in any way protested Stalin's machinations.

Since the bulk of available material covers the period before 1933, there are several important monographs dealing with the Russian Bolshevik nationality policy in the Ukraine before that time. On the Ukrainian side, perhaps the most outstanding in its interpretation and in its treatment is Sadovskyj's *Natsionalna Polityka Sovitiv na Ukraini.* The main weakness of this well-documented study is the fact that it limits itself to the political side of the national problem. Other valuable treatments of this earlier period, amply documented, but somewhat tinged with emotionalism, are Solovei's *Holhota Ukrainy,* and Kovalevskyj's *Ukraina Pid Chervonym Iarmom.*

On the Bolshevik side, the national problem in the Ukraine prior to 1933 is perhaps best presented in Girchak's *Na dva fronta v borbe s natsionalizmom.* The principal value of this work lies in the wealth of its documents and numerous quotations which, since 1933, have become unorthodox. Khvylia's *Natsionalnyi vopros na Ukraine,* though covering a shorter period, has a similar value.

In addition to these treatments of the earlier period of the Bolshevik nationality policy in the Ukraine, there are several important monographs on specific aspects of the problem. The educational and cultural policy of the Bolsheviks up to 1933 is well presented and documented in Siropolko's *Narodna Osvita na Sovetskij Ukraini.* Its statistics and charts are of great value. The history of the CP(b)U up to 1923, based on the theory that it was the outgrowth of both the Ukrainian and Russian Social Democratic movements—a theory which

was later condemned—is ably depicted in Ravich-Cherkasskii's *Istoriia
kommunisticheskoi partii (b-ov) Ukrainy*. Like most of the early Bolshevik treatments, the value of this work lies in the numerous documents it contains—documents which have since become "lost." The
tragedy of the *Borot'bisty* is very admirably treated by one of its former
members, in Majstrenko's *Borot'bism. A Chapter in the History of
Ukrainian Communism*. In addition to its generous documentation,
it provides useful biographical sketches of many *Borot'bisty*. Khvylovism, which which is considered by many Ukrainians as one of the most
significant expressions of Ukrainian resistance to Moscow, and considered by Moscow as one of the most dangerous, has received a re-
appraisal in Pliushch's *Pravda Pro Khvylovyzm*, which asserts that
Khvylovyj's goal was international Communism—not Ukrainian nationalism. The role of Ukrainian economy in that of the USSR, and
its effect on the nationality policy before the Second Five Year Plan,
has been ably and critically outlined by Glovinskyj, *et al.,* in *Suchasni
Problemy Ekonomiky Ukrainy*. Particularly valuable is the analogy it
draws between pre- and post-revolutionary economic policies and practices. Among the monographs dealing with the period since 1933, the
most outstanding, well-documented, and devoid of emotionalism, is
Holub's *Ukraina v Ob'ednanykh Natsiiakh,* in which the author treats
the UkSSR as one of Moscow's satellites rather than an integral part
of the USSR.

Most of the secondary accounts of the Russian Bolshevik nationality policy in the Ukraine have appeared in article form, some of which
treat the entire period, while others deal only with specific aspects of
that policy. The most outstanding among the former is perhaps Reshetar's "National Deviation in the Soviet Union." Another interesting
presentation is contained in Pap's "Soviet Difficulties in the Ukraine,"
wherein he argues that the tactics and the aims of Great Russian imperialism and Russian Bolshevik imperialism in the Ukraine bear a
striking resemblance.

The following selected bibliography includes only the most important and indispensable works for a study of Russian Bolshevik nationality policy in the Ukraine. It has been thought advisable to divide this
material into three general sections: I. *Sources,* which includes A)
Official Party and Government publications, and B) Speeches of responsible Party and Government spokesmen; II. *Secondary Accounts,*
which includes works that treat the problem either directly or indi-

rectly; and III. *Articles,* which emphasizes particular aspects of the problem.

Though not listed in the bibliography, extensive use was made of several Ukrainian and Russian newspapers and periodicals. Of particular value were *Pravda* (Moscow), *Izvestiia* (Moscow), *Bolshevik* (Moscow), and *Nova Ukraina* (Prague).

I. Sources

Bolshaia Sovetskaia Entsiklopediia. Soiuz Sovetskikh Sotsialisticheskikh Respublik. Moscow: Gosudarstvennyi Nauchnyi Instytut "Sovetskaia Entsiklopediia," 1948.

Comintern. *Ezhegodnik kominterna. Spravochnaia kniga po istorii mezhdunarodnogo rabochego, politicheskogo i professionalnogo dvizheniia, statistike i ekonomike vsekh stran mira na 1923 god.* Petrograd-Moscow: Kommunisticheskii Internatsional, 1923. 1047 pp.

——[Congress.] *Piatyi vsemirnyi kongress kommunisticheskogo internatsionala 17 iunia—8 iulia 1924 g. Stenograficheskii otchet.* Moscow: Gosizdat, 1925. 2 vols.

——*VI kongress kominterna. Mezhdunarodnoe polozhenie i zadachi kominterna. Stenograficheskii otchet.* Moscow: Gosizdat, 1929. vol. I.

——[Enlarged Executive.] *Erweiterte Exekutive der Kommunistischen Internationale Moskau, 17 Februar bis 15 März 1926. Protokoll.* Berlin: Carl Hoym Verlag, 1926. 672 pp.

CP(b)U. [Commission on the Study of the History of the October Revolution.] *Oktiabrskaia revolutsiia. Pervoe piatiletie.* Kharkov: Gosudarstvennoe Izdatelstvo Ukrainy, 1923. 663 pp.

——[Congress.] *Pervyi s'ezd kommunisticheskoi partii (bolshevikov) Ukrainy 5-12 iulia 1918 goda. K piatiletnomu iubileiu 1918-1923. Stati i protokoly s'ezda.* Kharkov: Gosudarstvennoe Izdatelstvo Ukrainy, 1923. 184 pp.

——*XVI Z'izd Komunistychnoi Partii (bilshovykiv) Ukrainy 25-28 Sichnia 1949 r. Materialy Z'izdu.* Kiev: Derzhavne Vydavnytstvo Politychnoi Literatury URSR, 1949, 255 pp.

CPSU. *Kommunisticheskaia partiia sovetskogo soiuza v rezolutsiiakh i resheniiakh s'ezdov, konferentsii i plenumov TsK, 1898-1953.* Moscow: Gosudarstvennoe Izdatelstvo Politicheskoi Literatury, 1953. vol. I.

Chubar, V[las] Ya. *Sovetskaia Ukraina.* Kharkov: "Proletarii," 1925. 55 pp.

Germany. Foreign Office. *Documents on German Foreign Policy, 1918-1945. Series D. (1937-1945). The Aftermath of Munich, October, 1938-March, 1939.* Washington: Government Printing Office, 1949-1951. vol. IV.

Khruschchev, N[ikita] S. *Najblyzhchi Zavdannia Pratsivnykiv Silskoho Hospodarstva Ukrainy.* Kiev: Derzhavne Vydavnytstvo Ukrainy, 1945. 27 pp.

———*O piatiletnem plane vosstanovleniia i razvitiia narodnogo khoziaistva USSR na 1946-1950 gg.* Kiev: Ukrainskoe Izdatelstvo Politicheskoi Literatury, 1946. 24 pp.

———*Osvobozhdenie ukrainskikh zemel ot nemetskikh zakhvatchikov i ocherednye zadachi vosstanovleniia narodnogo khoziaistva Sovetskoi Ukrainy.* Moscow: Gospolitzdat, 1944. 40 pp.

Kosior, S[tanislav] V. "Chotyry Roky Borot'by za Sotsializm ta Zavdannia Radianskoi Ukrainy," *Radianska Ukraina,* No. 2 (February, 1935), pp. 13-20.

———*Itogi noiabr'skogo plenuma TsK VKP(b) i zadachi kulturnogo stroitelstva na Ukraine.* Kharkov: Gosudastvennoe Izdatelstvo Ukrainy, 1929. 60 pp.

———*Konstitutsiia torzhestvuiushchego sotsializma.* Moscow: Partyzdat, 1936. 14 pp.

———*Statti i Promovy, 1933-1936.* Kiev: Partvydav, 1936. 511 pp.

Kuibyshev, V[alerian] V. *Vtoroi piatiletnyı plan. Doklad na XVII s'ezde VKP(b) 3-4 fevralia, 1934 g.* Moscow: Partyzdat, 1934. 64 pp.

Lenin, V[ladimir] I. *Leninskii sbornik.* Edited by L. B. Kamenev. Moscow-Leningrad: Institut Lenina pri TsK RCP(b), 1924-1940. 34 vols.

———*Sochineniia.* 4th ed. Moscow: Gosudarstvennoe Izdatelstvo Politcheskoi Literatury, 1941-1949. 35 vols.

Lenin i Stalin. *O borbe za ustanovlenie sovetskoi vlasti na Ukraine. Sbornik statei i dokumentov.* Kiev: Partyzdat, 1938. 94 pp.

Liubchenko, P[anas] P. "O proekte konstitutsii USSR," *Revolutsiia i Natsionalnosti*, No. 3 (March, 1937), pp. 30-7.

———*Stalinskaia konstitutsiia i sovetskaia Ukraina.* Moscow: Partyzdat, 1936, 29 pp.

Postyshev, P[avel] P. "Mobilizuemo Masy na Svoechasnu Postavku Zerna Derzhavi," *Hospodarstvo Ukrainy*, No. 5-6 (May-June, 1933), pp. 3-14.

———"Podniat rabotu marksistko-leninskikh nauchnykh institutov Ukrainy na uroven trebovanii nashei velikoi sotsialisticheskoi stroiki," *Bolshevik*, No. 3-4 (February, 1934), pp. 10-8.

———*Sovetskaia Ukraina na poroge 1936 goda.* Moscow: Partyzdat, 1936. 62 pp.

———*Tsvetet i krepnet industrialno-kolkhoznaia Ukraina.* Moscow: Partyzdat, 1935. 31 pp.

Postyshev, P. P. and S. V. Kosior. *Soviet Ukraine Today.* New York: International Publishers, 1934. 116 pp.

RCP(b). [Congress.] *VIII s'ezd rossiiskoi kommunisticheskoi partii (bolshevikov). Stenograficheskii otchet.* Saratov: Sovgrafiia, 1919. 163 pp.

———*X s'ezd rossiiskoi kommunisticheskoi partii (bolshevikov) 8-16 marta 1921 g. Stenograficheskii otchet.* Peterburg: Gosizdat, 1921. 203 pp.

———*XII s'ezd rossiiskoi kommunisticheskoi partii (bolshevikov), 17-25 aprelia 1923 g. Stenograficheskii otchet.* Moscow: Gosizdat, 1923. 705 pp.

———[Central Committee.] *Izvestiia tsentralnogo komiteta rossiiskoi kommunisticheskoi partii (bolshevikov).* Moscow: Izdatelskoe Otdelenie TsK RKP, 1922-1925.

RSFSR. [Commissariat for Foreign Affairs.] *Sbornik deistvuiushchikh dogovorov, soglashenii i konventsii RSFSR s inostrannymi gosudarstvami.* Peterburg: Gosizdat, 1922. 3 vols.

———[Commissariat for Justice.] *Sobranie uzakonenii i rasporiazhenii rabochego i krestianskogo pravitelstva RSFSR.* Moscow: Gosudarstvennoe Izdatelstvo, 1918-1923.

Savelev, M[aksimilian] A., and A. Poskrebyshev, eds. *Direktyvy VKP(b) po khoziaistvennym voprosam.* Moscow-Lenningrad: Gosizdat, 1931. 878 pp.

Skrypnyk, Mykola A. *Dzherela ta Prychyny Rozlamu v KPZU.* Kharkov: Derzhavne Vydavnytstvo Ukrainy, 1928. 150 pp.

———*Stati i Promovy.* Kharkov: Derzhavne Vydavnytstvo Ukrainy, 1930. 2 vols.

Stalin, I[osif] V. *Sochineniia.* Moscow: Gosudarstvennoe Izdatelstvo Politicheskoi Literatury, 1946-1953. 13 vols.

———*Voprosy Leninizma.* 10th ed. Moscow: Gosizdat, 1936. 655 pp.

———*Works.* Moscow: Foreign Languages Publishing House, 1948-1954. 9 vols.

VKP(b). [Central Committee.] *Izvestiia tsentralnogo komiteta vsesoiuznoi kommunisticheskoi partii (bolshevikov).* Moscow: Gosudarstvennoe Izdatelstvo, 1925-1929.

———[Congress.] *XV s'ezd vsesoiuznoi kommunisticheskoi partii (bolshevikov). Stenograficheskii otchet.* Moscow: Gosizdat, 1928. 1416 pp.

———*XVI s'ezd vsesoiuznoi kommunisticheskoi partii (bolshevikov). Stenograficheskii otchet.* Moscow: Gosizdat, 1930, 781 pp.

UkSSR. [Administration of Economic Outlook.] *Sotsialistychna Ukraina. Statystychnyj Zbirnyk.* Kiev: Derzhavne Vydavnytstvo Ukrainy, 1937. 238 pp.

———[Central Executive Committee.] *IX-j Vseukrainskyj Z'izd Rad Robitnychykh, Selianskykh ta Chervonoarmijskykh Deputativ. (Stenografichnyj Zvit).* Kharkov: Orgviddil VUTsVK, 1925. 413 pp.

———[Commissariat for Education.] *Pratsı Pershoho Z'izdu Doslidzhennia Produktsijnykh Syl ta Narodnoho Hospodarstva Ukrainy. Heolohiia.* Kharkov: Derzhavne Vydavnytstvo Ukrainy, 1926. vol. I.

———[Commissariat for Foreign Trade.] *Sbornik statei po voprosam vneshnei torgovli i ekonomiki, 7 noiabria 1917 g.-7 noiabria 1922 g.* Kharkov: Statistiko-ekonomichnyi Otdel Ukrvneshtorga, 1922. 171 pp.

———Gosplan. *Lehka Promyslovist Ukrainy Druhoi Piatyrichky.* Kharkov: "Hospodarstvo Ukrainy," 1932. 76 pp.

———*Materialy po raionirovaniiu Ukrainy.* Kharkov: Gosudarstvennoe Izdatelstvo Ukrainy, 1923. 200 pp.

———*Puti narodno-khoziaistvennogo razvitiia USSR. Materialy k postroeniiu piatiletnego plana.* Kharkov: Ukrgosplan, 1928. 488 pp.

————[Statistical Department.] *Ukraina. Statystychnyj Spravochnyk.* Kharkov: Derzhavne Vydavnytstvo Ukrainy, 1925. 516 pp.

U.S. Department of State. *Papers Relating to the Foreign Relations of the United States, 1918. Russia.* Washington: Government Printing Office, 1931. 3 vols.

USSR. Embassy (London). *The Sixteen Soviet Republics.* London: Embassy Press, 1945. 63 pp.

————Gosplan. *Gosudarstvennyi plan razvitiia narodnogo khoziaistva SSSR na 1941 god (Prilozheniia k postanovleniiam SNK SSSR i TsK VKP(b) No. 127 ot 17 ianuaria 1941 g.)* Baltimore: University Press for the American Council of Learned Societies, n.d. 746 pp.

————*Itogi vypolneniia vtorogo piatiletnego plana razvitiia narodnogo khoziaistva soiuza SSR.* Moscow: Gosplanizdat, 1939. 175 pp.

————*Piatiletnyi plan narodno-khoziaistvennogo stroitelstva SSSR.* Moscow: "Planovoe Khoziaistvo," 1930. 3 vols.

————*Tretii piatiletnyi plan razvitiia narodnogo khoziaistva soiuza SSSR (1938-1942 gg).* Moscow: Gosplanizdat, 1939. 240 pp.

II. SECONDARY ACCOUNTS

Akademiia Nauk URSR. *Vistnyk Akademii Nauk Ukrainskoi Radianskoi Sotsialistychnoi Respubliky.* Kiev: Akademiia Nauk, 1950. vol. XXII.

————Instytut Ekonomiky. *Narysy Rozvytku Narodnoho Hospodarstva Ukrainskoi RSR.* Kiev: Akademiia Nauk, 1949. 577 pp.

————*Pytannia Sotsialistychnoho Hospodarstva.* Kiev: Akademiia Nauk, 1940. No. 1-2.

————*Radianska Ukraina za 20 Rokiv.* Kiev: Partvydav, 1937. 109 pp.

————Instytut Istorii. *Istoriia Ukrainy. Korotkyj Kurs.* Kiev: Akademiia Nauk, 1941. 411 pp.

————Instytut Istorii i Arkheolohii. *Naukovi Zapysky.* Ufa: Vydavnytstvo Akademii Nauk, 1943. Bk. 1.

Allen, W[illiam]. E. D. *The Ukraine. A History.* Cambridge: The University Press, 1940. 404 pp.

All-Ukrainian Society for Cultural Relations with Foreign Countries. *Ukraine. A Short Sketch of Economic, Cultural and Social Constructive Work of the Ukrainian Socialist Soviet Republic.* Kharkov: All-Ukrainian Society for Cultural Relations with Foreign Countries, 1929. 100 pp.

Armstrong, John A. *Ukrainian Nationalism, 1939-1945.* New York: Columbia University Press, 1955. 322 pp.

Batsell, Walter Russell. *Soviet Rule in Russia.* New York: Macmillan, 1929. 857 pp.

Belousov, S[emen]. M. *Vozz'ednannia Ukrainskoho Narodu v Edynij Ukrainskij Radianskij Derzhavi.* Kiev: Akademiia Nauk, 1951. 166 pp.

Boiko, I. D. *Velyki Sotsialistychni Peremohy Ukrainskoho Narodu.* Kiev: Ukrainske Vydavnytstvo Politychnoi Literatury, 1948. 41 pp.

————*Vozz'ednannia Ukrainskoho Narodu v Edynij Ukrainskij Radianskij Derzhavi.* Kharkov: Knyzhkovo-Zhurnalno-Hazetne Vydavnytstvo, 1945. 24 pp.

Bregy, Pierre, and Prince Serge Obolensky. *The Ukraine—A Russian Land.* Translated by George Knupffer. London: Selwyn & Blount, 1940. 260 pp.

Butsenko, A[fanasij]. *Desiat Vseukrainskykh Z'izdiv Rad.* Kharkov: Derzhavne Vydavnytstvo Ukrainy, 1927. 100 pp.

Chamberlin, William Henry. *The Russian Revolution, 1917-1921.* New York: Macmillan, 1935. 2 vols.

————*Soviet Rule in Russia. A Living Record and a History.* Boston: Little, Brown & Co., 1931. 453 pp.

————*The Ukraine. A Submerged Nation.* New York: Macmillan, 1944. 91 pp.

Chervonenko, S. *Ukraina do Zhovtnevoi Revolutsii i v Roky Radianskoi Vlady.* Kiev: Derzhpolitvydav URSR, 1951. 115 pp.

Chubar, V[las Ya.]. *Do Novykh Peremoh.* Kharkov: "Proletarii," 1930. 102 pp.

Doroshenko, Dmytro. *Istoriia Ukrainy, 1917-1923.* Uzhhorod: n.p., 1932. 2 vols.

Dotsenko, Oleksander. *Zymovyj Pokhid.* Warsaw: Pratsi Ukrainskoho Naukovoho Instytutu, 1932. 240 pp.

Farberov, N. P. *O suverenitete soiuznykh respublik.* Moscow: "Pravda," 1946. 22 pp.

Fisher John. *Why They Behave Like Russians*. New York: Harper, 1947. 262 pp.

Girchak, E[vgenii]. F. *Na dva fronta v borbe s natsionalizmom*. Moscow: Gosizdat, 1930. 227 pp.

Gladkov, I. A. *Ocherki stroitelstva sovetskogo planovogo khoziaistva v 1917-1918 gg*. Moscow: Gospolitzdat, 1950. 362 pp.

Glovinskyj, E[vhen]., K. Matsievych, and V. Sadovskyj. *Suchasni Problemy Ekonomiky Ukrainy*. Warsaw: Pratsi Ukrainskoho Naukovoho Instytutu, 1931. 159 pp.

Grinko, G. T. *The Five Year Plan of the Soviet Union. A Political Interpretation*. New York: International Publishers, 1930. 340 pp.

Gurian, Waldemar, ed. *Soviet Imperialism. Its Origins and Tactics. A Symposium*. Notre Dame: University Press, 1953. 166 pp.

Halij, Mykola, and Bohdan Novytskyj. *Het' Masku! Natsionalna Polityka na Radianskij Ukraini v Svitli Dokumentiv*. Prague: "Vsetecka," 1934. 128 pp.

Hirchak, E. F. *Natsionalne Pytannia ta Pravyj Ukhyl*. Kharkov: Derzhavne Vydavnytstvo Ukrainy, 1930. 158 pp.

————*Shumskyizm i Rozlam v KPZU*. Kharkov: Derzhavne Vydavnytstvo Ukrainy, 1927. 247 pp.

————*Zavdannia Natsionalno-kulturnoho Budivnytstva*. Kharkov: "Proletarii," 1929. 47 pp.

Holub, Vsevolod. *Ukraina v Ob'ednanykh Natsiiakh*. Munich: "Suchasna Ukraina," 1953. 82 pp.

Khromov, P. A. *Promyslovist Ukrainy Pered Vitchyznianoiu Vijnoiu*. Kiev: Ukrainske Derzhavne Vydavnytstvo, 1945. 93 pp.

Khrystiuk, Pavlo. *Zamitky i Materialy do Ukrainskoi Revolutsii, 1917-1920*. Vienna: Ukrainskyj Sotsiologichnyj Instytut, 1921. 4 vols.

Khvylia, A[ndrei]. *Natsionalnyi vopros na Ukraine*. Kharkov: Gosudarstvennoe Izdatelstvo Ukrainy, 1926. 128 pp.

Kommunisticheskaia Akademiia. [Commission on the Study of the National Problem.] *Natsionalna politika VKP(b) v tsifrakh*. Moscow: Kommunisticheskaia Akademiia, 1930. 328 pp.

Kostiuk, Hryhory. *The Fall of Postyshev*. New York: Research Program on the U.S.S.R., 1954. 25 pp. Mimeographed Series No. 69.

Kovalevskyj, Mykola. *Ukraina Pid Chervonym Iarmom. Dokumenty i Fakty*. Warsaw-Lvov: "Skhid," 1936. 204 pp.

Lawrynenko, Jurij. *Ukrainian Communism and Soviet Russian Policy Toward the Ukraine. An Annotated Bibliography, 1917-1953.* New York: Research Program on the U.S.S.R., 1953. 454 pp.

Lorimer, Frank. *The Population of the Soviet Union: History and Prospects.* Geneva: League of Nations, 1946. 289 pp.

Majstrenko, Iwan. *Borot'bism. A Chapter in the History of Ukrainian Communism.* New York: Research Program on the U.S.S.R., 1954. 325 pp.

Manning, Clarence A. *Twentieth-Century Ukraine.* New York: Bookman Associates, 1951. 243 pp.

————*Ukraine Under the Soviets.* New York: Bookman Associates, 1953. 223 pp.

Miliukov, P[avel]. N. *Natsionalnyi vopros (Proiskhozhdenie natsionalnosti i natsionalnye voprosy v Rossii).* Prague: "Svobodnaia Rossiia," 1925. 192 pp.

Mirchuk, I[van]. ed. *Ukraine and Its People: A Handbook with Maps, Statistical Tables and Diagrams.* Munich: Ukrainian Free University Press, 1949. 280 pp.

Mirchuk, Petro. *Ukrainska Povstanska Armiia, 1942-1952.* Munich: n.p., 1953. 319 pp.

Nykolyshyn, S. *Kulturna Polityka Bolshevykiv i Ukrainskyj Kulturnyj Protses.* Na Chuzhyni: n.p., 1947. 119 pp.

Olezhko, Nestor. *Ahrarna Polityka Bolshevykiv (Sproba Istorychnoho Analizu).* Munich: "Nasha Knyhozbirnia," 1947. 103 pp.

Pliushch, Vasyl. *Pravda Pro Khvylovyzm.* Munich: Spilka Vyzvolennia Ukrainy, 1954. 63 pp.

Polonska-Vasilenko, N. *Ukrainska Akademiia Nauk (Narys Istorii) (1918-1930).* Munich: Institute for the Study of the History and Culture of the USSR, 1955. Part I. 148 pp.

Ravich-Cherkasskii, M[oisei]. *Istoriia kommunisticheskoi partii (b-ov) Ukrainy.* Kharkov: Gosudarstvennoe Izdatelstvo Ukrainy, 1923. 248 pp.

Reshetar, John S. Jr. *The Ukrainian Revolution, 1917-1920. A Study in Nationalism.* Princeton: University Press, 1952. 363 pp.

Richytskyj, And[rij]. *Do Problemy Likvidatsii Perezhytkiv Kolonialnosty ta Natsionalizmu.* Kharkov: Derzhavne Vydavnytstvo Ukrainy, 1928. 99 pp.

Sadovskyj, V[alentyn]. *Natsionalna Polityka Sovitiv na Ukraini.* Warsaw: Pratsi Ukrainskoho Naukovoho Instytutu, 1937. 174 pp.

Seredenko, M. *Vidbudova Promyslovosty Ukrainy.* Kiev: Ukrainske Derzhavne Vydavnytstvo, 1945. 44 pp.

Siropolko, S[tepan]. *Narodna Osvita na Sovetskij Ukraini.* Warsaw: Pratsi Ukrainskoho Instytutu, 1934. 240 pp.

Shapoval, M[ykyta]. *Bolshevyzm i Ukraina.* Prague: "Vilna Spilka," 1926. 60 pp.

————*Sotsiografiia Ukrainy. Sotsialna Struktura Ukrainy.* Prague: "Vilna Spilka," 1933. 2 vols.

Skrypnyk, Mykola. *Neprymyrenym Shliakhom.* Kharkov: Derzhavne Vydavnytstvo Ukrainy, 1929. 88 pp.

Smal-Stocki, Roman. *The Nationality Problem of the Soviet Union.* Milwaukee: Bruce Publishing Co., 1952. 474 pp.

Solovei, Dmytro. *Holhota Ukrainy.* Winnipeg: "Ukrainskyj Holos," 1953. vol. I.

Spilka Vyzvolennia Ukrainy. Kharkov: Derzhavne Vydavnytstvo Ukrainy, 1930. 97 pp.

Timoshenko, Voldemar. *Ukraine and Russia. A Survey of Their Economic Relations.* Washington: Friends of Ukraine, 1919. 14 pp.

Vashchenko, H. *Ukrainskyj Renesans XX Stolittia.* Toronto: "Na Varti," 1953. 80 pp.

Virnyk, D. F. *Ekonomichnyj Rozkvit Ukrainskoi RSR—Torzhestvo Leninsko-Stalinskoi Natsionalnoi Polityky.* Kiev: Akademiia Nauk, 1951. 96 pp.

————*Kompleksnoe narodnokhoziaistvennoe ispolzovanie vodnykh resursov Donbassa.* Kiev: Akademiia Nauk, 1940. 253 pp.

Voznesenskii, N[icolai]. *Voennaia ekonomika SSSR v period otechestvennoi voiny.* Moscow: Gosizdat, 1948. 192 pp.

Vseukrainska Akademiia Nauk. Istorychno-Arkheohrafichnyj Instytut. *Zapysky Istorychno-Arkheohrafichnoho Instytutu.* Kiev: Vseukrainska Akademiia Nauk, 1934. No. 1.

Vyshinsky, Andrei Ya. *The Law of the Soviet State.* Introduction by John N. Hazard. New York: Macmillan, 1948. 749 pp.

Wheeler-Bennett, John W. *The Forgotten Peace: Brest-Litovsk, March, 1918.* New York: William Morrow & Co., 1939. 478 pp.

Zatonskyj, Vol[odymyr]. P. *Natsionalna Problema na Ukraini. Dopovid na Plenumi TsK LKSMU (May, 1926).* Kharkov: Derzhavne Vydavnytstvo Ukrainy, 1926. 64 pp.

————*Natsionalno-kulturnoe stroitelstvo i borba protiv natsionalizma.* Kharkov: "Ukrainskyj Robitnyk, 1934. 84 pp.

III. Articles

Bondarchuk, S. "Ukraina v planakh germanskogo imperializma," *Borba Klassov*, No. 12 (December, 1933), pp. 12-23.

Butsenko, A[fanasij]. "Natsionalnye menshinstva na Ukraine," *Sovetskoe Stroitelstvo*, No. 4 (April, 1928), pp. 89-93.

——"Rabota sredi natsmenshinstv na Ukraine," *ibid.*, No. 1 (January, 1927), pp. 79-85.

Czubatyj, N[icolaus]. D. "The Ukrainians and the Polish-Russian Border Dispute," *The Ukrainian Quarterly*, No. 1 (October, 1944), pp. 57-71.

Danylovych, K. "III s'ezd KPZU," *Kommunisticheskii Internatsional*, No. 48 (November, 1928), pp. 18-26.

Enukidze, A. "K voprosu o natsionalnykh iazykakh," *Sovetskoe Stroitelstvo*, No. 1 (August, 1926), pp. 39-53.

Halahan, M[ykola]. "Likvidatsiia U.K.P.," *Nova Ukraina*, IV, No. 1 (May, 1925), pp. 26-38.

Hrynko, H. "Zapadnyi upor SSSR," *Khoziaistvo Ukrainy*, No. 10 (October, 1925), pp. 3-8.

Kats, S., and S. Horskii. "Osnovni Pidsumky Chystky Silpartorhanizatsii KP(b)U i Nashi Zavdannia," *Bilshovyk Ukrainy*, No. 5-6 (March, 1930), pp. 84-96.

Katsenelenbogen, Mikh[ail]. "Ob 'uklonakh' v natsionalnoi politike VKP(b)," *Bolshevik*, No. 22 (November 30, 1927), pp. 19-31.

Kosmin, Ev[genii]. "Ukrainskie plany polskogo fashizma," *ibid.*, No. 23-4 (December 31, 1928), pp. 112-25.

Krinitski, A. "K voprosu o natsionalnoi kulture," *ibid.*, No. 9 (May 1, 1927), pp. 51-63.

Larin, Iu. "Ob izvrashcheniiakh pri provedenii natsionalnoi politiki," *ibid.*, No. 23-4 (December 31, 1926, pp. 50-8; No. 1 (January 1, 1927), pp. 59-69.

Lednicki, Waclaw, and N. S. Timasheff. "The Russo-Polish Dispute," *The Review of Politics*, VI, No. 2 (April, 1944), pp. 151-92.

Levin, I. "Natsionalnyi vopros v Evrope i ugroza voiny," *Sovetskoe Gosudarstvo*, No. 4 (1934), pp. 16-30.

Litvin, K. "Ob istorii Ukrainskogo naroda," *Bolshevik*, No. 7 (April, 1947), pp. 41-56.

Pap, Michael. "Soviet Difficulties in the Ukraine," *The Review of Politics*, XIV, No. 2 (April, 1952), pp. 204-32.

Petrovskii, Nik[olai]. "Vossoedinenie ukrainskogo naroda v edinom ukrainskom gosudarstve," *Bolshevik,* No. 2 (January, 1944), pp. 42-55.

Popov, N[icolai]. N. "Ocherednye zadachi partii v natsionalnom voprose," *Kommunisticheskaia Revolutsiia,* No. 12 (July 1, 1923), pp. 65-78.

————"SSSR i natsionalnaia politika sovetskoi vlasti," *ibid.,* No. 4 (February 15, 1923), pp. 34-46.

Postolovskaia, T. "Borba za leninskuiu politiku na teoreticheskom fronte Ukrainy," *Vestnik Kommunisticheskoi Akademii,* No. 4 (1934), pp. 53-9.

Protsiuk, Stephen. "The Evacuation of Industry in 1941 and the Postwar Economy of Ukraine," *The Ukrainian Quarte*rly, V, No. 3 (Summer, 1949), pp. 210-18.

Reshetar, John S. Jr. "National Deviation in the Soviet Union," *The American Slavic and East European Review,* XII, No. 2 (April, 1953), pp. 162-74.

Sciborsky, Mykola. "The 'De-Ukrainianization' of the Ukraine by Soviet Russia," *The Trident,* IV, No. 1 (January-February, 1940), pp. 10-22.

————"Ukraine in Figures," *ibid.,* IV, No. 10 (December, 1940), pp. 30-8.

Serdiuk, Z. "Bilshovyky Ukrainy v Borot'bi za Vidbudovu i Pidnesennia Silskoho Hospodarstva," *Partrobitnyk Ukrainy,* No. 7 (July, 1946), pp. 56-61.

Shelkoplias, N. "K itogam borby na filosofskom fronte Ukrainy," *Pod Znamenem Marksizma,* No. 1 (1936), pp. 66-83.

Skrypnyk, N[icolai]. "Soiuz osvobozhdeniia Ukrainy," *Kommunist-icheskii Internatsional,* No. 11 (April, 1930), pp. 19-31.

Smirnov, A. "O natsionalisticheskikh izvrashcheniiakh v geograficheskoi nauke na Ukraine," *Pod Znamenem Marksizma,* No. 2 (1934), pp. 127-39.

Struve, Piotr. "Obshcherusskaia kultura i ukrainskii partikularizm," *Russkaia Mysl',* XXXIII (1912), pp. 65-86.

Suprunenko, N. I. "Obrazovanie ukrainskoi sovetskoi sotsialisticheskoi respubliki," *Voprosy Istorii,* No. 2 (February, 1954), pp. 20-40.

Tabolov, K. "O natsionalnoi kulture, ob ukrainizatsii i o literaturnoi esterike Vaganiana i Larina," *Bolshevik,* No. 11-2 (June 15, 1927), pp. 69-77.

Trainin, I. "Leninskaia partiia v borbe na dva fronta po natsional-nomu voprosu," *Sovetskoe Gosudarstvo,* No. 1 (1934), pp. 67-80.

Tun, Ia. "Problemy Narodno-hospodarskoho Budivnytstva na XI Z'izdi KP(b)U," *Hospodarstvo Ukrainy,* No. 5-6 (May-June, 1930), pp. 5-29.

Vlasenko, E. "Finansy Ukrainy," *Nova Ukraina,* VI, No. 12 (December, 1927), pp. 1-20.

Vlasenko, S. "O X vseukrainskom s'ezde sovetov," *Sovetskoe Stroitelstvo,* No. 5-6 (May-June, 1927), pp. 96-110.

Voitsekhivskyj, Iu. O. "Peremohy Leninsko-Stalinskoi Natsionalnoi Polityky Partii," *Radianska Ukraina,* No. 6 (June, 1935), pp. 15-9.

Volobuev, Mykhailo. "Do Problemy Ukrainskoi Ekonomiky," *Bilshovyk Ukrainy,* No. 2 (January, 1928), pp. 46-72; No. 3 (February, 1928), pp. 42-63.

————"Proty Ekonomichnoi Pliatformy Natsionalizmu," *ibid.,* No. 5-6 (March, 1930), pp. 54-69; No. 7 (April, 1930), pp. 28-40.

Vyhnanets, Ivan. [pseudonym]. "Vysoki Shkoly v Ukraini," *Siohochasne i Mynule,* III, No. 1 (1948), pp. 26-37.

Index

Africa, 250

Agriculture, Ukrainian: before World War I, 186; collectivization of, 133-4; Commissariat of, 69; destruction of, during World War I and II, 192, 212; disruption of, during collectivization, 133-4; during First Five Year Plan, 201-2; as foundation of Ukrainian economy, 196-7, 200; recovery of under NEP, 196-7. *See also* Collectivization, Economy, Five Year Plans, Industrialization, Peasantry

Air Force, Soviet, 165

All-Russian Central Executive Committee, 219

All-Russian Congress of Soviets, 194, 219

All-Russian Mining Congress, 193

All-Ukrainian Academy of Proletarian Literature, 92-3

All-Ukrainian Association of Marxist-Leninist Institutes, 151

All-Ukrainian Central Executive Committee, 70, 81, 219-20; jurisdiction of, 227; national composition of, 82; Ukrainization decree issued by, 88

All-Ukrainian Congress of Soviets: first meeting of, 30; jurisdiction of, 215; national composition of, 82-3; session of, 152

All-Ukrainian Revolutionary Committee, 47-8

All-Union Central Executive Committee, 65, 69; jurisdiction of, 217

All-Union Congress of Soviets, 155-6

Altai, 211

Amalgamation, 14, 17, 19, 21; Lenin on, 46-7; Stalin on, 132-3

Anti-Comintern Pact, 164

Arabia, 43

Armed Forces, Soviet, 163, 165, 172, 234

Armenia, 252

Artemovsk, 244

Asia, Central, 153, 199, 207, 238-9

Assimilation, 132

Austria-Hungary, 12, 20, 36-7

Autonomy, 13, 49

Autonomy Statute, 21-2

Azovstal, 208

Balkans, 5, 12, 27, 183

Baltic Region, 187-8, 193

Bazhan, M. P., 166

Belinsky, V. G., 93-4

Belorussian SSR, 133, 173

Beria, L. P., 250

Bessarabia, 167, 170

Bilshovyk Ukrainy, 117, 120

Black Hundreds, 15-6

Black Sea, 27, 183, 200

Bolsheviks, Russian: armed insurrection in Kiev by, 25; invasions of the Ukraine by, 31, 34-5, 191; misjudgment of Ukrainian problem by, 44; national policy of during 1920's, 122; need of Ukrainian resources by, 188-94; objectives of in Ukraine, 188; retreat from Ukraine by, 38; seizure of power in Russia by, 23-5; suspicion of Ukrainian intelligentsia by, 46; Ukrainian opposition to, 39; views on Ukraine by, 25. *See also* Lenin, National problem, RCP(b), RSDRP(b)

Border regions: Communist organizations in, 52; exploitation of, 117; Russia's dependence on, 48-50, 62; Stalin against separation of, 43; Stalin on, 65-6; Stalin on secession of, 48-9; Stalin on unity of Central Russia with, 49. *See also* RSFSR, Ukraine

Borot'bisty: CP(b)U's absorption of, 52, 238-9; dissatisfaction with Party

303

306